Mediating the South Korean Other

SERIES EDITORS: NOJIN KWAK AND YOUNGJU RYU

Perspectives on Contemporary Korea is devoted to scholarship that advances the understanding of critical issues in contemporary Korean society, culture, politics, and economy. The series is sponsored by The Nam Center for Korean Studies at the University of Michigan.

Hallyu 2.0: The Korean Wave in the Age of Social Media
  Sangjoon Lee and Abé Mark Nornes, editors

Smartland Korea: Mobile Communication, Culture, and Society
  Dal Yong Jin

Transgression in Korea: Beyond Resistance and Control
  Juhn Y. Ahn, editor

Cultures of Yusin: South Korea in the 1970s
  Youngju Ryu, editor

Entrepreneurial Seoulite: Culture and Subjectivity in Hongdae, Seoul
  Mihye Cho

Revisiting Minjung: New Perspectives on the Cultural History of 1980s South Korea
  Sunyoung Park, editor

Rediscovering Korean Cinema
  Sangjoon Lee, editor

Korean Families Yesterday and Today
  Hyunjoon Park and Hyeyoung Woo, editors

Mediating the South Korean Other: Representations and Discourses of Difference in the Post/Neocolonial Nation-State
  David C. Oh, editor

Mediating the South Korean Other

Representations and Discourses of Difference
in the Post/Neocolonial Nation-State

David C. Oh, Editor

UNIVERSITY OF MICHIGAN PRESS

Ann Arbor

Copyright © 2022 by David C. Oh
All rights reserved

For questions or permissions, please contact um.press.perms@umich.edu

Published in the United States of America by the
University of Michigan Press
Manufactured in the United States of America
Printed on acid-free paper
First published July 2022

A CIP catalog record for this book is available from the British Library.

Library of Congress Cataloging-in-Publication Data

Names: Oh, David C., editor.
Title: Mediating the South Korean other : representations and discourses of difference in the post/neocolonial nation-state / David C. Oh, editor.
Other titles: Perspectives on contemporary Korea
Description: Ann Arbor : University of Michigan Press, 2022. | Series: Perspectives on contemporary Korea | Includes bibliographical references and index.
Identifiers: LCCN 2022004666 (print) | LCCN 2022004667 (ebook) | ISBN 9780472075454 (hardcover) | ISBN 9780472055456 (paperback) | ISBN 9780472220373 (ebook)
Subjects: LCSH: Multiculturalism—Korea (South) | Postcolonialism—Korea (South) | Korea (South)—Ethnic relations.
Classification: LCC DS904.5 .M44 2022 (print) | LCC DS904.5 (ebook) | DDC 305.80095195—dc23/eng/20220401
LC record available at https://lccn.loc.gov/2022004666
LC ebook record available at https://lccn.loc.gov/2022004667

Contents

Acknowledgments   vii

Introduction   1
   David C. Oh

Part 1: Mediating the Racial and Ethnic Other

1. Aspirational Interraciality and Desirable Whiteness: South Korean Media Depictions of Interracial Intimacies between White Women and Cosmopolitan South Korean Men   27
Min Joo Lee

2. Strategic Blackness in South Korean Television   46
Benjamin M. Han

3. The Televised Korean Dream: *The Birth of a Great Star* and Racial/Ethnic Diversity in the Survival Audition Program in South Korea   66
Ji-Hyun Ahn

4. Narratives of Marginalized Otherness in Migrant Women: The South Korean films *Rosa* and *Thuy*   85
Eunbi Lee and Colby Y. Miyose

5. Two Sides of the "Other": Fear and Loving of Japanese Characters in Contemporary South Korean Cinema   103
Russell Edwards

Part 2: Mediating the Co-ethnic Other

6. "Truth? No One Cares about the Truth":
   On Marginalized Identities and Belonging
   in *The Bacchus Lady* ... 123
   Myoung-Sun Song

7. Staging North Korean Defections: Uncharted Borders,
   Ideological Disorientation, and Diasporic Conditions ... 141
   Miseong Woo

8. Enemy of the State: Cold War Rhetoric and Representation
   of North Korea/ns in *Hallyu* Films ... 159
   JongHwa Lee

9. Reframing the Difference of Co-ethnic Other in Japan:
   An Analysis of Representations and Identifications
   in the South Korean Documentary Film *Uri-Hakkyo* ... 178
   Min Wha Han

10. The Other at Home: A Comparative Analysis of Coverage
    of an Exiled Korean American K-Pop Star ... 197
    Alice Nahyeon Kim and Sherry S. Yu

Conclusion ... 216
   David C. Oh

Contributors ... 233

Index ... 237

Digital materials related to this title can be found on
the Fulcrum platform via the following citable URL:
https://doi.org/10.3998/mpub.11938487

Acknowledgments

The idea of this book had been percolating for several years, but I had largely abandoned it when a native Korean colleague backed out of co-editing the book. At that time, all of my previous Korea-based articles had been co-authored with a native Korean colleague because I did not want to be guilty of commenting on Korea as a US-raised academic without the deep insights and investments of lived experience. Because I am a second-generation Korean American, solo-editing seemed inappropriate, perhaps because I had internalized my own sense of inadequacy for several decades for speaking Korean with an accent. It was not until a conversation with Miseong Woo, Lili Kim, and Michael Prieler at a campus café on Yonsei University's campus that my perspective changed. I am especially indebted to Miseong Woo for expressing faith in my ability to credibly do the work. From that point forward, I took concrete action to intervene in the academic discourse of difference in Korea, which I have understood as too constrained by Western theories of how racism works in White supremacy.

The aforementioned conversation would not have happened in the first place if I had not been living in Seoul at the time on a Fulbright grant. Thus, I am also grateful to the Fulbright program for the opportunity to immerse myself in Korea for an extended period and to the Hankuk University of Foreign Studies (HUFS) for hosting me. It is because of my experiences in Korea and my conversations with colleagues such as Younghan Cho at HUFS, Minkyu Sung at the Ulsan National Institute of Technology, and Sunny Yoon at Hanyang University that I developed deeper insights, confidence, and commitment to turn my inchoate interests into a material book project.

Further, I am grateful for the institutions that have made the publication of the book possible. First, I would like to thank Ramapo College of New Jersey for providing a Faculty Development Fund grant, which allowed me to devote time in the summer to edit the contributions to this book. I would also like to thank the University of Michigan Press for their faith in the project and the three anonymous reviewers who provided support and intellectual direction. Their contributions were energizing for me and for the book's contributors. The contributors, of course, are the ones who made the book possible. I appreciate their enthusiasm, effort, and endurance. They made my job as an editor incredibly rewarding.

Finally, my deepest thanks go to my wonderful spouse and children, who accommodate my research plans and idiosyncratic writing habits. They enable me to be the best scholar and editor I can be.

Introduction

David C. Oh

In English-language conversations about otherness in South Korea (hereafter Korea), I have most commonly heard the term "racism" applied to the material and symbolic disadvantages and prejudice experienced by marginalized others. The use of "racism" as a translation for *injongchabyeol* (인종차별), the act or practice of othering, or *injongjuui* (인종주의), a system of othering, among Korean scholars or as an imported sociocultural logic by Westerners is prevalent. Because of "translation loss," the different connotative meanings attached to translated words (Sorby 2008), it is problematic because racism imposes a Western cultural logic that is less meaningful in a Korean context. With this in mind, this book is animated by a postcolonial impulse to develop locally meaningful theory, concepts, and language in order to avoid relying solely upon Western theoretical logics to explain Korea (Shome and Hegde 2002; Waisbord and Mellado 2014). As Shohat and Stam (1994) argue, Eurocentrism has become commonsensical in the academy, and this includes South Korean universities, whose faculty are largely trained in the United States. Indeed, in an influential article, Jeon (1999) argues that representational racism is sorely needed to understand *injong* in South Korea, and yet, even recently, Jae Kyun Kim (2015) argues that questions of racial formations in Korea are underdeveloped. The purpose of privileging local logics, however, is not an exercise to avoid Western knowledge for its own sake; indeed, Western-based theories and knowledge will meaningfully interact with the chapters in this book and in this introduction. However, when Western theories and/or concepts do not adequately explain the South Korean cultural terrain, then decolonizing knowledge is not only a political move but an intellectual one.

Using race and racism as explanatory logics is problematic because these were developed in the service of specifically Eurocentric taxonomies and hierarchies that reify White supremacy. Though it is beyond the scope of this introduction to explicate the development of race as a pseudoscientific concept and racism as a system that emerged in concert with it, a brief explanation is necessary to make the obvious point that the specific ideas of race and racism are not indigenous to Korea. For instance, Fredrickson (2003), an emeritus professor of history at Stanford University, noted in a contribution to a PBS documentary titled *Race: The Power of an Illusion*, "An ideological basis for explicit racism came to a unique fruition in the West during the modern period. No clear and unequivocal evidence of racism has been found in other cultures or in Europe before the Middle Ages." Indeed, early notions of race were rooted in a hierarchal Christian view of the world that was divided into three groups based on the descendants of Noah's children, with Europe at the top, Asia in the middle, and Africa at the bottom (Pieterse 1992).

With the Enlightenment, religious thinking was replaced with the pseudo-science of eugenics that rationalized existing prejudices and that created strict ahistorical taxonomies of human difference (Pieterse 1992). These beliefs acted as a justification for European colonialism. Employing a social Darwinist framework, Europeans could argue that its rule was "natural" and that they had a Christian duty to civilize the "savages" (Pieterse 1992), thus racializing colonialism (Stam and Shohat 2012). This racialization justified the possession of faraway lands (Said 1978) and the trading of African slaves (Shohat and Stam 1994). During the height of colonialism, Europe controlled 85 percent of the Earth's territory (Pieterse 1992) and spread racial logics along with its centuries-long domination. Even with the end of much of the colonial project, the continued geopolitical dominance of "the West" has resulted in a commonsensical understanding of racial difference (West 2004). It should be clear, then, that the concept of race itself is historically rooted in White supremacy (Almaguer 1994; Omi and Winant 1994). As a colonized nation, albeit by a non-White power, Korea would be not a beneficiary of racism but rather a victim of it.

That said, I do not subscribe to the view that only White people benefit from systemic racism and that people of color cannot be racist. This does not comport with even colonial histories in which the colonized internalize racial logics and hierarchies and employ it against marginalized others inside and outside their own societies. Even still, I strongly reject the idea of universalism—the idea that anyone or any nation can be equally racist as another. While the material and symbolic privileges of racism do not only accrue to White people, they are still racism's primary beneficiaries.

White supremacy has been globally advanced for centuries, and the West still controls much of the world's economic, military, and political power. In postcolonial nations, racism will always be more complicated when encountered and negotiated in local contexts than it would be in the West, in which the logic of White supremacy and its concomitant construction of race serves a simpler hegemonic function, to justify either European colonialism or European settler colonies. As Goldberg (2006) argues, racism is relational such that it travels to other places, transforming but not replacing existing logics of difference—who belongs and who does not, who is valued and who is marginalized.

That leads to a question of how race and racism have come to be understood in the Korean case and why I argue that othering in Korea cannot be reduced to racism. There is some disagreement about the time in which Western racial/racist ideology emerged on the peninsula with some scholars locating it in 1940s camptowns, where Koreans learned anti-Black racism from White American GIs and their insistence that Koreans provide segregated bars and sexual services (Gage 2014; K. Moon 1997; Seungsook Moon 2010).

> In short, the racist dimensions of American society were replicated and reenacted across the Pacific in the U.S. military camps, and the camptown residents interpellated by the U.S. military culture internalized anti-Black racism, which spilled over into Korean society at large and found its most vulnerable victims in Black Amerasians. (K. Lee 2015, 18)

Tikhonov (2013), on the other hand, argues that race as a conceptual category of human difference entered in the late nineteenth century, competing with the existing concept of an "ethnic nation." He argues that, since that time, racial classification systems were taught across Korea, blending a Sino-centric understanding of center and periphery, Social Darwinism, and local logics.

Because of Western military power and colonial control, White people came to be seen as the top of a racial hierarchy, adopting at least this tenet of White supremacy—racist hierarchy—yet Koreans could take solace in believing that other races existed below them (Tikhonov 2013). This view collapsed somewhat during the colonial era. Being colonized meant that Koreans developed a sense of inferiority to the more powerful Japanese (Em 2013) and saw themselves as similar to other colonized nations in the Global South (Jae Kyun Kim 2015). Seeing themselves as different and pushing toward modernization also meant creating collective psychic distance from the colonized nations and toward the West, producing anti-Black affect (Jae Kyun Kim 2015). Despite the differently argued time frames, it is clear that Western racial thinking has ossified since the mid-twentieth century, becoming a pervasive part of locally constructed hierarchies of human difference. The US's continued neocolonial domination and admired status have ensured that this is the case (A. Lee 2019; Hong and Kim 2010).

While places far from Korea were interpreted through a racist Western lens, there was only limited support for a "yellow" race with nearby Asian nations (Tikhonov 2013). Japan's brutal, colonial occupation of Korea made impossible the idea of shared racial kinship. Instead, the occupation animated its difference. Though there were existing discourses of ethnonational homogeneity, it was concretized in Koreans' resistance to Japanese cultural domination (G. Shin 2006; Cawley 2016; Em 2013; Lie 2014; Nora Kim 2014; H. Kim 2006). This was perhaps a co-optation of Japanese myths of its ethnonational homogeneity and the way the myth justifies Japanese beliefs in its superiority and its right to rule inferior others (Tai 2004). Though the myth of Korean ethnonational homogeneity is easily debunked (Jung 2016; H. Lim 2010), its political and social utility has led to its resilience as a hegemonic project (Ahn 2016; Seol and Seo 2014). As Kun Jong Lee (2015) writes, "Koreans' presumption of their ethnic purity might be seen as an expression of their yearning to maintain their integrity, honor, and self-respect especially in times of national crisis such as the Japanese colonization of Korea" (13). Even now as *damunhwa* (다문화, multiculturalism) has taken hold as state policy, folk notions of "shared blood" (*sunhyeoljuui*, pureblood-ism) still has strong appeal (Lie 2014; Gage 2014). The defensive nationalism helps protect the nation, but it also leans toward a tendency to essentialize Koreanness (Cho 1998), which leads to the legal and everyday mistreatment of "impure" Koreans, such as diasporic Koreans across Asia and Amerasians (Lie 2014). With the myth of ethnonational homogeneity intersecting with racial understandings of the globe, it creates a conflation of nation, race, and ethnicity in the Korean imagination (Nadia Kim 2006b). The point of this is that while Western racist logics matter in Korea, it is intermingled with local logics and lived experience.

Othering in Korea cannot be reduced to racism because it is not primarily racial difference that is the axis around which discrimination turns. Most notably, Japan and China have historically been considered different "races" because of Korea's intimate historical relationships with its neighbors (Nadia Kim 2014). This is not to say that racism is not manifest in Korea; it accrues benefits to people perceived as White or biracial Korean White (K. Lee 2015; Ahn 2015; Kang 2018; Nadia Kim 2006a; Geon-Soo Han 2007; Jinsook Kim 2017). Conversely, there are highly visible, racist comedy sketches that have used blackface (Gil-Soo Han 2015) and documentaries and informational television that represent Africa as primitive (Yoon 2015; Geon-Soo Han 2007). In the overheated English-teaching market (Lee, Han, and McKerrow 2010; Shim and Park 2008), there is also a racist disadvantage for teachers of color and a preference for White teachers, as English is associated with the West and the West is associated with Whiteness (Flynn 2017). Yet, still, it is arguable that Black American residents, for example, are relatively advantaged compared to Southeast Asian residents, Chinese Koreans, or North Korean refugees. In a recent survey of Korean schoolchildren, two of the three groups that they were least willing to accept as Koreans were Chinese Koreans and North Korean refugees (Nora Kim 2016). In this case, at least, it is neither racial nor ethnic difference that fits the cultural calculation of who is least acceptable.

The relative lack of emphasis on race compared to the West is unsurprising, as Korea has become a largely *intra*-regional receiving nation (Gaetano and Yeoh 2010). That is, in the global circuits of migration, immigrants to Korea come primarily from other parts of East and Southeast Asia (Geon-Soo Han 2007; A. Kim 2009; Kim and Oh 2011). Racially, then, most immigrants are also Asian. Their dissimilarity lies in their ethnic difference, national difference, and regional difference. In practice, othering carries similar kinds of discrimination and harms, which may be why it is difficult to let go of the concept of racism, as few words carry its rhetorical force. Yet, the distinction is an important conceptual one. It matters because by calling *injongchabyeol* or *injongjuui* "racism," it reifies universalist notions of racism that excuse and obscure White supremacy and colonial histories (Gilroy 2012). Indeed, it becomes discursively possible to shift racism to Asia and Korea while advancing post-racist myths that racism has been defeated in the West (Bonilla-Silva 2010).

Various attempts to explain othering in Korea, apart from racism, are worth addressing. The first is the claim of xenophobia, as rooted in the myth of ethnic homogeneity. The myth of "shared blood," a metaphor for ancestry, assumes Korea is ethnically, linguistically, and culturally homogenous (K. Han 2007; Chung and Kim 2012; Seungho Moon 2010; Hong and Kim 2010; Seol and Seo 2014; Cho 1998; Lie 2014). Though the specific claim about the myth leading to xenophobia is not manifest in scholarship, it is commonly heard in White foreign residents' discourses about

Korea (see Oh 2018, 2019; Oh and Oh 2017). Instead, scholars tend to argue that the myth of ethnic homogeneity is an obstacle to multiculturalism (Sookyung Kim 2012; M. Lee 2009; J. Shin 2019; Jinsook Kim 2017), excluding non-Koreans from conceptualizations of the nation (Kim and Oh 2011). While this explanation accounts for the fear or the marginalization of others based on ethnic and racial difference, it does not explain the marginalization of co-ethnic others, nor does it explain the privileged view of White Westerners in the cultural terrain.

A more interesting theory is Kyung-Koo Han's (2007) Confucian argument of self-development that is applied to the nation-state. This claim is predicated on the notion that Koreans view individuals as a metonym for their countries of origin such that foreign residents from an impoverished nation would be viewed as impoverished themselves and should seek assimilation into a culturally more advanced society. An alternative theory is that "neo-racism," not "neo-nationalism," explains Koreans' discriminatory attitudes (Lee, Jon, and Byun 2017). This explanation claims that viewing weaker nations as lower and more marginal than Korea shores up national identity and pride. Unlike the neocolonial racial and ethnic homogeneity arguments, both the Confucian and neo-racism arguments explain why co-ethnics who emigrate from non-industrialized countries are oppressed, and they also explain the elevated view of the West (as conflated with White racial difference). However, in a model that claims that national power or development is most valued, it does not explain why White people from less powerful nations are esteemed or why citizens of wealthy, non-White nations are not similarly esteemed as White people, for example, Japan or the United Arab Emirates. It also does not explain why non-White people from wealthy nations are not also beneficiaries of a Confucian logic. Further, as a practical matter, people do not have the cognitive energy to make sophisticated country-, ethnicity, or culture-specific judgments; rather, they are likely to draw generalized regional or racial meanings.

An unrelated criticism is that despite Kyung-Koo Han's (2007) progressive stand to challenge national demands for assimilation, the framework is not dissimilar from colorblind racism. His argument states that it is not race, national origin, or some other marker but rather a lack of intention to assimilate that generates animosity. It undervalues the adoption of Western racist hierarchies and local discriminatory logics, sharing the flaws of racial universalism while dressing up global racist hierarchy and local ethnonational hierarchy. Finally, and perhaps unintentionally, his Confucian claim is very similar to neoliberal multiculturalism, which places blame on the marginalized for not assimilating rather than on those oppressing.

Thus, no explanation fully captures the meaning-making involved in the process of othering. At this point, then, it is important to reconsider local meaning making that integrates Western racist logics, which have been adapted in the local terrain. So, then, returning to the opening paragraph, if othering in Korea cannot adequately be called racism, then what would a more accurate concept be? I think it is wise to consider the name Koreans themselves have given this form of othering, namely, *injongchabyeol*. Unlike racism, which signals a historically specific conceptualization of human difference based on hierarchical racial ontologies, *injongchabyeol* literally means "human-category-difference-distinction" when pulling apart the Chinese characters upon which the word is derived. In other words, *injongchabyeol* is discrimination based on perceived different human categories. This is a flexible type of discrimination that can include, but is not limited to, ethnic, racial, cultural, national, religious, and/or regional (e.g., Southeast Asian) difference. It is based on a multivariate calculation of who belongs and who is valued.

Because the term *injongchabyeol* itself is unlikely to be adopted by English-speaking scholars, I propose that, for lack of a more elegant term, it be called "anthrocategorism." For general purposes, I define this as a system of discrimination based on perceived human groupings. Specific to Korea, this refers to a system of othering that creates a hierarchical and concentric understanding of human difference. One purpose of the book is to map cultural logics of anthrocategorist cultural logics as articulated through media representation and discourse and to map cultural logics of anthrocategorist normality, which is the work of the book's conclusion. For this introduction, I argue that there is not a single unidimensional explanation—myth of ethnic homogeneity, neocolonial and postcolonial racism, or Confucianism—to understand othering in Korean society and media. Rather, there are at least two intersecting determinations: hierarchy, the linear, and normality, the concentric. For instance, while Whiteness may be understood hierarchically as desirable otherness, it is also perceived concentrically as a foreign other. While North Korean refugees may be considered hierarchically to be an undesirable other, they are perceived concentrically as a culturally unusual but ethnically similar other. In contrast, racism's hierarchies in the US are intertwined with concentric notions of normality. For instance, Whites are held in the highest regard along racist hierarchies (Shah and Thornton 1994) and considered "normal," the racial standard against which people of color are judged (Dyer

1997; Gabriel 1998; Lipsitz 1998; Nakayama and Krizek 1995; Shome 2000). Whiteness's racial superiority is contingent upon its racial normality, and its racial normality is dependent upon its invisibility (Nakayama and Krizek 1995; Dyer 1988). Anthrocategorism, in the Korean case, is a multidimensional system of discrimination and privilege. This should be expected, as "collectivistic"[1] cultures require more nuanced social calculations and obligations. It also means that Korean anthrocategorism secures and negotiates power in ways that are different from the racial logics of the West, particularly as it has a unique modern history as both a postcolonial state of a non-Western power, Japan, and a neocolonial state of a Western power, the US.

Anthrocategorism, Damunhwa, and Media in South Korea

Korea is an atypical postcolonial society. It was not colonized by a Western power, and it does not share the same ambivalence seen in other postcolonial states (Yoon 2015). However, it does have postcolonial structural legacies, including the forced relocation of Koreans to Japan, Manchuria, and Siberia. Korea's independence and the power vacuum that developed created the conditions for the US and the Soviet Union to claim influence over the peninsula. Ultimately, in the US's neocolonial domination, the US proposed a deal to the Soviet Union to divide the nation at the thirty-eighth parallel, creating the two Koreas; this happened without Koreans' input and despite Korea not being an enemy during World War II (Cumings 2005). When the US negotiated with Japan to end World War II, it did not invite or consult any Asian delegates, including Korean ones, during the signing of the San Francisco Peace Treaty. The treaty provided little satisfaction for previously colonized nations, provoking ideological tensions over history that intermittently boil over as unresolved conflicts. As such, Korea's legacy as a postcolonial state certainly matters in its view of others, particularly co-ethnics forcibly taken by the Japanese and co-ethnics divided by the US and its later civil war. Its view of Japan is also situated in an ambivalent understanding of Japan as a superior, somewhat familiar, though threatening other (Jung 2016).

Because Korea is also subordinated to the US, a Western power (Sumi Kim 2009), it is both a postcolonial state and a neocolonial state. As Höhn and Moon (2010) write, "Nowhere was the neocolonial character of the US presence more evident than in South Korea" (16). This has led to ambivalences that are typically seen in postcolonial countries. There is resentment because of the US's complicit support of tyrannical regimes, its reinstatement of Japanese sympathizers into positions of power, its lopsided Status of Forces Agreement (SOFA), and occasional cases of US soldiers' brutality, but the resentments sit alongside an aspirational and favorable view of the US. Indeed, the US is seen as a symbolic paternal figure from which Korea seeks to earn approval and acceptance (Oh and Oh 2016). Despite its postcolonial rupture from Japan, Korea manifests hybridity in its neocolonial relationship to the US as postcolonial states do with former colonizer nations. As such, contemporary Korean culture is shaped deeply by its relationship to the US and, more recently, by its relationship to the larger "international community," which generally means gaining acceptance by the powerful nations of the West (Seungho Moon 2010).

The desire for globalization accelerated with former president Kim Young Sam's policy of international market integration called *segyehwa* (세계화) (Ahn 2014; Shim 2014; A. Lee 2019), and it was furthered under the Lee Myung-bak administration's advancement of "Global Korea" (A. Lee 2019). This openness "created a climate in which the very self-identification of South Korea as a monocultural and monoethnic society was untenable" (Lie 2014, 19). With these globalization policies, Korea has become integrated into the global market by drawing upon neoliberal logics of open markets and flexible capital and labor flows. Like neoliberal economics in the West, which have leaked into social policy and ideologies, neoliberalism in Korea called upon citizens to become idealized subjects through their individual accrual of cosmopolitan social capital (Schattle 2015), most visible through international travel and study as well as English-language proficiency. This is manifest through the social capital accrued by demonstrating cosmopolitan sophistication as a neoliberal demonstration of global citizenry. Valued demonstrations of cosmopolitan social capital are manifest through tolerance for a multicultural society and global knowledge, which particularly fetishizes Europe and the US, which, as mentioned earlier, are conflated with Whiteness and with masculinity. In the local imagination, then, heterosexual White masculinity connotes strength, progressivism, and cosmopolitanism, particularly for heterosexual women disaffected by patriarchal obligations and oppression (Nadia Kim 2006a).

In mediated discourse, particularly with the increased visibility of foreign celebrities on variety programs, there has been a "preference for a white, male-centered global society" (Kang 2018, 10). Not only is there a preference, but Whiteness, and especially White masculinity, is represented as a desirable other (Ahn 2015). Oh (2020), for instance, refers to White foreign residents' representations on Korean television as "super-minorities." They are super because they are depicted as aspirational models of progressive cosmopolitanism but are minorities because of their cultural distance from "normal," authentic Koreanness. This desirability extends to their children, too. Though marginalized a few decades earlier as reminders of wartime trauma, mixed-race children and celebrities have found some degree of acceptance and desirability, especially children with White fathers (M. Lee 2009; Ahn 2015). In contrast, mixed-race Black Korean children are especially marginalized because their mothers are associated with sex work and because they are seen as the products of US neocolonialism (Lie 2014; Nadia Kim 2014).

In an influential early article about multiculturalism and Korean media, Cho (1998) writes, "The civilian government and the media are actively engaged in mobilizing and controlling popular voices, in some ways intervening deeply in the formulation of narratives on Koreanness" (84). For instance, Cha, Lee, and Park (2016) observe that on television, migrants from the West are interviewed in English while "Third World" women are interviewed in Korean, which shows them as less competent Koreans and less cosmopolitan. This is because of the symbolic capital invested in Whiteness, the West, and the English language. As Geon-Soo Han (2007) argues, there is a locally constructed hierarchy of migrants—"denizens" from the West, who occupy professional positions in the center of Seoul, and "margizens" from the Global South, who occupy low-status jobs and live in the periphery of the city. In addition to the favorable, though socially distant, representations of White foreign residents, neocolonialism is also manifest in the internalization and replication of Western racist tropes. For instance, Yoon (2015) finds that anthropologically centered documentaries often exoticize people from the Global South as primitive with "strange" customs. The shows dichotomize the world as modern—Korea and the West—and primitive—Global South (Yoon 2015).

These ideological meanings have existed alongside Korea's relatively recent policy of multiculturalism, referred to as *damunhwa* (다문화). The policy was seen as necessary, as Korea has become a receiving nation (Ahn 2014; Chung and Kim 2012; K. Han 2007; Nam-Kook Kim 2009). Korea is unique among its peer post/neocolonial states for this reason. With the influx of new residents, Korea is rapidly transforming into a multiethnic and multiracial society (Cawley 2016; Yoon, Kim, and Eom 2011; A. Kim 2009). The progressive, structural changes include the establishment of one hundred multicultural family support centers (Joon Kim 2011), the establishment of antidiscrimination laws, the official abandonment of the term "mixed blood" (혼혈) with "children of international marriage," and changes in school curriculum that have replaced ethnic homogeneity with "multiethnic and multicultural society" (Seungho Moon 2010; Yoon, Kim, and Eom 2011). Unlike in the West, where there has been a retreat from multiculturalism, in Korea there is growing acceptance and awareness of multiculturalism with intolerance framed as illiberal and regressive (Nora Kim 2015).

Despite "real and substantial" changes (Prey 2011, 121), the policy of multiculturalism is limited and, arguably, instrumental in its purposes (Nora Kim 2014). A criticism of *damunhwa* policy is that its purpose is not sincere but, rather, to demonstrate that it belongs among the powerful nations of the West, as globalization and multiculturalism are interpreted as signs of Western modernity and progress (A. Lee 2019). "Embracing the idea of multiculturalism allows the South Korean nation-state to assert its membership in the ranks of ethnically diverse and cosmopolitan global societies, implying that it has moved beyond the homogeneity and closed borders of the 'hermit kingdom' of yesteryears" (Cheng 2011, 1642). As such, Nadia Kim (2014) argues that the policy and the reality on the ground is multiethnicity rather than multiculturalism. This is because cultural difference is not celebrated; rather, the expectation is that immigrants, representing a multiethnic mosaic, will integrate into the Korean family and, by extension, the Korean nation-state. Despite this assimilationist tendency in *damunhwa*, Lim (2014) points out that the discourse creates space for a more socially just society: "It is easy to dismiss the introduction of multiculturalism in South Korea as little more than a cynical effort by the state to disguise a strongly, even coercive assimilationist and integrationist policy. But . . . the concept of multiculturalism cannot be entirely co-opted by the Korean state" (54).

In elite discourse, journalists have taken up governmental initiatives with support for *damunhwa* in their news pages, dismissing anti-foreigner sentiment as ignorant and xenophobic (Yi and Jung 2015). This was especially visible during Korea's celebration of the return to Seoul of former American football Super Bowl MVP Hines Ward. Writing about Korean media's reception of Ward's trip, Ahn (2014) says, "It connotes that Korea, too, welcomes racial diversity and will move forward to be a more open and global society where mixed-race individuals and racial minorities can achieve success as Hines Ward did in the USA" (403). In a strongly worded rebuke of this instrumentalism, Jun (2014) condemns the practice of *damunhwa*, stating that "the Korean discourse of tolerance is a narcissistic one shaped tremendously by the problematics of the self and its development" (83).

Another criticism is that *damunhwa* is a gendered state policy that favors the migration of women (Gaetano and Yeoh 2010; Chung and Kim 2012; Nadia Kim 2014). The reason is instrumental, as there is a state interest to counteract Korea's low birthrate, particularly in rural areas, without threatening the current patriarchal social order (Cheng 2011). The policy has facilitated international marriages as one of the few legal routes for immigration (Chung and Kim 2012), and this has opened the borders to an influx of women, particularly Korean Chinese women and also intra-regional spouses from China, Vietnam, Japan, the Philippines, and Mongolia (Seungho Moon 2010). The purpose of the policy, then, is to welcome more multicultural families by creating the ideological and structural space to accommodate desired demographic shifts while leaving out other groups (Cheng 2011; Chung and Kim 2012; Prey 2011).

The integration of the family into Korean society has been predicated on the family's assimilation rather than on Korean society's adaptation to a multicultural society. There is tolerance for embodied foreignness but not an accommodation of cultural difference (Joon Kim 2011; Jun 2014; Nora Kim 2014). This is similar to the desire for visible, superficial difference in Western countries that does not challenge existing structures or dominant culture. For foreign spouses and their children, the expectation is assimilation (Jun 2012; Geon-Soo Han 2007; Iwabuchi, Kim, and Hsia 2016). Kim and Oh (2011, 1577) write, "Policies designed to implicitly foster assimilation, rather than hastily spread the morals of multiculturalism, reflect the perception that international migration could be managed better through absorption than through changing the mindset of the majority population." The primary purpose of education programs is not to change Korea(ns) but to teach foreign spouses and refugees to understand and participate in society (Kim and Oh 2011; Sumi Kim 2009; Seungho Moon 2010). It is an unequal adjustment that exercises "no demand on the majority of Koreans to learn the cultures of other groups in the nation" (Choi 2010, 176). The assimilationist demands are justified by Confucian goals of "social harmony," which is emphasized over individual differences (Seungho Moon 2010).

Tolerance, which is contingent upon successful assimilation, is, for the non-White foreign resident woman, reified through television and film representation as well as news discourse. A frequent trope in the representation of multicultural families celebrates foreign wives for assimilating into the family and, as the family acts as a metaphor, into the nation (Jung 2016). Valorized women are also represented as seeking assimilation even, or perhaps especially, when it comes at the expense of cutting diasporic ties with their homeland cultures (Cha, Lee, and Park 2016). *Damunhwa*, then, is about the burden placed on the marginalized to not inconvenience the majority (Hundt, Walton, and Lee 2018, 447; Oh and Oh 2016). This common trope is problematic because it denies the necessity of systemic change and ideological transformation. As Cha, Lee, and Park (2016) write, "Media representations render foreign brides into docile subjects who must adapt to Korean patriarchal family culture to avoid being disciplined and punished" (1473).

In these portrayals, the disciplining into idealized Korean subjects is obscured by the representation of the happy family. The couples' loving relationships are presented as themselves transcending cultural differences and boundaries such that any structural barrier can be overcome; thus, the representations of happy families almost never depict racism, cultural isolation, domestic violence, and loss of agency (Cha, Lee, and Park 2016). Like neoliberal multiculturalism, these representations reduce racism to the interpersonal level, denying systemic oppression and the possibility of systemic remedies (Melamed 2006). In addition, migrant women are objectified to discipline sexually liberated Korean women by arguing that the migrant bride preserves traditional femininity, which is ironically gained through neoliberal globalization and modernization (Sumi Kim 2009).

To build hegemonic consent, media represent multicultural families as impoverished and pitiable (Cha, Lee, and Park 2016). Wives and children are frequently represented as helpless victims who need the paternal support and protection of the state and of Koreans (Sookyung Kim 2012; Oh and Oh 2016). While there certainly are enduring problems of discrimination (M. Lee 2009; G. Shin 2006; Lee, Jon, and Byun 2017), representations of victims often objectify marginalized groups, depriving them of agency. This is, however, better than the representation of foreign men laborers (from Southeast Asia), who are symbolically annihilated and made into a convenient scapegoat for social problems (Jirn 2014; Cha, Lee, and Park 2016). They do not fit a neoliberal, paternalistic, double assimilation narrative in which gendered, foreign others must make individual efforts to assimilate into the Korean family, while Koreans struggle to gain acceptance in the Western world order (Oh and Oh 2016). It is also preferable to the representation of *Joseonjok*, who are portrayed as ethnically similar but as having entrenched cultural difference (Yang 2010). Because of that difference, they are portrayed as a largely criminal underclass and an unnecessary source of conflict between the nation and China (Yang 2010).

This discussion leads to the second purpose of the book, which is to understand media's role in the ideological construction of otherness. Though there is a growing body of literature, there is urgency to develop a more holistic understanding of media representation that draws together different studies of otherness in an age of globalization and *damunhwa*. The book contributes to this area of the literature by shifting the lens such that other forms of otherness will be considered alongside migrant women, who have been the subject of most damunhwa research, and it contributes through its simultaneous engagement with neocolonial racial logics and local logics of difference. Because of the focused nature of journal articles, they have largely focused on one or the other, and it is the purpose of this book to map the ways difference is constructed in media discourse and representation. The book develops postcolonial theory through the elaboration of anthrocategorism (*injongchabyeol*), and it maps anthrocategorical logics. The chapters provide evidentiary grounds, with the conclusion providing a holistic integration of the studies to map anthrocategorism in Korean media culture. Like most critically informed cultural studies projects, the goal of studying media is not primarily to understand media themselves but, rather, to understand the ideological meanings upon which representations are formed and to understand the ideological meanings they articulate.

Preview of Chapters

The book is divided into two parts. The first is a collection of chapters that studies the mediated construction of racial and ethnic otherness, and the second part examines co-ethnic otherness. The chapters in the first part argue that Korea reimagines and reproduces racist hierarchies and the specific Black-White paradigm of the US. In Korea's reimagination, Blackness and Whiteness are both ambivalently represented, though the representations maintain the same general contours of neocolonial racist hierarchies. The chapters in the second part examine the mediated construction of same race, different ethnic otherness. The section is meaningful as it points to local meanings about difference that are rooted in Korea's intraregional histories with nearby Asian nations and with global meanings that divide the world into the "First World" and the "Third World." The three chapters in the third part argue that there are differences in the ways ethnic others have been received, with voluntary Korean American immigrants represented as desirable except when they are thought to abandon their homeland commitments and lumped with undesirable co-ethnic Koreans who have been forcibly removed or separated from the homeland and who are frequently represented as a contaminating presence. The final part examines the representations of co-ethnics on the peninsula who are othered and marginalized for their perceived threat, burden, or betrayal. These texts point to the continuing postcolonial legacies that find expression in media culture.

In chapter 1, Min Joo Lee[2] examines media discourses that privilege Korean men–White women heterosexual couples. She argues that Korean media purposefully formulate aspirational images of these interracial couples to advance the notion of Korean male cosmopolitanism and their global (heterosexual) desirability. Lee argues that mediated constructions of aspirational interracial relationships exemplify how South Korean culture is attempting to reformulate nationalism from one premised on ethnic/racial homogeneity to one that centers on masculinized cosmopolitanism, which elevates White femininity.

In chapter 2, Benjamin M. Han analyzes the representation of Black entertainers Sam Okyere and Hyun-min Han in their variety show appearances. Han argues that television representation uses "strategic blackness" as a cynical means of demonstrating an image of a multicultural, global Korea while simultaneously requiring that Blackness is tamed by valorizing superficial difference and assimilation into dominant Korean society. Their representational inclusion animates the dialectical tension between the domestication of Black entertainers via their competency in the Korean language and the media's strategic use of Blackness. It paradoxically upholds the dominant ideology of "ethnic homogeneity" by constructing Black entertainers as exceptional others while advancing a narrative of multiracial modernity.

In chapter 3, Ji-Hyun Ahn examines the first season of the reality competition show *Star Audition: The Great Birth* (MBC), focusing on the its coverage of Cheonggang Baek, an ethnic Korean Chinese (*Joseonjok*) winner. Ahn argues that because of the way Baek was celebrated as the first *foreigner* to win a competition talent show, his win works ideologically toward the project of a modern, multicultural "Korean Dream" narrative that is symbolically made tangible but materially withheld. His success on the show was portrayed as possible because of the mentoring and support he received from leading figures in the music industry and because of his performance of Koreanness. Yet, his popularity and inclusion have been contingent on fulfilling his role satisfactorily to exemplify the graciousness of the nation-state.

In chapter 4, Eunbi Lee and Colby Y. Miyose investigate race, ethnicity, and gender-based violence against migrant workers and marriage migrants in two independent films, *Rosa* (2012) and *Thuy* (2013). Like the reality show in the previous chapter, the films each point to migration and the cynical (im)possibilities of achieving the Korean Dream. *Rosa* depicts a White Uzbek woman who migrates to Korea to earn enough money to pursue her dream of being a ballerina but is forced into exotic dancing and sex trafficking. *Thuy* is the story of a marriage migrant from Vietnam who faithfully investigates her husband's mysterious death and is killed for revealing the depths of corruption in the town. The migrants' tragic lives also mark the different ways they are oppressed by patriarchal violence—Eastern European as an object of sexual desire and Southeast Asian as an object to benefit the Korean family.

In chapter 5, Russell Edwards explores the mediation of Korea's postcolonial relationship with Japan through the representation of the masculinized Japanese other and the feminized Japanese ally in *The Wailing* and *Anarchist from Colony*, respectively. He demonstrates that film represents the Japanese with more complexity than binary notions of good Koreans and bad Japanese would suggest. Japanese characters are represented as both sympathetic figures who support Korean liberation and as literal demonic others, whose presence corrupts and destroys Koreans from within. The moral rot caused by the presence of the Japanese other causes Koreans to turn against one another, becoming the more present danger.

In chapter 6, Myoung-Sun Song's analysis of the film *The Bacchus Lady* bridges this book's two parts—racial and ethnic othering as well as co-ethnic othering. The film centers around an elder sex worker and her relationships with marginalized others, including a transgender woman, a physically disabled man with a prosthetic leg, and a Korean Filipino boy who is left alone after his Filipino mother is arrested for stabbing his deadbeat Korean father. In the meantime, the protagonist struggles with her own marginalized identities as a current sex worker, a former sex worker in US camptowns, and a North Korean refugee. Song's analysis interrogates the relationships between the four characters and the (inter)dependence they have on one another in everyday survival, arguing that the film demonstrates that Korean society has prioritized and marked certain bodies as (un)desirable and in service of ethnonational, able-bodied, heteronormative patriarchy.

In chapter 7, Miseong Woo focuses in on the representation of North

Korean refugees, shifting from electronic media to the medium of the stage. Studying Eun-sung Kim's play *Sister Mok-rahn* and Mia Chung's play *You for Me for You*, Woo demonstrates the complexity in mediating co-ethnic others' sense of disorientation, literal and figurative border crossings, and their critical distance from neoliberal capitalist social conditions. Both films present South Korea as a dystopian space marked by the coldness of neoliberal capitalism. In these portrayals, North Korean refugees are humanized and presented as pitiable but sympathetic objects, as *Sister Mok-rahn* demonstrates the cruelty of South Korean society while *You for Me for You* narrates the US as a space of freedom and escape and North Korea as an oppressive regime.

In chapter 8, JongHwa Lee continues the attention on North Koreans, examining the rhetoric of two films, *The Spy Gone North* (2018) and *Confidential Assignment* (2017). Both films continue themes of shared kinship first popularized in *Joint Security Area*, but without the tragic consequences of that film. Instead, in mirrored fashion, the former features a South Korean spy who befriends and works with North Korean officials to prevent South Korean politicians' attempts to use North Korea for their political gain, while the latter features a North Korean spy who befriends a South Korean investigator to recover and eventually destroy counterfeit plates that were stolen by a North Korean criminal. These films challenge the rhetoric of the Cold War and the positioning of North Koreans as the "main enemy" of the state.

In chapter 9, Min Wha Han focuses her attention on the representation of Japan-residing Koreans in the documentary film *Uri-Hakkyo* (Our School, 2006). Han argues that Koreans in Japan who attend ethnic schools organized by the Chongryeon organization are represented simultaneously as a national other for their associations with Japan and North Korea and sympathetically as orphaned Koreans, abandoned by the paternal nation and victimized by Japan. Using *uri*, or "our-ness," as an ideograph, the documentary draws South Koreans into kinship with Korean Japanese, whose marginalization conjures shared postcolonial feelings of Japanese oppression.

In the final chapter, Alice Nahyeon Kim and Sherry S. Yu study the discursive representation of Steve Yoo, alternatively Yoo Seung-jun, in the Korean-language ethnic media in the US and the Korean-language dominant media in South Korea. A former K-pop idol, Yoo was transformed into a pariah in the Korean mediascape for pledging to fulfill his military obligations but renouncing his citizenship while visiting his family in Los Angeles. The analysis reveals that for Korean Americans, even those with native fluency like Yoo, his Koreanness was contingent upon his satisfactory performance of Korean duties. Yoo's liminality was articulated in the largely unsympathetic and vilifying coverage of him in the Korean press versus the more sympathetic coverage he received in the Korean ethnic press.

The book's conclusion brings together the findings of the ten contributions in order to understand them within the framework of anthrocategorism. The purpose, animated by a postcolonial drive to build upon local theory and understanding, is to map the cultural logics of othering in media culture in order to loosen the grip of Western knowledge production and to more fully represent the postcolonial and neocolonial nation.

NOTES

1. I put "collectivistic" in quotes because I dislike the Eurocentric implications of an individualistic-collectivistic framework, preferring concepts such as interdependent instead. However, in the interests of expediency, I use "collectivism," recognizing that it is a more widely understood, albeit problematic, term. Because my reservations are not substantive to this discussion at hand, I have used it reluctantly.

2. I have listed the authors' surnames last to fit with Western conventions. This is a problematic choice because it reifies Western naming conventions, but I make the choice to hopefully reduce confusion. There is a mix of Western names, Western first names with Korean surnames, and co-authors with Western first names and Korean first names, so for readers unfamiliar with naming conventions, I have problematically chosen clarity over ideological desirability.

REFERENCES

Ahn, Ji-Hyun. 2014. "Rearticulating Black Mixed-Race in the Era of Globalization: Hines Ward and the Struggle for Koreanness in Contemporary South Korean Media." *Cultural Studies* 28 (3): 391–417. https://doi.org/10.1080/09502386.2013.840665

Ahn, Ji-Hyun. 2015. "Desiring Biracial Whites: Cultural Consumption of White Mixed-Race Celebrities in South Korean Popular Media." *Media, Culture & Society* 37 (6): 937–47. https://doi.org/10.1177/0163443715593050

Ahn, Ji-Hyun. 2016. "Korean Multiculturalism and Its Discontents." In *Multiculturalism in East Asia: A Transnational Exploration of Japan, South Korea, and Taiwan*, edited by Koichi Iwabuchi, Hyun Mee Kim, and Hsiao-Chuan Hsia, 21–36. New York: Rowman & Littlefield.

Almaguer, Tomas. 1994. *Racial Fault Lines: The Historical Origins of White Supremacy in California*. Berkeley: University of California Press.

Bonilla-Silva, Eduardo. 2010. *Racism without Racists: Color-Blind Racism and Racial Inequality in Contemporary America*. Lanham, MD: Rowman & Littlefield.

Cawley, Kevin N. 2016. "*Back to the Future*: Recalibrating the *Myth* of Korea's Homogenous Ethnicity." *Asian Ethnicity* 17 (1): 150–60. https://doi.org/10.1080/14631369.2015.1051510

Cha, Na Young, Claire Shinhea Lee, and Ji Hoon Park. 2016. "Construction of Obedient Foreign Brides as Exotic Others: How Production Practices Construct the Images of Marriage Migrant Women on Korean Television." *International Journal of Communication* 10:1470–88.

Cheng, Sealing. 2011. "Sexual Protection, Citizenship and Nationhood: Prostituted Women and Migrant Wives in South Korea." *Journal of Ethnic and Migration Studies* 37 (10): 1627–48. https://doi.org/10.1080/1369183X.2011.613335

Cho, Hae-Joang. 1998. "Constructing and Deconstructing 'Koreanness.'" In *Making Majorities: Constituting the Nation in Japan, Korea, China, Malaysia, Fiji, Turkey, and the United States*, edited by Dru C. Gladney, 73–91. Stanford: Stanford University Press.

Choi, Jungsoon. 2010. "Educating Citizens in a Multicultural Society: The Case of South Korea." *Social Studies* 101 (4): 174–78. https://doi.org/10.1080/00377990903284153

Chung, Erin Aeran, and Daisy Kim. 2012. "Citizenship and Marriage in a Globalizing World: Multicultural Families and Monocultural Nationality Laws in Korea and Japan." *Indiana Journal of Global Legal Studies* 19 (1): 195–219.

Cumings, Bruce. 2005. *Korea's Place in the Sun: A Modern History*. Updated ed. New York: W. W. Norton.

Dyer, Richard. 1988. "White." *Screen* 29 (4): 44–64. https://doi.org/10.1093/screen/29.4.44

Dyer, Richard. 1997. *White*. New York: Routledge.

Em, Henry H. 2013. *The Great Enterprise: Sovereignty and Historiography in Modern Korea*. Durham: Duke University Press.

Flynn, Karen. 2017. "Reconfiguring Black Internationalism: English as Foreign Language Teachers of African Descent in South Korea." *Journal of African Diaspora Archaeology and Heritage* 6 (3): 262–83. https://doi.org/10.1080/21619441.2017.1385960

Fredrickson, George M. 2003. "The Historical Origins and Developments of Racism." *PBS*. https://www.pbs.org/race/000_About/002_04-background-02-01.htm. Accessed August 1, 2019.

Gabriel, John. 1998. *Whitewash: Racialized Politics and the Media*. New York: Routledge.

Gaetano, Arianne M., and Brenda S. A. Yeoh. 2010. "Introduction to the Special Issue on Women and Migration in Globalizing Asia: Gendered Experiences, Agency, and Activism." *International Migration* 48 (6): 1–12. https://doi.org/10.1111/j.1468-2435.2010.00648.x

Gage, Sue-Je L. 2014. "Almost Korean: Korean Amerasians in an Era of Multiculturalism." In *Multiethnic Korea? Multiculturalism, Migration, and Peoplehood Diversity in Contemporary South Korea*, edited by John Lie, 244–76. Berkeley: Institute of East Asian Studies.

Gilroy, Paul. 2012. "'My Britain Is Fuck All': Zombie Multiculturalism and the Race Politics of Citizenship." *Identities: Global Studies in Culture and Power* 19 (4): 380–97. https://doi.org/10.1080/1070289X.2012.725512

Goldberg, David Theo. 2006. "Racial Europeanization." *Ethnic and Racial Studies* 29 (2): 331–64. https://doi.org/10.1080/01419870500465611

Han, Geon-Soo. 2007. "Multicultural Korea: Celebration or Challenge of Multiethnic Shift in Contemporary Korea?" *Korea Journal* 47 (4): 32–63.

Han, Gil-Soo. 2015. "K-Pop Nationalism: Celebrities and Acting Blackface in the Korean Media." *Continuum: Journal of Media & Cultural Studies* 29 (1): 2–16. https://doi.org/10.1080/10304312.2014.968522

Han, Kyung-Koo. 2007. "The Archaeology of the Ethnically Homogeneous Nation-State and Multiculturalism in Korea." *Korea Journal* 47 (4): 8–31.

Höhn, Maria, and Seungsook Moon. 2010. "Introduction: The Politics of Gender, Sexuality, Race, and Class in the U.S. Military Empire." In *Over There: Living with the U.S. Military Empire from World War Two to the Present*, edited by Maria Höhn and Seungsook Moon, 1–36. Durham: Duke University Press.

Hong, Jia, and Hoonsoon Kim. 2010. "Dainjong gajeong jaehyeon tonghae bon Hanguksahwoeui damunhwa damnon TVdakyumenteori ingangeukjangeul jungshimeuro" 다인종 가정 재현을 통해 본 한국사외의 다문화 담론 TV다큐멘터리 인간극장을 중심으로 [The representation of multicultural discourse in Korean society: Analysis of TV documentary human theater]. *Hangukbangsonghakbo* 한국방송학보 [*Korean Journal of Broadcasting and Telecommunication Studies*] 24 (5): 544–83.

Hundt, David, Jessica Walton, and Soo Jung Elisha Lee. 2018. "The Politics of Conditional Citizenship in South Korea: An Analysis of the Print Media." *Journal of Contemporary Asia* 49 (3): 434–51. https://doi.org/10.1080/00472336.2018.1504111

Iwabuchi, Koichi, Hyun Mee Kim, and Hsiao-Chuan Hsia. 2016. "Rethinking Multiculturalism from a Trans-East-Asian Perspective." In *Multiculturalism in East Asia: A Transnational Exploration of Japan, South Korea and Taiwan*, edited by Koichi Iwabuchi, Hyun Mee Kim, and Hsiao-Chuan Hsia, 1–18. New York: Rowman & Littlefield.

Jeon, Gyu-Chan. 1999. "Injong'ui Hanguk munhwayeongunae baechie gwanhan gyebohwajeok gochal" 인종'의 한국 문화연구내 배치에 관한 계보화적 고찰 [A study on the place of "race" in Korean cultural studies]. *Hangukeonlonjeongbohakbo* 한국언론정보학보 [*Korean Journal of Communication*] 12:99–136.

Jirn, Jin Suh. 2014. "'Happy Seoul for Foreigners': Scenes from Multicultural Life in South Korea." *Inter-Asia Cultural Studies* 15 (2): 315–22. https://doi.org/10.1080/14649373.2014.918683

Jun, EuyRyung. 2012. "'We Have to Transform Ourselves First': The Ethics of Liberal Developmentalism and Multicultural Governance in South Korea." *Focaal: Journal of Global and Historical Anthropology* 64:99–112. https://doi.org/10.3167/fcl.2012.640109

Jun, EuyRyung. 2014. "Tolerance, *Tamunhwa*, and the Creating of the New Citizens." In *Multiethnic Korea? Multiculturalism, Migration, and Peoplehood Diversity in Contemporary South Korea*, edited by John Lie, 79–94. Berkeley: Institute of East Asian Studies, University of California, Berkeley.

Jung, Hyesil. 2016. "The Racialization of Multicultural Families by Media in a Multicultural Nation." In *Multiculturalism in East Asia: A Transnational Exploration of Japan, South Korea, and Taiwan*, edited by Koichi Iwabuchi, Hyun Mee Kim, and Hsiao-Chuan Hsia, 71–83. New York: Rowman & Littlefield.

Kang, Kyoung-Lae. 2018. "Talking Hospitality and Ethno-national Boundaries in Contemporary Korea: Considering Korean TV Shows Featuring Foreigners." *Television & New Media* 19 (1): 59–74. https://doi.org/10.1177/1527476417697196

Kim, Andrew Eungi. 2009. "Global Migration and South Korea: Foreign Workers, Foreign Brides, and the Making of a Multicultural Society." *Ethnic and Racial Studies* 32 (1): 70–92. https://doi.org/10.1080/01419870802044197

Kim, Hyuk-Rae, and Ingyu Oh. 2011. "Migration and Multicultural Contention in East Asia." *Journal of Ethnic and Migration Studies* 37 (10): 1563–81. https://doi.org/10.1080/1369183X.2011.613332

Kim, Hyun-Sook. 2006. "Hanmal 'minjok'ui tansaenggwa minjokjuui damnonui changchul minjokjuui yeoksaseosureul jungsimeuro." *Hangukdongyangjeongchisasangsayeongu* 한국동양정치사상사연구 [*Review of Korean and Asian Political Thought*] 5 (1): 117–40.

Kim, Jae Kyun. 2015. "Yellow over Black: History of Race in Korea and the New Study of Race and Empire." *Critical Sociology* 41 (2): 205–17. https://doi.org/10.1177/0896920513507787

Kim, Jinsook. 2017. "Rumors, Hatred, and the Politics of Multiculturalism: Unpacking Rumors about Jasmine Lee." *Communication, Culture, & Critique* 10:641–56. https://doi.org/10.1111/cccr.12174

Kim, Joon K. 2011. "The Politics of Culture in Multicultural Korea." *Journal of Ethnic and Migration Studies* 37 (10): 1583–1604. https://doi.org/10.1080/1369183X.2011.613333

Kim, Nadia Y. 2006a. "'Patriarchy Is So Third World': Korean Immigrant Women and 'Migrating' White Western Masculinity." *Social Problems* 53 (4): 519–36. https://doi.org/10.1525/sp.2006.53.4.519

Kim, Nadia Y. 2006b. "'Seoul—America' on America's 'Soul': South Koreans and Korean Immigrants Navigate Global White Racial Ideology." *Critical Sociology* 32 (2–3): 381–402. https://doi.org/10.1163/156916306777835231

Kim, Nadia Y. 2014. "Race-ing toward the Real South Korea: The Cases of Black-Korean Nationals and African Migrants." In *Multiethnic Korea? Multiculturalism, Migration, and Peoplehood Diversity in Contemporary South Korea*, edited by John Lie, 211–43. Berkeley: Institute of East Asian Studies.

Kim, Nam-Kook. 2009. "Multicultural Challenges in Korea: The Current Stage and a Prospect." *International Migration* 52 (2): 100–121. https://doi.org/10.1111/j.1468-2435.2009.00582.x

Kim, Nora Hui-Jung. 2014. "Korea: Multiethnic or Multicultural?" In *Multiethnic Korea? Multiculturalism, Migration, and Peoplehood Diversity in Contemporary South Korea*, edited by John Lie, 58–78. Berkeley, CA: Institute of East Asian Studies.

Kim, Nora Hui-Jung. 2015. "The Retreat of Multiculturalism? Explaining the South Korean Exception." *American Behavioral Scientist* 59 (6): 727–46. https://doi.org/10.1177/0002764214566497

Kim, Nora Hui-Jung. 2016. "Naturalizing Korean Ethnicity and Making 'Ethnic' Difference: A Comparison of North Korean Settlement and Foreign Bride Incorporation Policies in South Korea." *Asian Ethnicity* 17 (2): 185–98. https://doi.org/10.1080/14631369.2016.1151234

Kim, Sookyung. 2012. "Racism in the Global Era: Analysis of Korean Media Discourse around Migrants, 1990–2009." *Discourse & Society* 23 (6): 657–78. https://doi.org/10.1177/0957926512455381

Kim, Sumi. 2009. "Politics of Representation in the Era of Globalization: Discourse about Marriage Migrant Women in Two South Korean Films." *Asian Journal of Communication* 19 (2): 210–26. https://doi.org/10.1080/1292980902827086

Lee, Alex Jong-Seok. 2019. "Manly Colors: Masculinity and Mobility among Globalizing Korean Men." *Kalfou* 6 (2): 199–230. https://doi.org/10.15367/kf.v6i1.194

Lee, Jenny, Jae-Eun Jon, and Kiyong Byun. 2017. "Neo-racism and Neo-nationalism within East Asia: The Experiences of International Students in South Korea." *Journal of Studies in International Education* 21 (2): 136–55. https://doi.org/10.1177/1028315316669903

Lee, JongHwa, Min Wha Han, and Raymie E. McKerrow. 2010. "English or Perish: How Contemporary South Korea Received, Accommodated, and Internalized English and American Modernity." *Language and Intercultural Communication* 10 (4): 337–57. https://doi.org/10.1080/14708477.2010.497555

Lee, Kun Jong. 2015. "The Black Amerasian Experience in Korea: Representations of Black Amerasians in Korean and Korean American Narratives." *Korea Journal* 55 (1): 7–30.

Lee, Mary. 2009. "Mixed Race Peoples in the Korean National Imaginary and Family." *Korean Studies* 32:56–85. https://doi.org/10.1353/ks.0.0010

Lie, John. 2014. "Introduction: Multiethnic Korea." In *Multiethnic Korea? Multiculturalism, Migration, and Peoplehood Diversity in Contemporary South Korea*, edited by John Lie, 1–27. Berkeley, CA: Institute of East Asian Studies.

Lim, Hyung Baek. 2010. "Hanguginui jeongcheseongui damunhwajeok yoso: yeoksa-illyuhakjeok haeseok" 한국인의 정체성의 다문화적 요소: 역사-인류학적 해석 [A study on the multicultural factors of Koreans' identity: Historic-anthropological interpretation]. *Damunhwawa pyeonghwa* 다문화와 평화 [Multiculture & Peace] 4 (2): 10–43.

Lim, Timothy C. 2014. "Late Migration, Discourse, and the Politics of Multiculturalism in South Korea." In *Multiethnic Korea? Multiculturalism, Migration, and Peoplehood Diversity in Contemporary South Korea*, edited by John Lie, 31–57. Berkeley, CA: Institute of East Asian Studies.

Lipsitz, George. 1998. *The Possessive Investment in Whiteness: How White People Profit from Identity Politics*. Philadelphia: Temple University Press.

Melamed, Jodi. 2006. "The Spirit of Neoliberalism: From Racial Liberalism to Neoliberal Multiculturalism." *Social Text* 24 (4): 1–24. https://doi.org/10.1215/01642472-2006-009

Moon, Katharine H. S. 1997. *Sex among Allies: Military Prostitution in U.S.-Korea Relations*. New York: Columbia University Press.

Moon, Seungho. 2010. "Multicultural and Global Citizenship in the Transnational Age: The Case of South Korea." *International Journal of Multicultural Education* 12 (1): 1–15.

Moon, Seungsook. 2010. "Camptown Prostitution and the Imperial SOFA: Abuse and Violence against Transnational Camptown Women in South Korea." In *Over There: Living with the U.S. Military Empire from World War Two to the Present*, edited by Maria Höhn and Seungsook Moon, 337–65. Durham: Duke University Press.

Nakayama, Thomas K., and Robert L. Krizek. 1995. "Whiteness: A Strategic Rhetoric." *Quarterly Journal of Speech* 81 (3): 291–309. https://doi.org/10.1080/00335639509384117

Oh, David C. 2018. "'Racist Propaganda': Discursive Negotiations on YouTube of Perceived Anti-White Racism in South Korea." *Atlantic Journal of Communication* 26 (5): 306–17. https://doi.org/10.1080/15456870.2018.1517767

Oh, David C. 2019. "White Cyber-Protest in a Facebook Group: Articulating Colorblind Racialization in Response to Perceived South Korean Televised 'Xenophobia.'" *Journal of Asian Pacific Communication* 29 (2): 149–67.

Oh, David C. 2020. "Representing the Western Super-Minority: Desirable Cosmopolitanism and Homosocial Multiculturalism on a South Korean Talk Show." *Television & New Media* 21 (3): 260–77. https://doi.org/10.1177/1527467418789895

Oh, David C., and Chuyun Oh. 2016. "'Until *You* Are Able': South Korean Multiculturalism and Hierarchy in *My Little Hero*." *Communication, Culture, & Critique* 9 (2): 250–65. https://doi.org/10.1111/cccr.12104

Oh, David C., and Chuyun Oh. 2017. "Vlogging White Privilege Abroad: *Eat Your Kimchi*'s Eating and Spitting Out of the Korean Other on YouTube." *Communication, Culture, & Critique* 10 (4): 696–711. https://doi.org/10.1111/cccr.12180

Omi, Michael, and Howard Winant. 1994. *Racial Formations in the United States: From the 1960s to the 1990s*. 2nd ed. New York: Routledge.

Pieterse, Jan Nederveen. 1992. *White on Black: Images of Africa and Blacks in Western Popular Culture*. Translated by Jan Nederveen Pieterse. New Haven: Yale University Press.

Prey, Robert. 2011. "Different Takes—Migrant World Television and Multiculturalism in South Korea." *Global Media Journal—Canadian Edition* 4 (1): 109–25.

Said, Edward W. 1978. *Orientalism*. New York: Vintage Books.

Schattle, Hans. 2015. "Global Citizenship as a National Project: The Evolution of *Segye Shimin* in South Korean Public Discourse." *Citizenship Studies* 19 (1): 53–68. https://doi.org/10.1080/13621025.2014.883835

Seol, Dong-Hoon, and Jungmin Seo. 2014. "Dynamics of Ethnic Nationalism and Hierarchal Nationhood: Korean Nation and Its Otherness since the Late 1980s." *Korea Journal* 54 (2): 5–33.

Shah, Hemant, and Michael C. Thornton. 1994. "Racial Ideology in U.S. Mainstream News Magazine Coverage of Black-Latino Interaction, 1980–1992." *Critical Studies in Mass Communication* 11:141–61.

Shim, Doobo. 2014. "The Cyber Bullying of Pop Star Tablo and South Korean Society: Hegemonic Discourses on Educational Background and Military Service." *Acta Koreana* 17 (1): 479–504.

Shim, Doobo, and Joseph Sung-Yul Park. 2008. "The Language Politics of 'English Fever' in South Korea." *Korea Journal* 48 (2): 136–59.

Shin, Gi-Wook. 2006. *Ethnic Nationalism in Korea: Genealogy, Politics, and Legacy*. Stanford: Stanford University Press.

Shin, Jaran. 2019. "The Vortex of Multiculturalism in South Korea: A Critical Discourse Analysis of the Characterization of 'Multicultural Children' in Three Newspapers." *Communication and Critical/Cultural Studies* 16 (1): 61–81. https://doi.org/10.1080/14791420.2019.1590612

Shohat, Ella, and Robert Stam. 1994. *Unthinking Eurocentrism: Multiculturalism and the Media*. New York: Routledge.

Shome, Raka. 2000. "Outing Whiteness." *Critical Studies in Media Communication* 17 (3): 366–71. https://doi.org/10.1080/15295030009388402

Shome, Raka, and Radha S. Hegde. 2002. "Postcolonial Approaches to Communication: Charting the Terrain, Engaging the Intersections." *Communication Theory* 12 (3): 249–70. https://doi.org/10.1111/j.1468-2885.2002.tb00269.x

Sorby, Stella. 2008. "Translating News from English to Chinese: Complimentary and Derogatory Language Usage." *Babe* 54 (1): 19–35. https://doi.org/10.1075/babel.54.1.03sor

Stam, Robert, and Ella Shohat. 2012. "Whence and Whither Postcolonial Theory?" *New Literary History* 43 (2): 371–90. https://doi.org/10.1353/nlh.2012.0010

Tai, Eika. 2004. "'Korean Japanese': A New Identity Option for Resident Koreans in Japan." *Critical Asian Studies* 36 (3): 355–82. https://doi.org/10.1080/1467271042000241586

Tikhonov, Vladimir. 2013. "The Race and Racism Discourses in Modern Korea, 1890s–1910s." *Korean Studies* 36:31–57.

Waisbord, Silvio, and Claudia Mellado. 2014. "De-Westernizing Communication Studies: A Reassessment." *Communication Theory* 24 (4): 361–72. https://doi.org/10.1111/comt.12044

West, Cornel. 2004. "The New Cultural Politics of Difference." In *The Cultural Studies Reader*, 2nd ed., edited by Simon During, 257–67. New York: Routledge.

Yang, Eun-Kyung. 2010. "Minjogui yeogijuwa wigyejeok minjokseongui damnon guseong joseonilboui joseonjok damnon bunseok" 민족의 역이주와 위계적 민족성의 담론 구성 조선일보의 조선족 담론 분석 [Ethnic return migration and the discursive construction of hierarchical nationhood: The case of Korean-Chinese discourse on Chosun Ilbo]. *Hangukbangsonghakbo* 한국방송학보 [Korean Journal of Broadcasting and Telecommunication Studies] 9:194–237.

Yi, Joseph, and Gowoon Jung. 2015. "Debating Multicultural Korea: Media Discourse on Migrants and Minorities in South Korea." *Journal of Ethnic and Migration Studies* 41 (6): 985–1013. https://doi.org/10.1080/1369183X.2014.1002202

Yoon, Sunny. 2015. "Taming the Primitive: Multiculturalism and the Anthropological Vision of South Korean Media." *Visual Anthropology* 28:422–37. https://doi.org/10.1080/08949468.2015.1086209

Yoon, Tae-Il, Kyung-Hee Kim, and Han-Jin Eom. 2011. "The Border-Crossing of Habitus: Media Consumption, Motives, and Reading Strategies among Asian Immigrant Women in South Korea." *Media, Culture & Society* 33 (3): 415–31. https://doi.org/10.1177/0163443710394901

PART 1

Mediating the Racial and Ethnic Other

1

Aspirational Interraciality and Desirable Whiteness

South Korean Media Depictions of Interracial Intimacies between White Women and Cosmopolitan South Korean Men

Min Joo Lee

In the twenty-first century, mainstream Korean television entertainment programs have been portraying certain interracial relationships as aspirational and laudatory. These interracial relationships involve cosmopolitan Korean men and Western White women. In this chapter, I critically analyze Korean mainstream media depictions of three interracial couples: rapper Beenzino and his German girlfriend, Stephanie Michova; soccer player Joo-ho Park and his Swiss wife, Anna Park; and singer Hyun-joon Kim and his Italian wife, Christina Confalonieri. I argue that media representations construct these White women as desirable "others" and the men as successful cosmopolitans. In contrast to the prevalent discourse of impurity and shame, which have been associated with interracial and interethnic relationships throughout Korean history, these three relationships are portrayed as pinnacles of modernity that others—particularly Korean men—should aspire toward. I ask the question, Why and how do media portray these relationships as aspirational? I suggest that the glorified depictions of these interracial relationships are interconnected with particularly salient misogyny that has plagued women in Korea since the early twenty-first century.

As an ethnic Korean female scholar who resides in the US, my contact with Korean culture mainly occurs in two ways: via conversations with friends and relatives residing in Korea and through the internet. Throughout the years, as I talked to my friends and relatives, they noted the rise in the use of new misogynistic terminology in Korean online forums. When I browsed various Korean websites that feature user-generated content, I also noticed an uptick in the use of misogynistic terminology.

Internet forums in Korea popularized many derogatory terms regarding women of Korean ethnicity. For instance, the nickname *Doenjang-nyeo* (된장녀), meaning soybean paste girl, stigmatizes young Korean women as vain and materialistic. These women are characterized as enjoying expensive Starbucks coffee that costs as much as a meal, dressing up in foreign luxury brands, and maintaining such vain lifestyles by leeching off of their boyfriends because they personally lack the finances to maintain such luxurious lifestyles (Jinsook Kim 2018). Similarly, the derogatory nickname *Kimchi-nyeo* (김치녀) refers to "Korean women who appeal to men and encroach on men's rights while insisting on gender equality" (158). The proliferation of such judgmental terminology indicates some Koreans' extreme dissatisfaction with contemporary Korean femininity. These terms imply that Korean women are burdensome to men and detrimental to society at large. I suggest that mainstream television entertainment programs cater to these gendered frictions by pointing to interracial relationships as ideal types of relationships and to Western White women as perfect partners for cosmopolitan Korean men.

Mainstream media idealize Western White women by juxtaposing them with Korean women, who are portrayed as inadequate subjects for Korean men's affection. Korean women are portrayed in one of two ways: one, as women who, in pursuit of modern femininity, have lost their "traditional" feminine ways, and two, as women who were never modern enough to be suitable partners for cosmopolitan Korean men. Meanwhile, Western White women are seen as modern women who can strike a perfect balance between tradition and modernity. Women are pitted against each other to satisfy patriarchal notions of ideal femininity that is positioned somewhere in between modernity and tradition. Amy Sueyoshi (2018) notes how, throughout history, US media used essentialist images of Asian women to deter the burgeoning feminist movement among White American women. These media juxtaposed stereotypes of Asian women as docile "geishas" who revere and honor their husbands with stereotypes of White feminists as angry and anti-patriarchal (Sueyoshi 2018). The media also portrayed White men in relationships with Asian women in order to discipline White American women and to warn them that, if they do not embody femininity that is more pleasing to patriarchy, they will no longer be desirable to White men (Marchetti 1994; Sueyoshi 2018). In the Korean media that I analyze in this chapter, such cross-racial comparison between White women and Asian women is happening in reverse: rather than criticizing White femininity, the media serve to uphold White femininity as ideal and Korean femininity as deficient. In the following section, I contextualize my argument by examining the history of interracial relationships in Korea and how they shaped femininity and masculinity.

Masculinity, Race, and Interracial Intimacy

Throughout Korean history, women were subject to more transnational intimacies than men. During Japanese colonialism, transnationally intimate relationships meant those between Japanese men and Korean women, and later they referred to those between Korean women and US soldiers stationed in Korea. Many folks comprehend these relationships as symbolic of Korea's—particularly men's—powerlessness and women's defilement, as they "often reminded South Koreans of foreign invasion or a betrayal of nationalism" (M. Kim 2014, 304). These negative connotations are, in part, due to misogynistic nationalism, which defines women as "carriers of nationalist wombs to deliver heirs and potential warriors who can defend the nation" (Moon 1998, 52). In such discourse, women's value as human beings is boiled down to their reproductive abilities. To deliver "pure" Korean heirs, women are expected to be "chaste and vigilant against foreign males and, by extension, masculine foreign power" (Kim and Choi 2012, 14). Masculinity is also influenced by such misogynistic nationalism, which views women as property that men should "protect" from foreign men.

Discourses of Korean masculinity are formulated through transnational and transracial comparisons to foreign masculinity (Creighton 2009). For instance, in Elisabeth Schober's research (2014), Korean men complained that US soldiers did not treat them as real men. Popular culture also makes a note of the transracial masculine competitions between Korean men and foreign men. A popular music video entitled "Itaewon Freedom," featuring the famous comedian Se-yoon Yu, shows Korean women rejecting Korean men's sexual advances for that of foreign men (Schober 2014, 48). The music video portrays women's rejection of Korean men in comedic fashion, but in reality Korean women who have intimate relations with foreign men are often deemed as traitors who spurned

Korean men (Soh 2004). For instance, throughout Korean history, women who engaged in interracial and interethnic relationships were called various derogatory names, including *Yang-gongju* (양공주), meaning Yankee whore, and *Hwanhyang-nyeo* (환향녀), meaning women who returned to Korea after they were taken abroad and defiled by foreign men. In these ways, discourses of Korean masculinity have been formulated in relation to foreign masculinity and the real and assumed power hierarchy between these masculinities; this hierarchy is based on which group of men has easier sexual access to women. In such a hierarchical masculine model, Western men are victors who conquered and gained access to Korean women, while Korean men are the defeated ones who figuratively lost their women. Such a sentiment of masculine defeat is the context within which contemporary media formulate discourses of interracial relationships between Korean men and foreign women.

While women who have intimate relations with foreign men are deemed traitors, men who have relations with foreign women are deemed national heroes:

> Korean men who have sex with foreign women may beam with (national) pride—"sticking the Korean flag pole (on a foreign land)" *(taekukirulkotda)* is a popular phrase to endorse such a feat. Furthermore, sex with a white woman, popularly known as "riding a white horse" *(paekmarultada)* remains the fantasy of many Korean men. (Cheng 2000, 67)

Korean men are exalted as those who won the sexual competition against Western men. Some men describe their one-night stands with foreign women as a means of getting even with Western men, who for a long time had intimate access to Korean women (M. Lee 2020). According to a survey conducted by Joon Kim and May Fu (2008), a majority of their Korean male participants claimed to favor White women as intimate partners above women of other races and ethnicities. According to Kim and Fu, "Many Korean men actively seek out Russian women because they satisfy not only their desire for dominance over exotic females but also the latent psychological need to overcome a racial inferiority complex" (2008, 512). As per Kim and Fu's assertion, racial inferiority complex may be one of the driving forces for interracial relationships between Korean men and White women. However, I do not believe that it is the sole factor. I suggest that the sexual and racial politics of interracial relationships between Korean men and White women extend beyond the framework of racial inferiority.

Due to rapid economic development, modernization, and the transnational popularity of Korean popular culture, Koreanness now centers around a sense of pride and superiority rather than presumed inferiority to other nations or cultures (Jeongmee Kim 2014; M. Lee 2021). Therefore, a discourse of racial inferiority complex in mainstream media is limited. Rather, in the television programs that I will analyze in this chapter, Korean men's interracial intimacies with White women are portrayed as proof of their—and, by extent, the Korean nation's—global competence and appeal.

In the introduction to this book, David Oh states that Korean notions of cosmopolitanism are intertwined with Whiteness and masculinity, whereby Western White men become epitomes of cosmopolitanism, modernity, and strength. I agree with Oh's claim. Research studies on Korean media examine how they portray Western men as ideal cosmopolitan subjects (Oh 2020; Yoon 2015; Ahn 2015). At the same time, I suggest that Western White men are not the only group of people who are defined as pinnacles of cosmopolitanism; many Koreans see themselves as increasingly cosmopolitan (Cho 2012; H. Lee 2011). Reflecting these popular sentiments, in mainstream media, which I will analyze in the following sections, Korean men are portrayed to be just as cosmopolitan as Western White men. Their cosmopolitanism is marked by their successful transnational education, their career, their romantic and non-patriarchal behaviors, and, most importantly, their ability to woo Western White women.

The White female partners to the cosmopolitan Korean men are portrayed as those who admire the supposedly cosmopolitan Korean men and who further help shape them into global citizens. These women are not described through assimilationist discourses. Rather, they are deemed to be valuable to Korea and Korean men because of their transnational backgrounds, which make them stand apart from Korean women. The women I analyze in this chapter have some resemblance to those who are called WAGS (wives and girlfriends of sports stars). Existing scholarship on WAGS analyzes these group of women through the intersection of gender and class (Clayton and Harris 2004; Marks 2019; Millican and Emmers-Sommer 2020). However, few research studies examine such relationships through the framework of race. I employ the intersection of race and gender as a focal framework through which to critically analyze media depictions of interracial relationships between Korean men and Western White women.

Cosmopolitan Romance with a Devoted White Girlfriend

Beenzino is a rapper who revealed his intimate relationship with German model Stefanie Michova to the public. After that, whenever he made an appearance on a television talk show, he was coerced into discussing the details of his interracial relationship. For example, when Beenzino appears as a special guest on the television program *Video Star* (MBC Every 1 2019), one of the four female hosts asks Beenzino, "I heard that you advise other male celebrities who are contemplating going public about their romantic relationships to become their girlfriends' dog. Is that true?"[1] All four female hosts stare at Beenzino with curiosity as Beenzino responds, "As men, when our relationships become public, our images do not suffer. For women, it is a different story. They have to be courageous to have publicly open relationships. That is why men need to be devoted and good to their girlfriends as if we are their dogs." One of the female hosts says, "You really know your way toward women's hearts!" The female hosts interpret Beenzino's recommendation that boyfriends be subordinate to their girlfriends as a sign of his romanticism.

Romance is often associated with cultural refinement: "It has long been taken for granted that romantic love is the fruit of cultural refinements and not an experience readily available or accessible to non-Westerners in general. . . . The hidden inference of this assumption may be that romantic love is the prize or reward of true culture" (Jankowiak 1997, 1). More specifically, men's romantic love has been defined as a marker of cultural modernity (Lipset 2004). In Korea, men's romantic behaviors have been defined as representative of modernity and as the antithesis of patriarchy and cultural backwardness (N. Kim 2006). The Korean women whom Nadia Kim (2006) interviewed claimed that they aspired to be in relationships with White American men based on their assumption that White men are more modern and thereby more romantic compared to patriarchal Korean men. By portraying Beenzino as romantically subordinate, the television program implied that he was non-patriarchal and thereby a properly modernized subject.

At the same time, the television program noted that his romantic behaviors were for women who were worthy of them. One of the female hosts asks Beenzino, "What made you fall in love with her?" Beenzino chuckles sheepishly and says, "I think it was because of her rustic mannerisms." A male guest on the program who is also a friend of Beenzino adds, "What he means to say is that she is humble and frugal." Beenzino describes how they went shopping in New York; he wanted to buy her some expensive presents, but she started to cry and said that she did not like expensive presents or an exuberant lifestyle. While Beenzino is talking, the camera zooms in on the female hosts' faces as they appear shocked at hearing that a woman would cry and refuse an expensive present from a boyfriend. With wide eyes and mouth agape, one of the female hosts mutters, "There are women like that?" Beenzino smiles and says, "That is the trip where I fell in love with her; I realized that she is not superficial." The female hosts tell each other, "Yes, that is how women should be. We should learn from her." The program compared Michova's frugality with Korean women's purported extravagance. *Video Star* juxtaposed Korean women, represented by the four female hosts, with Michova to suggest that Korean women are inadequate to be partners to cosmopolitan and romantic men such as Beenzino because of their superficial behaviors.

The television program, Beenzino, and the female hosts juxtaposed Michova's frugality and economic independence (i.e., not asking Beenzino for gifts) with the popular critique of Korean women as gold diggers. As I mentioned at the beginning of this chapter, in recent years, Korean women have been lumped together as a group and critiqued for supposedly maintaining exuberant Westernized lifestyles beyond their means, often at their boyfriends' expense (Jinsook Kim 2018). The television program indicates that such *doenjang-nyeo* and *kimchi-nyeo*, who receive expensive gifts from their boyfriends, should relearn proper modern femininity (i.e., economic independence) from Western White women such as Michova. These comparisons especially critique Korean women's power as consumers: they are portrayed as those who not only expend too much on luxury goods but also extort expensive gifts from their boyfriends. Discourses about these women portray them as excessive and problematic consumers who assert their rights as consumers without bearing the duties (i.e., paying for the items they purchase). Such discourse that portrays Korean women as asserting their rights without carrying out their duties repeats itself regarding issues of the Korean mandatory military service.

In Korea, only men are required to fulfill the compulsory military service; women are exempt from it. Such gender disparity has long been a source of anti-feminist resentment (Han, Lee, and Park 2017; S. Kim 2015). Some Korean men claim that Korean women are "opportunistic types who abandon traditional responsibilities and only pursue their own interests" (Han, Lee, and Park 2017, 73). These men claim that Korean women are a group of selfish women who neither contribute to Korea's advancement nor share men's burden of sustaining national safety and prosperity.

In direct contrast, the media defined Michova as a loyal and dedicated girlfriend who supported her boyfriend through hardship. She is portrayed as embodying loyal and dedicated femininity, which Korean women supposedly no longer abide by. For example, a popular entertainment news program begins its news story of Beenzino and Michova with a grainy video taken on someone's cell phone (SBS Entertainment 2019). In the video, Beenzino gives Michova a pair of Korean traditional rubber shoes and explains the meaning of the gift: "Never wear these shoes the other way. In Korea, that means a girlfriend will cheat on her boyfriend who went to the military." Michova chuckles and says, "Oh, okay," while staring at the rubber shoes in Beenzino's hands. They speak in English, which serves as a direct contrast to how Southeast Asian marriage migrants to Korea are expected to speak in Korean. The Southeast Asian migrant brides are often coerced to swiftly and fully assimilate into Korean culture (Lim 2010). Through social pressure and surveillance, these migrant brides are forced to change their names, renounce their cultural heritage, and abide by Korean norms of domesticity and motherhood (Lee, Kim, and Lee 2015). Those who are unsuccessful in their assimilation into Korean culture are heavily chastised by society at large (Shin 2019). The migrant brides, their multiethnic children, and the presumed social problems that arise due to multiculturalism are deemed inevitable outcomes of Korean women's selfishness and the low birthrate in contemporary Korea. In contrast, the newscaster did not comment on how Beenzino and Michova were communicating in English; the news program seemed to take it for granted that the couple should communicate in English rather than Michova assimilating into Korean culture and speaking in Korean. Their English dialogue served to affirm Beenzino's cosmopolitanism.

The scene changes to a montage of photos of Beenzino in uniform, and the male newscaster claims that Beenzino successfully fulfilled his mandatory military service because of Michova's assurance that she will not cheat on him. The news clip shows Michova's Instagram posts, where she professed her longing for Beenzino. The newscaster states, "Michova is wholeheartedly empathizing with Beenzino and sharing his burden. . . . She is amazing because Michova stood by Beenzino even though it must have been difficult for her to understand why Korean men have to fulfill their mandatory military service." The news program described Michova as a loyal girlfriend who shared in Beenzino's duties as a Korean citizen by remaining loyal and providing him with emotional support throughout his mandatory military service. These discourses directly juxtaposed Michova against popular critique of Korean women that describes them as selfish women who only reap the benefits of citizenship without bearing the responsibilities.

Michova is characterized as someone who is deserving of cosmopolitan Korean men's romantic behaviors due to her divergence from the discourses of selfish Korean femininity. Rather than being required to assimilate into Korean culture, she is positioned as someone who can teach Korean women about being proper (i.e., frugal and loyal) spouses for Korean men. Michova's Whiteness makes her appear modern, and at the same time the television programs emphasize her traditionalism. She appears to fulfill the double bind that many women face of having to appear modern and traditional at the same time. Through media depictions, Michova becomes an ideal woman who, as a popular model, could have had other intimate partners, including White men, but instead chose Beenzino. The media discourses portray her choice of a Korean partner as legitimating Korean men's cosmopolitanism and erotic desirability. As I analyze further in this chapter, Michova is not the only Western White woman whom television programs portray as an ideal spouse to cosmopolitan Korean men; many Western White women are depicted as modern women who simultaneously embody "traditionally" feminine qualities. They are juxtaposed with Korean women, who are portrayed as either too backward or, ironically, too Westernized to be appealing to cosmopolitan Korean men.

Korean Men's Sexual Desirability and White Women's Sexual Availability

Christina Confalonieri is an Italian woman married to a Korean classical singer. She gained popularity in mainstream media due to her humor, Korean fluency, and hypersexuality. In her appearance on the popular television program *Radio Star*, one of the male hosts asks her how she ended up in Korea (MBC Entertainment 2013). Confalonieri describes the sacrifices she had to make for love:

> Since young, I had a dream to go work for an international organization. I went to Belgium and actually managed to get a job at the UN, but at that moment, I met the love of my life. . . . The time came that my husband finished studying and had to return to Korea. So at that point, I had to choose between love and work. I captured love.

The price of loving a Korean man is equated with a dream job at the UN. When Confalonieri explains that her husband is a musical elite who went to Italy to study classical music, the hosts nod in approval and claim that he is indeed an elite and cosmopolitan man who is worthy of such sacrifice. The camera zooms in on the male guests and the hosts clapping at her story of sacrifice. Similar to Michova, whom the television programs described through a discourse of sacrifice and loyalty, Confalonieri is also lauded as a woman who knows when to make sacrifices to capture a chance at a romantic relationship with a cosmopolitan Korean man. Her television appearance serves to emphasize the desirability of Korean men as intimate partners to Western White women.

On television programs where she appeared alongside her husband, Confalonieri is portrayed as a hypersexual partner who always sexually pursues her stoic husband. On the television program *Always a Guest* (*Baek-nyeon Sonnim*), the male hosts express gleefulness and envy while observing Confalonieri seducing her husband (SBS Entertainment 2018a). Typically, the program entails a panel of observers in a studio watching and commenting on a husband who visits and spends time at his in-laws' home. The viewers and the observers make fun of the awkwardness between the husbands and the in-laws. However, when Confalonieri and her husband appeared as guests on the show, instead of visiting Confalonieri's parents, they visited an elderly Korean couple's home in a rural part of Korea. While the original format of the program is geared toward ridiculing the husbands, in Confalonieri's case, the program reconfigured its format so that the husband was not the object of the humor. Rather, the program focused on the interactions between the old Korean couple and Confalonieri. In one of the scenes, the old couple, their son-in-law, Confalonieri, and her husband sit around a dinner table and Confalonieri feeds her husband a piece of Korean pancake (SBS Entertainment 2018b). The camera captures the shocked reactions from the old couple. The elderly woman attempts to dispel the awkwardness by commenting to Confalonieri, "Your husband looks so young. He looks as though he is a high school student." Confalonieri retorts, "He looks so young because I treat him well." Hearing this, the elderly woman's son-in-law states that the elderly woman should learn from Confalonieri about how to treat her husband well. Confalonieri recommends that the elderly woman begin by expressing intimacy with her husband. The elderly woman shakes her head and shuts her eyes as if to remove herself from the situation, but the son-in-law and Confalonieri insist that she be intimate with her husband. The elderly woman shouts that she is not used to such acts and does not want to express intimacy. However, the camera shows a close-up of the elderly husband, and the subtitle on-screen under his face says, "I can be good at intimacy," as if to imply that the husband is actually looking forward to his wife's expressions of intimacy but that the wife is rejecting his desires.[2] Confalonieri states that in Italy old couples pat each other's behinds as signs of affection and encourages the elderly couple to do the same. When the elderly woman shows no desire to engage in such intimate behavior, her husband approaches her and pats her on her behind. Here, the elderly woman is portrayed as ignoring her husband's desires for intimacy and being too sexually restrained. The television program shows Confalonieri teaching a Korean woman how to express intimacy.

In Korea, public displays of sexuality are taboo (M. Kim 2014), which may explain the elderly woman's aversion to engaging in intimate behavior in front of her son-in-law, another couple, and the entire television camera crew. However, instead of applauding the woman's sexually reserved attitude that abides by Korean social norms, the program problematizes her stoicism. As if to contrast the elderly woman's sexual rejection of her husband to Confalonieri's hypersexuality, the next scene of the television program depicts Confalonieri and her husband in their room. As soon as they enter the room, she jumps into her husband's arms and showers him with kisses and hugs. The men in the studio who are observing the couple let out gleeful shouts at Confalonieri's sexual assertiveness. The program uses computer graphics to insert pinkish hues onto the male observers' cheeks as if they are blushing. While her husband is sitting on the bed, she sits on top of his outstretched legs and inches closer to his torso and bounces up and down in a very sexual pose. The background music changes into a sticky tune as the observers in the studio—particularly the Korean men—shout and clap in shock and envy while the female observers ask, "Is she allowed to do that on television?" On-screen, as if to respond to the female observers' queries, the subtitle states, "One does not need social permission to show intimacy." In the program, the Korean women in the studio, as well as the elderly Korean woman, are portrayed as prudish women who are not sexual enough to satisfy Korean men.

Feminist research studies have indicated that non-Western cultures police their women's chastity by pointing to Western women as hypersexual and immoral women (Espiritu 2001; Nader 1989). According to these studies, non-Western cultures use gendered and moralist discourse to critique Western cultures and to position their own cultures as morally superior to Western culture based on women's sexual chastity. However, in Korean mainstream television programs, Western White women, rather than being critiqued for their hypersexuality, were lauded for their sexuality. Furthermore, these Western White women were upheld as ideal women whom Korean women should emulate and learn from in order to become ideal intimate partners who can sexually satisfy Korean men.

The effect of television programs portraying Confalonieri's sexuality is twofold. First, as represented by the scene where Confalonieri teaches the elderly woman about expressing affection toward her husband, the program problematized Korean women's sexual reserve. Second, by juxtaposing Confalonieri's hypersexuality with the relatively more subdued behavior of her husband, the television program portrayed Confalonieri as actively pursuing cosmopolitan Korean men because of their desirability. One's ability to be desirable to women has long been a mark of successful heterosexual masculinity (M. Kim 2014; Creighton 2009). The television programs, *Always a Guest?* and *Radio Star*, suggest that cosmopolitan Korean men are globally desirable intimate partners and that Western White women truly know how to appreciate Korean men's value.

Thus far, I have analyzed media depictions of interracial relationships where the couples do not have multiracial children. Throughout history, multiracial Koreans have been among the most stigmatized groups of individuals because of their supposed ethnic "impurity." This begs the question: How do television entertainment programs portray Western White women as maternal figures? Are they portrayed in an equally favorable light as the women I have analyzed thus far in the chapter?

The Western White "Wise Mother and Good Wife" and Her Cosmopolitan Interracial Children

Joo-ho Park is a soccer player who played in the European league. Although he was already popular among soccer fans, he garnered mainstream popularity when he appeared on the popular television entertainment program *Return of Superman*. From the program, the viewers found out that he was married to a Swiss woman, Anna Park, and had three interracial children named Naeun, Gunhoo, and Jinwoo. Through the depiction of this family, the program emphasizes the benefits of interracial relationships. More specifically, the program emphasizes White women's beauty and how they educate their children to become independent and cosmopolitan subjects (KBS Antenna 2019). The camera voyeuristically shows Naeun, the couple's daughter, waking up in the morning and making her way to the living room. Her face is covered by her long curly brown hair. When she arrives in the living room and turns her face toward the camera in slow motion, the program captures her in a manner that is similar to the way romantic comedies portray female protagonists from the love-struck male protagonists' gaze. The commentators on the show, a married Korean couple, describe her as a "Suri Cruise lookalike."[3] Suri Cruise's photo appears beside Naeun's photograph on-screen. Looking at the photos, the male commentator states, "Wait, I think Naeun is actually better-looking than Suri Cruise. Her face is like a piece of art." He looks at his wife and says, "If we have a daughter, she is not going to be as beautiful as Naeun, is she?" The wife says, "Absolutely not. You should wish for something realistic." Naeun, a mixed-race girl, is portrayed as aesthetically superior to both the Western White girl—Suri Cruise—and Korean girls. Her multiraciality is portrayed not as a detriment but as something that improves upon monoethnic femininity.

Not only is Naeun portrayed as aesthetically superior to monoethnic girls, but the program also emphasizes how cosmopolitan she is at such a young age. The family sits around a table to eat breakfast. The program portrays a montage of conversations between different members of the family and keeps a tally of how many languages they speak at the table. When the filming crew asks Anna Park about Naeun's multilingualism, she responds, "She can speak German, she speaks English, and since April, she's been talking in Korean with her Korean family, and with my family, she speaks in Spanish mostly with my mother. We are not pushing her to learn all the languages. She is just learning through her daily life." Repeatedly, through consecutive episodes, the program emphasizes Naeun's multilingualism by having her interact with her father's foreign colleagues as well as tourists from different countries.

Naeun's multilingualism and beauty are mostly credited to her mother. The program introduces Anna Park as a multilingual and multicultural woman who can speak Spanish, English, French, Korean, German, and Italian. There is a parallel in how the program emphasizes Anna Park's beauty and Naeun's beauty. Anna Park awakes from sleep and walks into the living room. The camera captures her in slow motion, and the subtitle on-screen states, "Even when she just awoke from sleep, she looks beautiful enough to be in a commercial." The narrators say in an astonished tone, "Wow, she does not look like a mother to two children." The scene resembles the way the camera captured Naeun and the ways in which the narrators gushed at her beauty.

Not only is Anna Park valued for her beautiful appearance, but she is also portrayed as an ideal wife and mother who embodies modernity and traditionalism at the same time. She is viewed as the epitome of the traditional female ideal of "wise mother and good wife" (현모양처). The program emphasizes how Anna Park, a "wise mother," raises her children in "European style." After the family finishes breakfast, Anna Park asks Naeun to help clean the table. The narrators state, "In Europe, they teach children these practical life skills so they can grow to be independent individuals." Naeun wipes the dishes dry while her mother washes them. The program utilizes sound effects of people oohing and aahing as if in admiration of how capable Naeun is at domestic work at such a young age. Asking children to help with house chores is not necessarily a European child-rearing technique per se. Nonetheless, the television program claims that Anna Park's child-rearing approach is a "Western" style that specializes in nurturing children's independence. She is admired for bringing such a modern perspective into child-rearing. In other words, her different cultural background is perceived to be beneficial to her children.

Academic research has indicated that marriage migrants to Korea often experience precarious motherhood. For example, "when a child enters school, the existence of a 'foreign' mother would show up in the official documents; they had often heard that children were discriminated against in school, so these women consider acquiring citizenship before their children's entry to school" (Lee, Kim, and Lee 2015, 418). Newspaper reports describe multicultural Korean children as somehow deficient (Shin 2019). Various "problems" that the mixed-race or multicultural children may have, including their lack of Korean language fluency or problematic behaviors, are all attributed to the marriage migrants from developing nations, who are perceived as inadequate mothers (Lee, Kim, and Lee 2015). Their child-rearing techniques and motherhood are questioned continuously by media and the culture at large out of fear that they are somehow raising and populating Korea with inadequately modernized Koreans. On the contrary, the mainstream television entertainment program *Return of Superman* portrays Anna Park as the ideal mother to raise future generation of cosmopolitan Koreans. She is seen as someone who brings advanced Western child-rearing knowledge to Korea. Her Whiteness and European affiliations grant her the status as an ideal and modernized mother in media.

While Anna Park abides by the so-called Western child-rearing doctrine, the program also emphasizes how she teaches her children to be proper Koreans. For example, at the breakfast table, Naeun calls out to the camera crew to sit next to her at the table. However, instead of using honorific Korean, as is appropriate for addressing older people, Naeun rudely says to the camera crew, "Come to me and sit." The moment those words leave her mouth, the camera zooms in on Joo-ho Park and Anna Park as they tell Naeun in unison to say instead "Please sit here." They both correct Naeun's rude behavior. The subtitle on-screen states, "They are strict in teaching Naeun Korean honorifics." Anna Park, while advocating "Western" child-rearing philosophy, is also portrayed as a mother who teaches her children how to be respectful Koreans. The implication here is that although they are a cosmopolitan and modern family, their Koreanness is not compromised.

The program not only portrays Anna Park educating Naeun about proper Korean manners but also depicts her expertly cooking Korean food as a "good wife" should do for her husband. As Anna Park cooks, the program's background music turns into a tune from the transnationally popular television drama *Jewel in the Palace* (*Daejanggeum*)—a program credited with popularizing Korean food around the world. The camera captures a close-up of Anna Park frying egg whites and yolks and cutting them into thin slices. The male narrator of the show states, "She has quite a bit of Korean cooking skill," while the female narrator remarks, "I agree. It is tough to get fried egg whites and yolks to have that vivid of a color." As Anna Park pours rice cakes into a steaming bowl of broth, the subtitle on the screen states that she is a "Blond Janggeum." Janggeum is the name of the female protagonist in the *Jewel in the Palace*. By this comparison, the program implies that Anna Park, albeit phenotypically different from "typical" Korean women, is an expert at Korean cuisine. Both the female and the male narrators applaud her Korean culinary skills. She becomes the prototypical image of the "wise mother and good wife" (현모양처) who is good at raising well-behaved children and knows how to cook for her husband.

The relationship between Anna Park and Joo-ho Park is framed through discourses of the Western White woman sacrificing her career in order to maintain her intimacy with the Korean man. Joo-ho Park explains that Anna Park "married me at a young age of twenty-three and gave up her dreams. She became a mother at a young age and had to bear the burden of raising two children alone because I am away from home for months at a time during the soccer season." Romantic love and women's ability to choose their romantic partners have been associated with modernity, liberalism, and individualism (M. Lee 2019). In Korea, during the Enlightenment period, individuals who chose their romantic partners as opposed to abiding by familial expectations and arrangements were deemed modernized subjects (Kwon 2005). Therefore, by emphasizing how they made their romantic choices, the television programs emphasize Anna Park's and Christina Confalonieri's modernity. At the same time, the women are portrayed as "traditionally" feminine in that they sacrificed their careers for romance. The television programs describe their romantic choices through discourses of sacrifice—the kind of sacrifice that contemporary Korean women are supposedly refusing to make nowadays. Hence, through discourses of romantic choice and sacrifice, Western White women are cast as ideal women who are the new embodiments of the "wise mother and good wife."

Conclusion

In this chapter, I critically analyzed the depictions of three interracial couples on television entertainment programs. Through these examples, I argued that contemporary Korean media portrayed interracial relationships between Korean men and Western White women as ideal forms of intimacy. These interracial relationships were not defined through discourses of the defilement of Korean ethnic purity. Rather, they were portrayed as a means to help Korea expand its boundaries of national influence. Here, Western White women were not portrayed as those who made Korea a modern nation; Korean men were credited with such a feat. Korean men were portrayed as cosmopolitan and successful men who were erotically appealing and competitive on the global stage. Their interracial relationships with White women served as proof of their cosmopolitanism, and at the same time, through these relationships, they were seen as benefitting Korea at large by bringing their White female partners to Korea as role models who can show other Koreans—especially Korean women—ways of becoming proper cosmopolitan subjects. While Korean men were seen as appropriately modern subjects, Korean women were portrayed as those who needed to be reeducated about proper modernity because they were either too traditional (e.g., too sexually reserved) or over-the-top modern (e.g., irreverent of patriarchy).

The mainstream media's idealization of interracial relationships and Western White women indicates how Korea's prioritization of ethnic purity has given way to a form of national identity that revolves around desires to be a modern and cosmopolitan nation. It is important to note that such desires for cosmopolitan nationhood specifically revolve around Korea's aspirations to integrate only White and Western subjects (particularly Western White women) as opposed to people from different racial, ethnic, and national backgrounds.

The men in the mediatized interracial relationships serve as models of aspirational masculinity that the audiences are encouraged to aspire toward and emulate. These aspirations are actually regressive patriarchal policing of women masked as Korea's steps toward modernity. These men are portrayed as cosmopolitan subjects who are capable of dating Western White women and viewed as aspirational because of their power to make these women "voluntarily" perform traditional femininity. In other words, they are portrayed as men who are so popular and desirable as intimate partners that they do not have to tolerate women who do not cater to their expectations of "traditional" femininity.

I am not implying that the Korean men I have examined in this chapter are patriarchal or that their interracial relationships are somehow untoward. Rather, I am pointing to a much broader problem with media discourses. I am suggesting that the media discourses surrounding these men conflated their cosmopolitanism with their heteropatriarchal power over women (both Western and Korean). While Korean men were encouraged to aspire to interracial relationships rather than tolerating Korean women's "bad" femininity, through the same media depictions, Korean women were encouraged to return to a form of "traditional" femininity of sacrifice and sexual availability that caters to cosmopolitan Korean men's desires.

NOTES

1. I translated Korean dialogue and subtitles into English.
2. Korean television programs frequently use subtitles to enhance comedic effects. In particular, Korean television entertainment programs use subtitles to infer the inner thoughts and feelings of the people on-screen. These subtitles may not even be accurate reflections of what the people on-screen may be feeling. These subtitles are inserted by the subtitle writers and editors at their own discretion to enhance the entertainment value of the program.
3. Suri Cruise is the daughter of Hollywood actors Tom Cruise and Katie Holmes.

REFERENCES

Ahn, Ji-Hyun. 2015. "Desiring Biracial Whites: Cultural Consumption of White Mixed-Race Celebrities in South Korean Popular Media." *Media, Culture & Society* 37 (6): 937–47. https://doi.org/10.1177/0163443715593050

Cheng, Sea-ling. 2000. "Assuming Manhood: Prostitution and Patriotic Passions in Korea." *East Asia* 18 (4): 40–78.

Cho, John. 2012. "Global Fatigue: Transnational Markets, Linguistic Capital, and Korean-American Male English Teachers in South Korea." *Journal of Sociolinguistics* 16 (2): 218–37.

Clayton, Ben, and John Harris. 2004. "Footballers' Wives: The Role of the Soccer Player's Partner in the Construction of Idealized Masculinity." *Soccer & Society* 5 (3): 317–35.

Creighton, Millie. 2009. "Japanese Surfing the Korean Wave: Drama Tourism, Nationalism, and Gender via Ethnic Eroticisms." *Southeast Review of Asian Studies* 31:10–38.

Espiritu, Yen Le. 2001. "'We Don't Sleep Around Like White Girls Do': Family, Culture, and Gender in Filipina American Lives." *Signs: Journal of Women in Culture and Society* 26 (2): 415–40.

Han, Woori, Claire Shinhea Lee, and Ji Hoon Park. 2017. "Gendering the Authenticity of the Military Experience: Male Audience Responses to the Korean Reality Show Real Men." *Media, Culture & Society* 39 (1): 62–76.

Jankowiak, William. 1997. "Introduction." In *Romantic Passion: A Universal Experience?*, edited by William Jankowiak, 1–20. New York: Columbia University Press.

Kim, Elaine H., and Chungmoo Choi. 2012. *Dangerous Women: Gender and Korean Nationalism*. New York: Routledge.

Kim, Jeongmee. 2014. "Say *Hallyu*, Wave Goodbye: The Rise and Fall of Korean Wave Drama." In *Reading Asian Television Drama: Crossing Borders and Breaking Boundaries*, edited by Jeongmee Kim, 239–62. London: I.B. Tauris.

Kim, Jinsook. 2018. "Misogyny for Male Solidarity: Online Hate Discourse against Women in South Korea." In *Mediating Misogyny: Gender, Technology, and Harassment*, edited by Jacqueline Ryan Vickery and Tracy Everbach, 151–69. London: Palgrave Macmillan.

Kim, Joon K., and May Fu. 2008. "International Women in South Korea's Sex Industry: A New Commodity Frontier." *Asian Survey* 48 (3): 492–513.

Kim, Minjeong. 2014. "South Korean Rural Husbands, Compensatory Masculinity, and International Marriage." *Journal of Korean Studies* 19 (2): 291–325.

Kim, Nadia Y. 2006. "'Patriarchy Is So Third World': Korean Immigrant Women and 'Migrating' White Western Masculinity." *Social Problems* 53 (4): 519–36.

Kim, Sooah. 2015. "온라인상의 여성 혐오 표현." 페미니즘 연구 15 (2): 279–317.

Kwon, Boduerae. 2005. "The Paradoxical Structure of Modern 'Love' in Korea: Yeonae and Its Possibilities." *Korea Journal* 45 (3): 185–208.

Lee, Euna, Seung-kyung Kim, and Jae Kyung Lee. 2015. "Precarious Motherhood: Lives of Southeast Asian Marriage Migrant Women in Korea." *Asian Journal of Women's Studies* 21 (4): 409–30.

Lee, Hyun-Jung. 2011. "해외원조의 새로운 윤리적 시각: 세계시민주의." 윤리연구 82:193–212.

Lee, Min Joo. 2019. "Romantic Love: Mechanism for Feminist Empowerment or Orientalist Legacy?" *SARE: South Asian Review of English* 56 (2) (Special Issue on Love): 26–42.

Lee, Min Joo. 2020. "Transnational Intimacies: Korean Television Dramas, Romance, Erotics, and Race." PhD diss., University of California, Los Angeles.

Lee, Min Joo. 2021. "Branding Korea: Food, Cosmopolitanism, and Nationalism on Korean Television." *Situations: Cultural Studies in the Asian Context* 14 (1): 53–76.

Lim, Timothy. 2010. "Rethinking Belongingness in Korea: Transnational Migration, 'Migrant Marriages,' and the Politics of Multiculturalism." *Pacific Affairs* 83 (1): 51–71.

Lipset, David. 2004. "Modernity without Romance? Masculinity and Desire in Courtship Stories Told by Young Papua New Guinean Men." *American Ethnologist* 31 (2): 205–24.

Marchetti, Gina. 1994. *Romance and the "Yellow Peril": Race, Sex, and Discursive Strategies in Hollywood Fiction.* Berkeley: University of California Press.
Marks, Shawna. 2019. "Cinderella at the (Foot) Ball: Wives and Girlfriends in Australian Rules Football." *Continuum* 33 (4): 435–45.
Millican, Kaitlyn M., and Tara M. Emmers-Sommer. 2020. "A Content Analysis of Identity Expressions from Female Cast Members on the Reality Television Series WAGs (Wives and Girlfriends of Sports Stars): A Case Study." *Atlantic Journal of Communication* (ahead-of-print), 1–16. https://doi.org/10.1080/15456870.2020.1825219
Moon, Seung Sook. 1998. "Begetting the Nation: The Androcentric Discourse of National History and Tradition in South Korea." In *Dangerous Women: Gender and Korean Nationalism*, edited by Elaine H. Kim and Chungmoo Choi, chap. 3. New York: Routledge.
Nader, Laura. 1989. "Orientalism, Occidentalism and the Control of Women." *Cultural Dynamics* 2 (3): 323–55.
Oh, David C. 2020. "Representing the Western Super-Minority: Desirable Cosmopolitanism and Homosocial Multiculturalism on a South Korean Talk Show." *Television & New Media* 21 (3): 260–77.
Schober, Elisabeth. 2014. "Itaewon's Suspense: Masculinities, Place-Making and the US Armed Forces in a Seoul Entertainment District." *Social Anthropology* 22 (1): 36–51.
Shin, Jaran. 2019. "The Vortex of Multiculturalism in South Korea: A Critical Discourse Analysis of the Characterization of 'Multicultural Children' in Three Newspapers." *Communication and Critical/Cultural Studies* 16 (1): 61–81.
Soh, Chung-Hee. 2004. "Women's Sexual Labor and State in Korean History." *Journal of Women's History* 15 (4): 170–77.
Sueyoshi, Amy. 2018. *Discriminating Sex: White Leisure and the Making of the American "Oriental."* Chicago: University of Illinois Press.
Yoon, Sunny. 2015. "Taming the Primitive: Multiculturalism and the Anthropological Vision of South Korean Media." *Visual Anthropology* 28 (5): 422–37.

MULTIMEDIA SOURCES

KBS Antenna. 2019. "[Legend of *Return of Superman*] Naeun and Gun-hoo's First Appearance on the Program." In *Return of Superman*. YouTube.
MBC Entertainment. 2013. "*Radio Star*: Why Did Christina Come to Korea? Because of Her Romance with Her Student." In *Radio Star*. YouTube.
MBC Every 1. 2019. "Romantic Beenzino's Love Story: Video Star Episode 25." In *Video Star*. YouTube.
SBS Entertainment. 2018a. "Christina Couple, Married Twelve Years, Are as Romantic as Ever @ Forever Guest Episode 417 [Baeknyeon Sonnim Jagiya]." In *Always a Guest*. YouTube.
SBS Entertainment. 2018b. "Christina Lectures Embarrassed Chunja Lee on Intimacy @ Forever Guest [Baeknyeon Sonnim Jagiya] Episode 417." In *Always a Guest*. YouTube.
SBS Entertainment. 2019. "You Lose If You Are Jealous: Beenzino's Girlfriend Stephanie Michova @ Evening Entertainment News Episode 97." In *Evening Entertainment News [Bongyeok Yeonae Hanbam]*. YouTube.

2
Strategic Blackness in South Korean Television

Benjamin M. Han

In a 2013 episode of *Hello Counselor* (*Annyeonghaseyo*, KBS), a Korean TV show in which regular people are invited as guests to share a problem with celebrity hosts and the audience, a young Black migrant from Africa shared his personal stories of racial discrimination and struggles in South Korea. In the episode, a student from Ghana named Sam Okyere also appeared as the guest's friend and drew attention for his fluency in the Korean language and his sense of humor. This appearance was Okyere's debut on South Korean television, and he later became known as the most famous Black person in Korea. Despite the growing visibility of Black entertainers in the South Korean media such as Han Hyun-min and Jonathan Tona, the television industry has shown a commitment to African migrants over African Americans.

The media's interest in Black entertainers aligns with the evolving discourse of *damunhwa* and the influx of foreigners in the form of migrant workers, brides, and international students who are making valuable contributions to the Korean economy. In April 2006, the South Korean government announced the "Plan for Promoting the Social Integration of Migrant Women, Biracial People, and Immigrants." This initiative was significant because it signaled the first phase of integrating migrant workers into society and moving toward a multicultural society. On the surface, the plan was considered a positive step toward a more inclusive society. However, the policy highlighted the state's efforts to incorporate the idea of a "mono-ethnic nation" without damaging its national identity (Ahn 2018, 104). More specifically, the government used the rhetoric of multiculturalism as a branding strategy to strengthen the image of the nation

(S. Kim 2015). The state's policies have led to an increasing number of foreigners and mixed-race Koreans on television. For example, between 2005 and 2012, among the 512 dramas aired on three major terrestrial TV networks (KBS, MBC, and SBS), 33 (6.4 percent) of them cast a foreigner (Ju and Noh 2013, 354). Hence, the government's cultural policies have shaped Black representational politics in the media, further paralleling the state's narrow definition of *damunhwa* "based on principles of distinction and exclusion and selective assimilation" (Lim 2020, 349).

Nevertheless, the growing visibility of Black entertainers from Africa on television does not correspond to the small population of Africans in Korea. While the most recent population census gathered by the Ministry of Justice does not include any statistics on registered foreigners from Africa, in 2005, there were only 947 registered foreigners from Nigeria (A. Kim 2009, 78). Despite their low number compared to other ethnic groups such as Chinese and Vietnamese, between 2004 and 2009, the number of African migrants grew by 80 percent (Geon-soo Han 2003). Furthermore, the shifting geopolitical relations between South Korea and Africa have informed the representation of Black entertainers on television. During President Roh Moo-hyun's tenure, the South Korean government collaborated with African nations, including Egypt and Nigeria, to help them adopt the economic model that led to Korea's compressed modernity. In addition, in 2006, Roh announced the "Africa Development Initiative" to foster greater partnerships with Korea and African nations. And in November 2006, the Roh administration announced that Korea would "triple its economic assistance" to Africa through the Korea International Cooperation Agency, prompting corporations, including Samsung, to make significant investments in the continent (Bone and Kim 2019). Most recently, the Moon Jae-in administration has continued to display its geopolitical interest in Africa as it aims to develop both economic and commercial alliances with the continent (Bone and Kim 2019). But more importantly, the government's foreign policies spanning the Roh and the current administrations are firmly embedded in assisting the African nations to achieve the same economic status as South Korea in order to cement the global status of Korea as both a technologically and an economically advanced nation.

In this chapter, I examine the representations of blackness in the form of popular Black and Black Korean biracial entertainers on television, focusing on Han Hyun-min and Sam Okyere as two primary case studies. In analyzing their representation in diverse genres of commercial television, I explore how the institutional discourse or what Timothy Havens

(2013) terms "industry lore" around blackness materializes into a coherent and consistent racial narrative manifested in domestication, which I describe as "strategic blackness." In other words, I argue that the TV industry deploys strategic blackness as an explicit marker of diversity to strengthen the image of global Korea and further legitimize the Korean Wave as a global phenomenon. The use of strategic blackness, which claims Black figures as authentic Koreans, highlights how Korea has made advancements in race relations in translating blackness as nonthreatening to the homogenous ethnic makeup of the nation. As William H. Bridges (2020) notes in his study of blackness in postwar Japanese literature, it is more productive to think of how blackness is translated than to be trapped in the "assumption that writing blackness means always representing the black other" (7). Therefore, the chapter is invested in how television translates blackness for Koreans instead of exploring it only as an othering process. It is also in dialogue with the other chapters in this volume that examine how the media mobilizes race and identity to engage with the Korean Dream, interracial relationships, and transnational identities (see this vol., Ahn, chap. 3; Lee, chap. 8; Kim and Yu, chap. 10).

Strategic Blackness and the Korean TV Industry

In her book *Postracial Resistance*, Ralina Joseph (2018) defines "strategic ambiguity" as a "different, necessarily subtle form of resistance and risk that balances on an escape hatch of deniability" (3). Joseph further argues that Black female cultural producers, including celebrities and showrunners, utilize a subtle form of defiance in the form of "coded resistance" without making explicit references to racism. She writes, "[Strategic ambiguity is] a way of pushing back against that discrimination anyway through a coded resistance to postracial ideologies. It entails foregrounding crossover appeal, courting multiple publics, speaking in coded language, and smoothing and soothing fears of difference as simply an incidental sidenote" (3).

On the one hand, strategic ambiguity is an iteration of resistance against racism that grants agency to Black cultural producers as active-speaking subjects whose coded language is often only understood and interpreted by the individuals who belong to the same racial or ethnic community. On the other hand, strategic blackness transfers power from individuals to institutions, such as the media industry, to create and shape particular forms of Black representation that appeal to the TV audience.

Accordingly, the TV industry shies away from culturally specific and nuanced depictions of Africans as it strategically represents blackness in juxtaposition with Korean celebrities to strengthen narratives of Korean modernity, which stands in stark opposition to the peripheral modernity of Africa. Furthermore, strategic blackness functions as the legitimization of Korea's acceptance of blackness as a positive ramification of Korea-Africa geopolitical relations, the Korean Wave, and a progressive understanding of race and ethnicity.

While strategic ambiguity and strategic blackness stand at opposite ends of the spectrum, the intertwining link between them is that both are subtle and gendered manifestations of power that are less apparent to the mainstream than the ethnic audience. Strategic ambiguity is considered a bottom-up approach used by individual cultural producers while strategic blackness operates more on an institutional (top-down) level to assert power over Blacks through exploitative and commodified mechanisms. In other words, strategic ambiguity aims to challenge cultural industries that systemically oppress Black female writers, actors, and showrunners. On the contrary, strategic blackness is the media industry's carefully orchestrated tactics to render Blacks as conditionally acceptable if they assert their Koreanness, further undermining their agency and autonomy as cultural producers, as well as making their blackness illegible to the general audience.

Additionally, strategic blackness advances Catherine R. Squires's (2014) notion of "hipster racism," where entertainment embedded in comedy, humor, and jokes around ethnic and racial characters is viewed not only as both progressive and regressive but also as a "hip way of pushing boundaries" (6). While Squires's description of hipster racism is limited to fictional TV characters in narrative serials, the Korean TV industry deploys it strategically in reality TV and variety shows to disguise the continuing marginalization of Black entertainers and simultaneously to assert dominance over them. Hence, strategic blackness offers a false illusion of Korea's progressive racial politics through othering that benefits the media as a response "to demands by activists for diversity in programming and production" to further demonstrate the persistent problem of how the media industry equates progressive representational politics with demography (Gray 2016). In the case of Korean television, strategic blackness is a mere illusion of the industry's efforts to expand the national rhetoric and policy of *damunhwa* beyond "families consisting of a Korean national and a foreign spouse" via Black visibility and legibility (Yi and Jung 2015). Accordingly, strategic blackness does not translate into the social empowerment of Black entertainers but uses them as valuable assets that contribute to the global circulation of Korean media and culture.

Black Entertainers in the Korean Media

The visibility of Black entertainers in Korean television is confined to specific genres such as reality TV, documentaries, and variety shows that successfully construct them as exemplary neoliberal subjects whose individual success and achievement in the form of stardom are credited to their hard work, self-enterprising efforts, and guidance from other ethnic celebrities. Despite the experience of racism by Black entertainers as othered subjects, the media capitalizes on the narrative of overcoming personal struggles to dismiss the larger social conditions that continue to structure racial and ethnic disparities in Korean society. The TV industry's inclination toward Black entertainers from the African continent, such as Ghana and Nigeria, facilitates the efficacy of strategic blackness, given Korea's tumultuous racialized past under US imperialism and its shameful historical treatment of mixed-race Koreans known as *honhyeol*, particularly Black Korean biracial children. In contrast to African American soldiers, who were deployed to Korea under US military occupation and were considered sojourners, Black residents from the African continent have voluntarily arrived in Korea as immigrants, underscoring their affective desires to stay permanently in the country. Nevertheless, Africans in pursuit of better economic opportunities are still viewed as "the most inferior of blood lines" (N. Kim 2014, 218). Similarly, anthropologist Geonsoo Han (2003) argues that the economic advancement of Korea enables the nation to construct its own "Other" as an object of comparison and pity (161).

Throughout the history of Korean television, Black Korean biracial entertainers have been sporadically visible with figures such as Insooni, Park Il-joon, Yoon Mi-rae, Sonya, and Michelle Lee. While most of them are musicians and women, they also embody the specter of US military occupation. As Gil-Soo Han (2016) writes, "Prior to globalization in the 1990s, the legacy of African American soldiers in Korea and Korean beliefs in pure-bloodism were enough justification for some to ridicule black Americans" (144). More specifically, mixed-race children stemming from an interracial marriage between a Black father and a Korean mother have occupied a hostile position in modern Korean history. If mixed-race people have been visible at all, their representations have been confined to TV documentaries in which they are portrayed as overcoming their struggles and assimilating successfully into Korean society. But more importantly, as Nadia Kim (2014) explains, the dissemination of European-American racial ideologies under Japanese colonization and the absence of antiracist movements in Korea's history have shaped Korea's racial ideologies concerning blackness. Nadia Kim (2014) writes, "These factors factored into Koreans for the White-over-Black institutional order imported by [the US] military beginning in 1945" (217). After the conclusion of the Korean War in 1953, President Syngman Rhee instituted directives to remove all mixed-race children from the nation (Woo 2019). According to historian Susie Woo (2019), this was attempted via international adoption because "mixed-raced children hampered Korean claims to independence and were troubling reminders of American empire," further rendering them as "stateless subjects" (150).

Despite the negative perception and the traumatic historical past imbued in US militarism that Korea wanted to break away from, the circulating narratives around mixed-race children and adoption often made the (Korean) mother absent because both Americans and Koreans disavowed them (Woo 2019). Accordingly, Korean mothers and mixed-raced children occupied a liminal space between Korea and the US. Regardless of where they resided, they were a "phantom presence," an excess of the American empire and Korean nationalism that threatened both if made too visible (173). However, the rise of anti-Black sentiment is not the sole outcome of US imperialism, as it is grounded in a longer history. Sociologist Jae Kyun Kim (2015) explains that the construction of Korean identity during the precolonial and postcolonial periods "required racial otherness in the form of antiblackness" (209). Kim explains that the Korean imaginary of Africa as backward and hopeless contributed to its national identity and offered hope for independence from the Japanese empire in the absence of actual physical interaction with the Black race. And the West's Eurocentric understanding of otherness firmly rooted in racial hierarchies in which Blacks were seen as the most inferior race further informed the discourse of blackness in Korea (J. Kim 2015).

Therefore, not only did the hidden manifestation of anti-Black sentiment shape Korea's attitude and treatment of Blacks, but also the media played an instrumental role in reinforcing anti-Black rhetoric. In the 1980s, many Korean comedians performed in blackface on television without public scrutiny or criticism. They were viewed as a regular act of comedy without any ill intention toward any particular ethnic group (Gil-Soo Han 2015). However, with the wide circulation of Korean popular culture across the globe, Korean entertainers' use of blackface is no longer acceptable, as both the domestic and the international communities have expressed their criticisms of the racist practice. More specifically, two different responses to blackface performance have emerged. Some netizens are more forgiving of the act, as they see it stemming from Koreans' lack of cultural awareness and interactions with Black people, while others criticize it for being simply ignorant, disrespectful, and racist, having little to do with the issue of cultural sensitivity (Gil-Soo Han 2015). These diverging reactions illustrate how the use of blackface mimicry in Korean sketch comedy attests to the ambivalent ways that television has negotiated and translated blackness for its viewers. The racialized past has not only informed and shaped the Black representational politics in Korea but also offered bleak opportunities for Blacks. Nevertheless, more contemporary representations of blackness have improved somewhat dramatically on the surface, not only from negative to positive images but also in the degree to which the TV industry makes them more legible for Koreans.

Han Hyun-min and the Illegibility of Blackness

Among the most visible Black Korean biracial entertainers is Han Hyun-min, a Korean Nigerian teenage model who rose to fame when *Time* magazine selected him as one of the world's top thirty influential teen figures of 2017. Ever since his name made it on the list, he has drawn public attention and appeared on many Korean television programs, including news, variety shows, and reality TV. Despite his markers of racial excess and extraordinariness defined by his dark skin shade and hair that inform the politics of Black visibility and aesthetics, he has showcased his "authentic" Korean side through his native fluency in the Korean language and love for traditional dishes.

Therefore, despite the othering of Hyun-min's status as a *honhyeol*, the fact that he is a byproduct of a marriage between a Nigerian father and a Korean mother breaks away from the past consistent racial narratives around being mixed-race. While mothers have been invisible within the narrative of mixed-race children, in the case of Hyun-min, his Nigerian father remains in the background, appearing on television as a nonassertive and nonthreatening patriarchal figure, while his mother is foregrounded as an influential matriarch responsible for her biracial son's bright character and success. Thus, Hyun-min is not represented as a typical *honhyeol*, having neither a dark past nor a need for empathy from society. As a result, the family story of Hyun-min and his mother is an appealing mixed-race narrative to the media industry. Hyun-min's blackness, in conjunction with his Koreanness, becomes legible as it is foregrounded in his innocence and naivete as a nineteen-year-old still under the caring wings of his mother.

Hyun-min's increasing presence on Korean television, especially his appearance on the JTBC reality TV program *Stranger* (*Ibangin*, 2018) as a regular cast member, deserves critical analysis. The reality show documents the diasporic lives of Korean celebrities living away from their homeland and of foreigners residing in Korea. The show provides access to their daily lives and activities not often seen in front of the camera. In episode 12, Hyun-min is introduced to the audience for the first time after joining the show as a regular cast member. Even though Hyun-min was born in Korea and has lived his entire life there, his casting in the show illustrates how the media still aims to construct him as the other. In this episode, we witness him speaking in the form of a confession video, a mode of expression common in the observational reality TV genre, which involves intimate and personal moments when cast members disclose their thoughts and feelings in front of the camera. In the introductory video, the screen caption reads "Nationality: 100% Korean," followed by his explanation that he wants to demonstrate that he is "fully Korean." The representation of Black entertainers, including Hyun-min, on Korean television is embedded in a consistent racial narrative that requires them to showcase and perform their authenticity as Korean. Whether it is Hyun-min's TV interviews with news programs on YTN, KBS, and Channel A or other entertainment programs, the media's narrative of his inclusion in *Time* magazine is constructed as not only a personal but also a national achievement in an attempt to underscore his Korean ethnic identity and make his blackness illegible for the Korean audience. As Ji-Hyun Ahn argues in the next chapter, racial and ethnic diversity is mobilized to showcase television's global engagement while legitimizing Korea's social progress. In contrast to Hines Ward, a biracial former NFL football player, who represents a successful Korean American returnee, Hyun-min is an emerging homegrown star who embodies the Koreanness attached to his Black body, elevating him to "a mythical text that stands for social/racial integration in contemporary Korea" (Ahn 2014, 402). Thus, the Korean TV industry's exhaustion of the narrative around Hyun-min's accomplishment as the first Korean teen model selected in a reputable global magazine cements his status as a transnational Korean star instead of a Black figure who threatens the monoethnic construction of the nation.

In episode 12 of *Stranger*, the introductory confession video proceeds with a scene in which Hyun-min appears as a typical and ordinary Korean high school student in a classroom surrounded by his classmates. Although he is a native Korean speaker, his fluency and mastery of the Korean language are a welcome surprise to the audience, making it easier for the Korean media to domesticate him and portray him as more affable. Hyun-min's use of culturally specific words and his knowledge of Korean history construct him as a more ordinary and intimate figure for domestic audiences. In the ensuing segment, Hyun-min and his classmates, including a Mexican friend, visit a nearby *bunsikjeom*, a popular restaurant among students that sells inexpensive Korean dishes, which further indicates how he has firmly cemented his status as fully Korean despite the racial markers inscribed in his blackness and provides an opportunity him to perform his Koreanness, which the TV show can exploit.

The most exciting segment of the episode occurs when Hyun-min meets a fellow Black celebrity named Sam Okyere. In contrast to Hyun-min, Sam is a foreigner from Ghana who speaks Korean fluently. More specifically, Sam is an embodiment of a positive geopolitical relationship between South Korea and Ghana. He was able to migrate to Korea and study at Sogang University as a computer science major under the auspices of the Korean government, which offered him an educational scholarship and even granted permanent residency. Thus, Korean television capitalizes on this exchange as a form of strategic blackness by highlighting Korea's contribution to Sam's success and stardom while underscoring his full-fledged transformation into an "authentic" Korean in order to promote a positive image of a global Korea that is invested in diversity and inclusion.

In the episode, Hyun-min and Sam meet in a neighborhood known as Haebangchon, which is in close proximity to Itaewon, a district in Seoul that is often considered a multiethnic enclave with diverse ethnic restaurants, gay bars, and foreign residents. More specifically, Itaewon is also known as a neighborhood where many African migrants, mostly from Nigeria and Ghana, first settled in Korea. Africans migrated to Korea to "draw on the Asian Tiger as a model for developing their own country's economy" (N. Kim 2014, 229–30). Nigerians constituted the largest population of African migrants in the Yongsan district before many were forced out due to rising rent prices and discrimination (N. Kim 2014). The neighborhood of Haebangchon, located close to the Yongsan US military base, attracted many migrants as it developed into a new industrial zone with many job opportunities, low living costs, and proximity to Seoul (Križnik and Cho 2017).

As Hyun-min and Sam are walking on the streets of Haebangchon, Hyun-min recollects his early childhood memories of growing up in the area and observes that nothing has changed since then. These scenes that trace Hyun-min's past childhood contribute to the media's framing and construction of Hyun-min's citizenship and ethnic status as Korean through shared collective experience and nostalgic longing for sweet and innocent school days, which resonate with the local audience. In the episode, Sam takes Hyun-min to his favorite African restaurant in Itaewon. The restaurant, including the atmosphere, appears somewhat foreign to Hyun-min since he has never visited Nigeria, his father's homeland. The episode strategically highlights his incompetent knowledge in Nigerian history and culture, as it is Sam, an immigrant from Ghana, who assumes the role of educating him about Nigeria, which is the most affluent nation in Africa and boasts an emerging vibrant film industry known as Nollywood to instill pride in Hyun-min's Nigerian ethnic identity. Even though Sam expresses dismay to Hyun-min for his lack of knowledge about his Nigerian roots and heritage, Sam assumes the role of a cultural educator as a native African, and the show continues to represent Sam within the boundaries of conditional acceptance because he uses the Korean language to educate both Hyun-min and the audience about Africa.

As Sam is educating Hyun-min about Africa in general, an edited montage consisting of images of Nigeria and Africa is inserted, which presents a primitive and underdeveloped simulacrum of Africa as emblematic of peripheral modernity in stark contrast to the compressed modernity of South Korea. Africa in Korea has been imagined as an object of exoticism grounded in poverty and difficult lives even though it has been the subject of a number of TV programs, including documentaries, educational programs, and telethons (Kim, Chae, and Jung 2014). In particular, television has documented Africa through a postcolonial practice, imitating the Western colonial view as it is depicted as primitive and "the other end of Western modernization" (Yoon 2015, 431).

Despite the progressive outlook of the reality show *Stranger* in its feature of two Black men engaged in an open conversation around different topics, the way that the show presents Africa for its domestic audience affirms the unwillingness of the media industry to engage in earnest representations of Black people. One topic that Hyun-min and Sam discuss during their conversation over lunch is race. Sam asks Hyun-min whether it was difficult for him to grow up in Korea as a Black Korean. The candid discussion between the two Black individuals about race relations in Korean society provides a solemn moment in the show, shifting the humorous and comedic tone of the episode. Hyun-min explains that he was in kindergarten when he came to the full realization that he is, in fact, different from other Koreans because of his skin color and provides many anecdotes about being a victim of racism. Yet what is noteworthy about this particular scene is that it is structured as a self-reflection in which both Black celebrities can only revisit and openly discuss their past given their current achievements and popularity and the fact that they overcame racism and discrimination. Hence, the conversation ends expectedly and disappointingly when Sam credits his experiences as a motivation for him to achieve success in the entertainment industry. Sam adds that this is why he needs to demonstrate both his love for Korea as a Ghanaian and his ability to intermingle harmoniously with Koreans despite their racialization of him as a Black foreigner. *Stranger*, therefore, constructs Sam as a neoliberal subject whose ability to overcome racism stems from his hard work and efforts in self-enterprise, which lend to the depiction of racism as an individual act bestowed on others.

As Squires notes cogently, "Post-racial discourses obfuscate institutional racism and blame continuing racial inequalities on individuals who make poor choices for themselves or their families" (2014, 6). The candid conversation about race in Korea between Hyun-min and Sam ends not only on an optimistic note but also as expected when the episode shows Sam verifying Hyun-min's star status by pointing to a large billboard featuring Hyun-min hanging outside Doota, also known as Doosan Tower, an eight-floor shopping mall in the popular fashion district of Dongdaemun. Sam uses this billboard featuring a Black Korean teenage model as proof of Korea's significant progress in racial and ethnic equality. Nonetheless, the episode fails to point out how the logic of capitalism informing the Korean television industry exploits Hyun-min's blackness for commodification and branding purposes. Thus, the dissemination of television narratives that equate stardom with racial progress continues to privilege Black entertainers as exemplary neoliberal subjects. Furthermore, *Stranger* only offers a glimpse of what the life of a Black teenage male model entails when we see how Hyun-min lives with two other Korean male models in a crowded apartment; they feed on instant ramen noodles and conform to the demands of the Korean fashion industry, which capitalizes on their precarious labor and, more problematically, Hyun-min's Black exotic attributes such as his Afro hairstyle.

The commodification of Hyun-min's visible markers of blackness continues to serve the commercial interests of the TV industry. In a later episode of *Stranger*, the audience witnesses Sam and Hyun-min visiting a gym, exposing the configuration of their blackness through hypermasculine bodies, as Sam displays his well-trained muscular body while Hyun-min, with the help of a personal trainer, aspires to achieve a similar body type. These affordances of strategic blackness that the reality TV show focuses on further indicate how it shies away from more nuanced representations of Black celebrities that are grounded in ethnic and cultural specificity. The representation of blackness that is marked by Sam and Hyun-min's racial and ethnic excess is reinforced through the disciplining of the men's natural bodies under the expert guidance of a Korean personal trainer to transform themselves into Black hypermasculine men whom the media desires to commodify as a marker of Black authenticity. More importantly, after the conclusion of the workout at the gym, Hyun-min introduces Sam to his favorite Korean dish, *soondaeguk*. They enjoy the blood sausage soup, and Hyun-min slurps it, further asserting their Korean authenticity. More specifically, their consumption of a local Korean dish also perpetuates their status as ordinary, everyday citizens despite their star status, further domesticating them and rendering them more intimate and appealing to the Korean audience. While one can claim that this particular episode offers a nuanced representation of blackness that is not confined to the positive/negative binary, the TV industry exploits these moments of cultural interaction and assimilation to highlight Hyun-min's Korean authenticity and to make his homeland (African) food more foreign than local food, further rendering Nigerian culture less intimate and comfortable. The TV show's attempt to define Hyun-min's authenticity as Korean through localism, language, and food is a common feature of strategic blackness that the Korean media industry deploys to obliterate the legible traits of blackness, with the show failing to highlight how blackness contributes to Hyun-min's unstable and complex racial, ethnic, and cultural identity formation. Indeed, strategic blackness does not provide space for a critique of anti-blackness, as the issue is always centered and framed on what transforms Black Koreans into more authentic Koreans or even on how much Koreanness they embody themselves.

The emphasis on Koreanness over blackness also instills nationalistic sentiment in the Korean audience as they witness how much these racialized Black figures have become just like them through their acceptance of Korean culture. In particular, the construction of Koreanness as national identity contributes to narratives of Korean modernity via Black racial projects in order to uphold ethnic nationalism and the ideology of *minjok*, "a category inclusive of every Korean without regard to age, gender, or status distinctions" (Em 1999, 339; J. Kim 2015). This particular iteration of nationalism sets up the Korean media as if it condemns racial discrimination in Korean society but is "nevertheless unsure as to how to welcome or involve those foreigners politically, culturally, and economically" (Gil-Soo Han 2016, 145). In other words, strategic blackness operates as a covert act of nationalism that marks Korea's global status as a progressive and modernized nation while avoiding the need to address the social conditions that continue to discriminate against Blacks.

The Most Famous Black Man in Korea: Sam Okyere

Similar to Hyun-min Han, Sam Okyere has catapulted into stardom through his appearances on Korean television, establishing himself as one of the most recognizable Black men in Korea. In contrast to his guest appearances on numerous reality TV and variety shows, Okyere made regular appearances on the reality TV show *My Little Old Boy* (*Miun Uri Saekki*, SBS, 2016-present). The reality TV program features single, middle-aged male celebrities as it documents their daily lives. The show also features a panel consisting of hosts, a celebrity guest, and mothers of the celebrities, who add commentary for extra entertainment as they too observe what is unveiled in front of the camera. In episode 59 of *My Little Old Boy*, Tony, a former member of the famous boy band HOT, and Kangnam, a Japanese Korean singer, visit Okyere's home to celebrate a holiday. The episode documents Tony making traditional Korean holiday dishes from instant food he purchased at a convenience store. As Tony, Kangnam, and Sam prepare a wide array of dishes, they also engage in conversation on different topics. For example, Tony asks Kangnam what they eat in Japan on holidays. The same question is then asked to Sam.

During the conversation, Sam explains that he has a busy schedule when he visits his native country, cementing his celebrity status in Ghana. Kangnam then abruptly asks Sam whether there are TVs in Ghana. Sam is dismayed, and his facial expression changes in response to Kangnam's ignorant question. Kangnam further asks whether there are TV stations such as SBS or MBC in Ghana, illustrating his obliviousness to other nations and cultures, particularly Africa. Sam responds sarcastically that there are buses, airplanes, and even lions in Ghana. He adds that if you visit a city in Ghana, it looks very similar to Seoul. After the episode was broadcast, several newspapers, including *Joongang Daily* and *Donga Ilbo*, criticized Kangnam's racist questions. Some newspapers even criticized the cable channel JTBC for including the segment in the broadcast of its episode. While Kangnam's ignorance stems from his image of Africa, which is rooted in primitive, savage, underdeveloped, and colonial discourses, it also translates into covert racism, which the TV show strategically frames as entertainment, leaving it for the viewers decide whether to interpret it as scripted humor.

More significantly, this mode of entertainment is an iteration of hipster racism as a "form of scripted humor that accommodates simultaneous and contradictory calls to racial, ethnic, gender, and sexual difference and bias" (Molina-Guzmán 2018, 55). More specifically, "hipster racism in post-racial comedies is then produced through conscious, unconscious, and implied verbal and nonverbal putdowns as well as slapstick and physical comedy that make fun of race, ethnic, gender and sexual difference" (13). Hence, the burden of interpreting racism, sexism, and homophobia rests on the audience. Whether Kangnam made the insensitive comments consciously or unconsciously, the TV show's playful use of his rendition of hipster racism in which Kangnam uses offensive questions somewhat ironically makes him stand out among the guests through the perpetuation of his blunt persona and adds more entertainment value to the show.

Despite the show's ability to edit out the racist segment, the fact that it kept it in testifies to how the media deploys different versions of hipster racism by pushing the boundaries of what they consider to be jokes made by a celebrity born and raised in Japan. In other words, Kangnam's offensive and inappropriate comments could also imply the opposite, as dry humor meant to amuse the audience. Hence, the degree of amusement that Kangnam's version of hipster racism elicits "depends on audiences' own comfort and relationship to racism, sexism, homophobia, and xenophobia" (Molina-Guzmán 2018, 13). Some audiences familiar with Kangnam's persona constructed through his "blunt" behaviors displayed in his past TV appearances would interpret his action as more funny than shocking and attribute it to his lack of cultural sophistication. Nevertheless, the deployment of a multicultural cast within the episode makes the use of hipster racism less apparent to the audience. Additionally, the publicized racist incident functions as an asset to the show, as it serves as a catalyst to the content development of several future episodes in which Sam and his Korean celebrity friends, particularly Kangnam, not only travel to Ghana to be educated on its culture but also make Africa and its people an object of comparison to Korea through the use of strategic blackness.

Indeed, in episode 68 of *My Little Old Boy*, Tony, Kangnam, Boom (a multifaceted entertainer), and Sam visit Ghana. The Korean celebrities comment on how their archaic perception of Ghana is changing as they witness a far more modernized country than they imagined. As they ride in a car on their way to visit Sam's families, the vehicle comes to a traffic stop, and they encounter many street vendors attempting to sell a wide array of items. One of the hosts of the show, comedian Shin Dong-yup, finds resonance with the image of the street vendors as it evokes a familiar scene of Korea in the past, implying how Ghana is still far from achieving full modernity even though the show depicts many modern aspects of the African nation. The dissonance between the images of Ghana displayed on the reality TV show and the commentaries positions Korea as a superior nation. In fact, this is a manifestation of strategic blackness in which the TV show presents itself as offering an accurate representation of Africa while the commentaries interspersed throughout the episode continue to situate Africa as underdeveloped, enabling the Korean audience to feel more comfortable with and receptive to Black entertainers, particularly Sam Okyere. And the panelists' commentary that Korea is like Ghana in the past perpetuates what Wilk (2002) describes as "colonial time," that is, a "system that merges time with physical distance and cultural difference" (177). The affirmation by the panelists that Ghana is lagging years or even decades behind Korea in terms of economic and technological advancements and cultural trends is further validation of how television asserts power over Africans.

Moreover, the deployment of strategic blackness in the media is aligned with Korea's investment in its global image through the transnational distribution of its media and culture across many continents, including Africa. Thus, the display of African entertainers on television aspires to establish connection and identification between Koreans and Africans in order to legitimize the cultural power of the Korean Wave in Africa despite their lack of shared cultural affinity and geo-linguistic proximity. The visibility of Black entertainers on Korean television lends itself to greater transnational and transcultural affinities, further prompting Africans to develop connections with Korean culture. This is a strategy that the Korean television industry embraces, as an increasing number of episodes of reality TV shows and dramas are being shot outside Korea, including Europe, Latin America, and even Africa. For example, in episode 70 of *My Little Old Boy*, Sam, Tony, Kangnam, and Boom participate in a facilities tour of a local Ghanaian TV network and observe the live broadcast of a popular talk show. As they participate in the live talk show as audience members in the studio, the producer invites them to appear on the show on the spot.

Sam's appearance alongside his Korean celebrity friends on a local Ghanaian TV show legitimizes the global influence of the Korean Wave as it even makes inroads into an African nation. Sam is elevated to become an informal African spokesman of Korea, whose personal narratives about its culture and society strengthen the transnational flow of Korean media and culture, as well as its global image in Ghana.

In the next episode, Sam leaves his homeland because of his busy schedule in Korea, but his friends remain in the foreign country. They are introduced to Sam's female friends, who serve as tour guides. The climactic moment of the episode occurs when they visit a local eatery that turns out to be a Korean restaurant. The fact that a Korean restaurant exists in Ghana surprises both the Korean celebrities visiting the country and the panelists in the studio. The rest of the episode is devoted to cultural interactions between Sam's Ghanaian female friends and the Korean male celebrities through the active consumption of Korean dishes such as bulgogi, pork belly, spicy squid, and even *choongmoo kimbap*, a dish popular among Koreans but exotic to Ghanaians. More significantly, the entire episode's segment featuring Sam's female friends continues to reinforce the gendered dynamics manifested in heterosexual romance not only via foreign food consumption but also in the essentializing of Ghanaian women as romantic figures through their exotic physical attributes, accent, and cultural norms. The show represents Ghanaian women as objects and victims of male desire and romanticization, as perpetuated in many Korean TV shows featuring foreign brides, such as *Love in Asia* and *Global Talk Show* (Kim, Park, and Yi 2009).

Moreover, the hypervisibility of Korean cuisine in this episode does not aim to educate Koreans about African culture and society but instead validates the Korean Wave's global reach for the domestic audience. Sam's Ghanaian female friends' participation in and embrace of their cultural immersion in Korean food attest to how legitimization gains its affordance when Africans are domesticated for the Korean audience, subsuming any markers of racial excess in the form of skin color and language. Michelle Cho (2017), in her examination of Korean Wave stars on domestic television, claims that domestic television assumes the role of a vital "theater" for "K-pop celebrities, a medium in which they must constantly perform their approachability to maintain a semblance of intimacy with Korean viewers" (2309). Cho further explains that "the familiar televisual stage offers intimate access to the performers to domesticate their transnational pop idol personae" (2311). In the case of *My Little Old Boy*, racialized Blacks are domesticated, and the show demands that they continue to perform their authentic Koreanness to assert themselves as less threatening to Korea's monoethnic configuration and to penetrate global cultural industries and markets.

Conclusion

In 2020, a yearbook photo of five students at Uijeongbu High School parodying Ghana's dancing pallbearers in blackface began circulating on the internet. In response to the photo, Sam Okyere criticized the act as derogatory and offensive on his Instagram account. The post drew public backlash as internet users commented on Okyere's use of the words "educate" and "ignorance," which they interpreted as a criticism of Korean education. Amid the controversy, a photo of Okyere making the slanted-eyes gesture in an episode of the talk show *Non Summit* in 2015 quickly disseminated online. As the backlash against Okyere intensified, he removed his original Instagram post and apologized to the public. The incident had a trigger effect, as Okyere disappeared from the television scene. More specifically, it illustrates how the media exploits either his Koreanness or blackness when they are seen as beneficial or threatening to the nation. It further speaks to how "blackness does more than simply denote a racial category—it determines what kind of human being a person is" (Bridges 2020, 13). Even though his slanted-eyes gesture at the time was acceptable as entertainment television, it accrues an explicitly racist meaning in the context of a Black man's critique of blackface.

The use of strategic blackness has continued in fictional TV series such as *Goodbye to Goodbye* (*Ibyeori Tteonatda*, MBC, 2018) and *Itaewon Class* (JTBC, 2020) through the characters of Bikila (Joel Roberts) and Toni Kim (Chris Lyon), respectively. Strategic blackness is also visible in cinema, most recently in *Swing Kids* (2018), starring actor Jared Grimes as Sergeant Jackson, who starts a tap-dancing group at a prisoner of war camp in Geoje during the Korean War. Jackson's development of empathy for the North Korean prisoners through his own experience as a Black man serving in the US military is foregrounded to counter Korea's othering of African American soldiers with ties to US militarism and to elicit progressive sentiments toward the Black Korean imaginary. These examples further point out how the domestication of Black entertainers to resonate with the Korean audience is gendered, as it is more effective when it involves men than women. Men are more appealing and attractive to the female audience, as ethnic women in the form of foreign brides have fallen prey as victims of romanticized interracial romance and marriage in the media.

In sum, strategic blackness in the Korean media highlights the expansion of the discourse of *damunhwa* while disguising both the exploitation and the commodification of blackness. The media strategically domesticates Black entertainers through their perpetual performance and validation of their Korean cultural identity. Their conditional acceptance is susceptible to rendering their blackness illegible while making Koreanness more pronounced for the audience. Therefore, strategic blackness strengthens the logic of multiculturalism with a few selective and accomplished Black entertainers who are considered valuable resources for the media industry in terms of content diversification and expansion into other national markets.

REFERENCES

Ahn, Ji-Hyun. 2014. "Rearticulating Black Mixed-Race in the Era of Globalization." *Cultural Studies* 28 (3): 391–417. https://doi.org/10.1080/09502386.2013.840665

Ahn, Ji-Hyun. 2018. *Mixed-Race Politics and Neoliberal Multiculturalism in South Korean Media*. Cham: Palgrave MacMillan.

Bone, R. Maxwell, and Matthew Minsoo Kim. 2019. "South Korea's Africa Outreach: Tracing South Korea's Approach to the Continent under 4 Presidents." *The Diplomat*, August 2. https://thediplomat.com/2019/08/south-koreas-africa-outreach/

Bridges, William H. 2020. *Playing in the Shadows: Fictions of Race and Blackness in Postwar Japanese Literature*. Ann Arbor: University of Michigan Press.

Cho, Michelle. 2017. "Domestic *Hallyu*: K-Pop Metatexts and the Media's Self-Reflexive Gesture." *International Journal of Communication* 11:2308–31.

Em, Henry H. 1999. "Minjok as a Modern and Democratic Construct: Sin Ch'aeho's Historiography." In *Colonial Modernity in Korea*, edited by Gi-Wook Shin and Michael Robinson, 337–61. Cambridge, MA: Harvard University Press.

Gray, Herman. 2016. "Precarious Diversity: Representation and Demography." In *Precarious Creativity: Global Media, Local Labor*, edited by Michael Curtin and Kevin Sanson, 241–53. Oakland: University of California Press.

Han, Geon-soo. 2003. "African Migrant Workers' Views of Korean People and Culture." *Koreana Journal* 43 (1): 154–73.

Han, Gil-Soo. 2015. "K-Pop Nationalism: Celebrities and Acting Blackface in the Korean Media." *Continuum: Journal of Media & Cultural Studies* 29 (1): 2–16. https://doi.org/10.1080/10304312.2014.968522

Han, Gil-Soo. 2016. *Nouveau-riche Nationalism and Multiculturalism in Korea*. Abingdon: Routledge.

Havens, Timothy. 2013. *Black Television Travels: African American Media around the Globe* (Critical Cultural Communication). New York: New York University Press.

Joseph, Ralina. 2018. *Postracial Resistance: Black Women, Media, and the Uses of Strategic Ambiguity*. New York: New York University Press.

Ju, Hye Yeon, and Kang Woo Noh. 2013. "Deurama soke jaehyeonndoen oegugingwa hangukui damunhwajuui." *Manhwaaenimeisyeonyeongu Tongkwon* 32:335–61. http://dx.doi.org/10.7230/KOSCAS.2013.32.335

Kim, Andrew Engi. 2009. "Global Migration and South Korea: Foreign Workers, Foreign Brides and the Making of a Multicultural Society." *Ethnic and Racial Studies* 32 (1): 70–92. https://doi.org/10.1080/01419870802044197

Kim, Chun-sik, Youn-gil Chae, and Nak-won Jeong. 2014. *Hanguk Midieoui Apeurika Jaehyeon Bangsikkwa Suyongja Insik Josa*. Seoul: Save the Children.

Kim, Hyeran. 2017. "Kangnam, Sam Okyeree 'Ghana TV isseo?' musi baleon nonran . . . yeoja bihaneun susiro?" *Dong-A Ilbo*, October 23. http://www.donga.com/news/article/all/20171023/86912120/2

Kim, In-yeong, Kwang-yeong Bak, and In-hui Yi. 2009. "TV Peurogeuraeme Natanan Hangukjeok Damunhwajuuiui Teuksuseonge Kwanhan Midieo Damron: KBS Reobeu in Asiawa Minyeodeului Sudareul Jungsimeuro." *Oughtopia: The Journal of Social Paradigm Studies* 24 (2) (Winter): 69–96.

Kim, Jae Kyun. 2015. "Yellow over Black: History of Race in Korea and the New Study of Race and Empire." *Critical Sociology* 41 (2): 205–17.

Kim, Nadia. 2014. "Race-ing Toward the Real South Korea: The Cases of Black-Korean Nationals and African Migrants." In *Multiethnic Korea? Multiculturalism, Migration, and Peoplehood Diversity in Contemporary South Korea*, edited by John Lie, 211–43. Berkeley: Institute of East Asian Studies.

Kim, Sookyung. 2015. "Soft Talk, Hard Realities: Multiculturalism as the South Korean Government's Decoupled Response to International Migration." *Asian Pacific Migration Journal* 24 (1): 51–78. https://doi.org/10.1177/0117196814565165

Križnik, Blaž, and Ha-young Cho. 2017. "Comparing Transformation of Deprived Mixed-Use Areas in Seoul: Community Building in Traditional Industrial Clusters." In *The Entrepreneurial City: 10th Conference of the International Forum on Urbanism*, edited by Hendrik Tieben, Yan Geng, and Francesco Rossini. Rotterdam: International Forum on Urbanism.

Kwon, Sungeol. 2017. "Sam Okyere 'hanguk saramdeuli Kangname daesin hwanaego sakwahaejueo gamdong.'" *Insight*, December 29. https://www.insight.co.kr/news/132571

Lim, Timothy C. 2020. "'It's Not Just Talk': Ideas, Discourse, and the Prospects for Transformational Change in a Homogeneous Nation-State." *Asian Ethnicity* 21 (3): 348–72. https://doi.org/10.1080/14631369.2019.1698283

Molina-Guzmán, Isabel. 2018. *Latinas & Latinos on TV: Colorblind Comedy in the Post-Racial Network Era*. Tucson: University of Arizona Press.

Squires, Catherine R. 2014. *Postracial Mystique Media and Race in the 21st Century*. New York: New York University Press.

Wilk, Richard R. 2002. "Television, Time, and the National Imaginary in Belize." In *Media Worlds: Anthropology on New Terrain*, edited by Faye D. Ginsburg, Lila Abu-Lughod, and Brian Larkin, 171–88. Berkeley: University of California Press.

Woo, Susie. 2019. *Framed by War: Korean Children and Women at the Crossroads of US Empire*. New York: New York University Press.

Yeo, Hyun-goo. 2017. "Sam Okyere Hyanghan Kangnamui 'Injongchabyeoljeok' Baleon Nonran." *Korea JoongAng Daily*. October 23. https://news.joins.com/article/22041439

Yi, Joseph, and Go-woon Jung. 2015. "Debating Multicultural Korea: Media Discourse on Migrants and Minorities in South Korea." *Journal of Ethnic and Migration Studies* 41 (6): 985–1013. https://doi.org/10.1080/1369183X.2014.1002202

Yoon, Sunny. 2015. "Taming the Primitive: Multiculturalism and the Anthropological Vision of South Korean Media." *Visual Anthropology* 28 (5): 422–37.

3
The Televised Korean Dream

The Birth of a Great Star and Racial/Ethnic Diversity in the Survival Audition Program in South Korea

Ji-Hyun Ahn

On May 27, 2011, it was announced that Cheonggang Baek, an ethnically Korean Chinese national (*Joseonjok*), had won the first season of *The Birth of a Great Star* (*Widaehan Tansaeng*, MBC, 2010–13; hereafter *BGS*), a survival audition program for which Baek received significant media attention as the first foreign national to win such a competition in Korea in the more than twenty years that audition programs have been popular. So-called multicultural programs featuring casts made up primarily of foreign residents and immigrants have also become popular on Korean television during this period with the construction and production of a multicultural reality involving carefully crafted visual representations of foreigners, immigrants, and ethnic Koreans (Ahn 2018; Kim and Kim 2018).

In the specific case of audition programs, the trend toward recruiting participants from countries around the world has been coincident with the trend in K-pop toward increasing globalization and hybridization in terms of both production and consumption. A handful of foreign participants—including Brad Moore[1] of the popular indie band Busker Busker in *Super Star K* (season 3, 2011) and Longguo Jin[2] in *Produce 101* (season 2, 2017)—have attracted considerable media attention. Though many Korean survival audition programs have included foreign participants as a novelty to pique audiences' interest, none has yet produced a second foreign winner, even a decade after Baek's achievement. In this context, Baek's unique first-place showing in the first season of *BGS* merits an in-depth analysis as an example of an audition program assuming the status of a national media event and of the narration of the "Korean Dream" through the lens of racial and ethnic diversity.

According to reality TV scholars (Orbe 2008; Sen 2012; Murray and Ouellette 2009), it is not uncommon for this genre to appropriate cultural diversity to attract larger audiences. Korean survival audition programs actively embrace participants' diversity in terms of race, gender, class, sexuality, disability, and other lines of difference to dramatize their personal stories. Examining the global circulation of the *Idol* format, Sen (2012) astutely argues that "reality television's appetite for difference helps make it the global format *par excellence*, because globalization itself is fundamentally based on the category of difference" (207). Indeed, in the era of neoliberal capitalism, culture is commodifiable, and both cultural diversity and racial/ethnic difference serve as (cultural) resources to maximize profit. In Korea, the appearance of ethnic Korean nationals of other nations and other foreigners on audition programs serves to illustrate the shows' global engagement.

While it is apparent that neoliberal capitalism incorporates cultural diversity in the form of reality TV, a relatively small number of studies have specifically examined racial politics in reality TV (Orbe 2008). Some emblematic studies in the American context include racialized representations of White men and women of color in *The Bachelor* (Dubrofsky 2006), the commodification of gendered racial identity in *America's Next Top Model* (Hasinoff 2008), racial conflicts between rural Whites and urban Blacks in *The Real World* (Kraszewski 2009), and the construction of a postracial narrative in *Survivor* (Drew 2011), to name a few.

Even with the growing literature on race and reality TV, however, the gap in literature is even more startling when considering the global circulation of the reality TV format, because a critical analysis of race and reality TV within a specific local context is significantly lacking in global TV studies. Except for a couple of studies that examine how the *Idol* format of a competition show constructs a new national identity in the era of globalization in postcolonial multiracial/cultural societies—for example, *Malaysian Idol* (Lim 2008) and *New Zealand Idol* (De Bruin 2012)—the traveling narrative of race in reality TV is relatively understudied in global TV studies.

In the Korean context, critical media scholars, who have explored reality programs as part of a local and global nexus, assert the need for contextualized and historicized studies on reality television and its cultural meanings (Sujeong Kim 2010; Kim and Park 2006; Young-Chan Kim 2005; Choi and

Kang 2012; Choi and Kim 2010). These studies use close textual analysis to explicate the implications of reality television in contemporary Korean television within the context of social changes and media industrial changes. Yet, important gaps remain. Little research addresses the articulation of racial politics and the global circulation of the reality television format in the context of Korea's neoliberal globalization.

This chapter calls attention to how a localized survival audition program mediates racial/ethnic diversity to project the idea of a global Korea. Specifically, it examines how season 1 of the Korean survival audition program *BGS* narrates and constructs the Korean Dream through Baek's case and interrogates the broader social implications of this representation. In so doing, this study aims to fill an important gap in television studies scholarship by contemplating how Baek's ethnic background as a Korean Chinese is mediated in the audition program genre in Korea.

The chapter proceeds in four sections. It begins by reviewing the literature on reality television in general and Korean reality television in particular to identify a gap filled by this study: the need to analyze the articulation of racial politics in the global circulation of the reality television format under neoliberal globalization. I critically review the rise of the *Idol* format in the global television industry and contextualize the recent increase in audition programs in Korean television in relation to the globalization of Korean popular music (or K-pop). Second, I introduce season 1 of *BGS* in detail and analyze its localization practices in relation to its format. Third, I examine how the show produces Baek's victory as a national event through an analysis of the hero narrative and the mentor school system, a format that the show implemented to dramatize the mentor-mentee relationship. I explain how these tropes are linked to a larger social transformation. Fourth, I argue that *BGS*'s season 1 formulates a particular ideological construction of the Korean Dream through the image of Korea that it presents. I also demonstrate a paradox of the Korean Dream by pointing out its impossibility.

The *Idol* Franchise, Cultural Diversity, and the Globalization of K-Pop

The reality TV genre became a popular staple of television programming worldwide over two decades ago (Hill 2005; McMurria 2009; Orbe 2008; Murray and Ouellette 2009; Oren and Shahaf 2012). The genre took off in the UK and the US in the late 1990s and has since become one of the most profitable TV formats in the global television market due to its cheap production costs and flexible program formats. Studies that examine local variations and different cultural practices in the reality TV format have recently been introduced in the field of global TV format studies (see Moran 2009; Oren and Shahaf 2012).

Specifically, survival audition programs have been one of the most successful subgenres worldwide. This subgenre is exemplified by shows such as *American Idol* (Fox, 2002–16; ABC, 2018–present) and *Britain's Got Talent* (ITV, 2007–present), both of which achieved international popularity. The *Idol* format also provides the basis for hundreds of other talent competitions in local markets (Oren and Shahaf 2012, 13). According to Bochanty-Aguero (2012), *American Idol* has been distributed in 130 countries and the *Idol* format has been licensed to over forty media territories. Studies on the local adaptation of the *Idol* format have investigated its broader social and cultural implications in a global context and show that locals utilize the format to (re)construct national and/or regional identities (Kraidy and Sender 2011; Oren and Shahaf 2012; Lim 2008; Tay 2011).

Several studies argue that the *Idol* program has functioned as a televisual nation-building project in many countries around the world, including Malaysia (Lim 2008), India (Sen 2012), and New Zealand (De Bruin 2012). Analyzing *Malaysian Idol* and *New Zealand Idol*, respectively, Lim (2008) and De Bruin (2012) argue that though the programs are basically a singing competition, participants' vocal ability is not the primary criterion for their selection as a (national) idol. Instead, the correspondence between a participant's talent or character and the dominant society's image of the national ideal is determinative.

As a growing regional media hub for globalizing Asian media and popular culture, Korea is also deeply involved with a global *Idol* format. The cable TV channel Mnet first brought the *Idol* format to Korea through the survival audition program *Super Star K* (Mnet, 2009–16), one of the most popular and long-running survival audition programs in Korea. The first two seasons of *Super Star K* achieved the highest audience rating in the history of cable TV (with a national rating of 8.3 percent for the first season and 14.5 percent for the second season). Deeply influenced by Mnet's success, Korea's national television networks launched their own survival audition programs in the early 2000s: *BGS* (MBC, 2010–13), *Top Band* (KBS-2, 2011–12), and *K-Pop Star* (SBS, 2011–17).

This recent boom in *Idol*-formatted survival audition programs and music competition shows on Korean television has been supported by the recent regional and global success of the Korean Wave (*hallyu*), or the global diffusion of Korean popular culture, especially K-pop. As K-pop has become more and more visible and accessible in the global pop market, the national aspiration to produce "K-pop stars" has deepened both domestic and international viewers' interest in survival audition programs. Though K-pop is a distinctly Korean genre, in recent years, entertainment agencies have begun to recruit multinational trainees from other Asian countries such as China and Thailand to create global idol groups that can appeal to other Asian and Western markets. In the process, the content of K-pop has been increasingly hybridized and globalized (Ahn and Lin 2019; Hong and Lee 2010; Huang 2011).

BGS, Season 1: A Global Star Audition?

Capitalizing on the increasing popularity of K-pop in the global market and the national boom of audition programs in the late 2000s, *BGS* first aired on November 5, 2010, and lasted until 2013, broadcasting three annual seasons. To compete with the already successful cable TV show *Super Star K*, *BGS*, in season 1, increased its final prize as well as the scale of the show. The winner received a high-end sedan, 100 million won (about $90,000) in prize money, and 200 million won (about $180,000) to finance an album release. In addition, the show distinguished itself as global (rather than national) in scale, holding preliminary auditions that recruited participants from other nations, such as Japan, China, America, and Thailand.

As a result of global recruitment, five of the top-twelve contestants who made it to the live performance stage had originally auditioned abroad (see table 3.1). These participants' "foreignness" was not a detriment to their national popularity but instead affirmed a global interest in K-pop. *BGS* localized the *Idol* format by introducing new rules such as requiring the participants to sing at least one Korean song for the preliminary rounds of the show. Though other survival audition programs such as *Super Star K* and *K-Pop Star* did not place strict language requirements on songs, Korean language competency was important in *BGS*.[3] This is because *BGS* based its criteria on local sensibilities, a factor that distinguished the show from *American Idol* and other similar programs, while keeping its global appeal through international auditions, which attracted foreign participants and overseas Korean diasporas.

In terms of format, the show consisted of four stages: (1) preliminary

TABLE 3.1. The Names of the Top 12 Participants with National Origin or Residence Outside Korea

Participant	Rank	Race/ethnicity	Nationality	Residence
Cheonggang Baek	Top 1	4th generation Korean-Chinese (*joseonjok*)	China	China
Shayne Orok	Top 3	Vietnamese-Canadian (biracial White)	Canada	Canada
David Oh	Top 5	Korean-American	America	America
Seeun Baek	Top 10	Korean	Korea	Japan
Rise Kwon[a]	Top 12	4th generation Korean-Japanese (*zainichi*)	Korea	Japan

[a] After gaining some popularity through the show, Rise Kwon and David Oh from *Great Birth* were cast as a new (virtually) married couple on another reality program, *We Got Married* (MBC, 2008–2017). Kwon also successfully joined a female idol group called Ladies' Code in 2013. However, on September 3, 2014, Kwon and another group member were killed in a car accident.

round, (2) training camp, (3) mentor school, and (4) top-twelve live performances. In the preliminary round, the program selected 300 participants/teams, a number that was narrowed to 120 in the second round (100 participants/teams from Korea and 20 participants/teams from abroad and YouTube [episodes 1–7]).[4] After participating in a three-day and two-night training camp, the contestants went through various challenges, and twenty teams were selected for the pre–live broadcasting round (episodes 8–13). Those twenty teams were divided into five groups, each led by five mentors or judges who were professional singers, producers, and composers. After spending two weeks training under the mentor-mentee system (which the program calls the "mentor school system"), the top-twelve participants/teams were selected for the live broadcast (episodes 14–18). During the live performance period, the show eliminated two participants/teams per week (episodes 19–21) and then one per week (episodes 22–26) until Cheonggang Baek finally became the season's winner (episode 27).

Aside from its first few weeks of broadcast, season 1 of *BGS* was commercially successful, holding on to a fairly high audience rating throughout the season. The ratings ranged from 10 percent to 20 percent or above nationwide. Especially, the ratings reached their peak (23 percent) during the live performance period as the show's viewers willingly incurred a fee for voting via text messages (costing 100 won per message). On the day of the first live stage competition, for instance, the total cost of the text messages the program received was over 170 million won (about $150,000), a record for audition programs.

Korean Chinese in Korea's National Imagination

Baek's background as an ethnically Korean Chinese national means that the media buzz around his win was unusual. Historically speaking, Korean Chinese are Koreans who moved to China to escape Japanese colonial rule (1910–45) and settled in the specialized Korean districts in Northeast China. Though believed to share a blood tie with other Koreans, this group has historically been excluded from Koreanness due to their different nationality (Chinese citizenship) and long separation from mainland Korea (H. Park 2011). The issue of Korean Chinese immigrants in Korea (re)entered the public consciousness as Korea began to import foreign labor in the 1980s. Over the subsequent decades, China's post-socialist transformation, combined with Korea's higher wages, resulted in an increase in this immigrant population (Seol and Seo 2014). In search of a better lifestyle and better paid jobs, Korean Chinese adults (massively) migrated to Korea, creating a "Korean Wind" for those who live in Yanbian Korean Autonomous Prefecture in northern China close to the North Korean border, where roughly one-third of the population is of Korean ethnicity (Kwon 2015).

Ever since Korea and China established diplomatic ties in 1992, the number of Korean Chinese migrants has been continuously increasing in Korea, quickly becoming one of the largest ethnic groups in the country (Yoon 2010). In 2012, among all marriage migrants who married Korean spouses, Korean Chinese migrants made up 32.1 percent of that population, constituting the largest ethnic group, followed by (Han) Chinese (21.1 percent) and Vietnamese (18.3 percent) (MOGEF 2013). In addition, the total number of Korean Chinese migrants living in Korea reached 701,098 by the end of 2019, accounting for approximately 28 percent of all foreign residents (KOSIS 2020). In short, from childcare and restaurant work to construction jobs, Korea's industrial and service sectors now rely on Korean Chinese as a source of inexpensive labor.

Initially, the nation welcomed Korean Chinese because of their similarities to Koreans in language and physical appearance (Moon 2000, 157). As Yoon (2010) rightly puts it, however, "though Korean-Chinese seem to occupy privileged positions in Korea compared to other migrant worker groups, they are equally low-skilled workers and clustered at the lower classes" (537). Because they mostly joined the lowest rungs of Korea's job markets in the so-called 3-D (dirty, difficult, and dangerous) menial jobs shunned by affluent Koreans, they soon were located at the bottom of the racial/ethnic hierarchy in Korean society (Seol and Seo 2014). Studying hierarchal nationhood among different minority groups in Korea, Seol and Seo (2014) demonstrate that the ways in which the nation treats or governs ethnic/social minorities have changed from including and excluding certain groups to creating a hierarchy among those minority groups. They also found that Korean Chinese rank second to last in terms of legal and social rights in Korea among the nine different ethnic/social minorities, including mixed-race people, North Korean refugees, and sexual minorities. Furthermore, as discussed in other chapters of this book, discrimination against racial/ethnic minorities and such hierarchical visual representations on them in contemporary Korean visual culture generate particular narratives around their racial and cultural differences.

Due to the social discrimination and hostility that Korean Chinese experience during their stay in Korea, some Korean Chinese, despite their Korean blood ties, indicated that their return home migration experience to South Korea ended up reinforcing their Chinese identity (Hong, Song, and Park 2013).[5] Furthermore, the popular mainstream media's representation of Korean Chinese as cruel, inhumane, and greedy, coupled with the increasing crime rate among this group (see Yoon 2010, 538), furthered the othering process of Korean Chinese in Korean society (N. Kim 2014). In short, echoing what Oh addressed in the introduction to this volume; othering practices in Korea do not necessarily work through the concept of race. Even though Korean Chinese are ethnically Korean, they have been racialized as second-class citizens, deepening social antagonism between Koreans and Korean Chinese.

Narrating the Korean Dream

Under this social context, it is somewhat surprising that Korean audiences showed incredibly strong support for Baek: two of his online fan clubs combined had over twenty thousand members while he was on the show in 2011. He had more fan club members than any other participant in any season of *BGS*. When Baek eventually won first place, the Korean mainstream media was quick to frame his win as the "Korean Dream come true" (Kim and Jeong 2011; G. Park 2012). Indeed, Baek's reality TV win sparked a national conversation, positing that the Korean Dream was attainable by Korean Chinese and other migrants, including those from less-developed Southeast Asian countries.

In the beginning of the episode that depicted the preliminary round held in China (episode 6), the show described Baek as a "diamond in the rough." As a twenty-one-year-old man who loved K-pop and dreamed of becoming a singer in Korea, Baek was able to succeed through each round of the show despite being a fourth-generation Korean Chinese. In fact, the show embraced his nationality as a non-Korean citizen as a marker of its own (cultural) diversity and fairness. Because the Korean mainstream media normally represents Korean Chinese through negative stereotypes—as bloodless money-grubbers or heinous criminals (Se Ryoung Kim 2012; N. Kim 2014)—Baek's first-place win on a commercial audition program was unexpected. However, the show's Korean Dream narrative that portrays Korea as an ideal place for Korean Chinese to fulfill their dreams and achieve success went beyond its embrace of ethnic diversity and Baek's first-place win.

Similar to the colloquial use of the term "American Dream," the term "Korean Dream" "implies a certain desire for equation between Korea and America as a destination for immigrants and migrants, as the term Korean Dream recognizes Korea's new place in the global hierarchy as a semiperipheral metropole" (Lee 2010, 214). Specifically, it locates Korea in an imaginative place where it promises fulfillment of migrants' desire to be (economically) successful and where their (social) well-being is guaranteed as long as they are talented and work hard. This narrative that projects a particular image onto Korea needs to be (re)narrated and (re)invented not only for (im)migrants but also for general Koreans through various social apparatuses, including popular culture and media, in order to effectively govern and suture racial antagonism among different racial/ethnic groups as the number of ethnic minorities increases. Therefore, it is important to understand how shows like *BGS* construct the Korean Dream narrative: specifically, how the show produced Baek as a final winner and what this signifies for Korean popular culture.

Hero Narrative

The narrative structure of the survival audition program—the premise that anybody can audition and that ordinary people (just like us) can become celebrity heroes—is an attractive element for audiences (Choi and Kang 2012). Viewers get vicarious pleasure from watching participants' emotional journeys as they achieve their dreams through the show.

Contemporary reality television has evolved from a documentary format and focus (Corner 2002; Kilborn 1994, 2003; Nichols 1994; Hill 2007), so contemporary reality audition programs have increased the audience's dramatic interest by emphasizing the participants' life stories and by documenting an unscripted competition. The shows have highlighted unique or dramatic features of the participants' life stories, such as physical disabilities or life hardships such as extreme poverty or familial problems. Many winners of survival audition programs have been people who overcame great difficulty in their past. For instance, Donggeun Han, the winner of *BGS*, season 3, has epilepsy. Gak Heo, the winner of *Super Star K*, season 2, was not able to finish high school for economic reasons. Heo worked as a ventilator repairman to earn money while pursuing his singing career at a night club, a story that touched audiences' hearts and made him the eventual winner of his season.

Yet *BGS*, season 1, is distinct from other survival audition programs in that in addition to providing broad Korean audiences with vicarious satisfaction by dramatizing the winner's story of transformation and triumph, it also provides a narrative of the Korean Dream specifically targeting Asian immigrants, particularly Korean Chinese. Baek's personal life story is woven into the show's narrative as the story of a "great birth." His personal story as a Korean Chinese, who lived in China his whole life, follows a hero narrative in the sense that he overcomes difficulties with the help of a mentor to eventually win the top prize (Choi and Kang 2012). For instance, in his personal interview on the show, Baek said that he has lived on his own since the age of nine, when his parents went abroad to Russia and Korea to earn money. Because he was poor, Baek ate ramen (a cheap instant noodle dish in Korea) daily to save money. Despite these difficult circumstances, Baek did not give up on his dream to be a singer in Korea. Instead, he took a thirty-six-hour train ride to audition for *BGS* in Chungdo, China. Baek's dramatic success story was not only highlighted by the survival audition program but also later circulated on the national level via television, print, and online media.

The show articulated Baek's Korean Chinese identity to dramatize his victory. In the ordinary manner of survival audition programs, the show constructed a hero narrative that presented Baek as a young man in his early twenties who overcame challenges such as family poverty and his minority ethnic background through his passion for achieving the goal of becoming a singer in Korea. Instead of making him even more foreign and unrelatable to a Korean audience, Baek's ethnic minority status provided a reason to support him because it was tied to his economic struggles, the backdrop for his ultimate success.

Mentor School System

While the hero narrative is crucial to understanding the Korean Dream narrative surrounding Baek's dramatic personal story, that alone does not explain Baek's popularity because he is not the only contestant who overcame hardships that the show dramatized. Instead, his popularity grew during the mentor school system, a device introduced by *BGS*. Unlike other *Idol* formats, which generally cast three judges, season 1 of *BGS* casts five mentors.[6] By calling them "mentors" instead of "judges," the show redefined the relationship between judge and participant, emphasizing the mentors' participation in helping to create the participants' "great birth." As Kim and Kim (2012) point out, this was a marker of television format localization, where the show attempted to create *jeong* (the Korean notion of affection) between mentors and mentees. By highlighting affection, the show increased opportunities for dramatic relational moments while maintaining the basic format of the show as a competition program. The enactment of the value of *jeong* allowed audience members to feel that they were participating in the contestants' success (through their voting) and that the Korean Dream was nobler than a cutthroat capitalist system that determines success based on superficial factors like an individual's appearance or economic background.

Baek's celebrity cannot be fully understood without first understanding his close relationship to his mentor, Taewon Kim. As the former lead guitarist of the famous Korean rock band *Buhwal* ("revival"), Kim embodied a narrative of revival as he himself was once imprisoned for drug use. Yet by the time he was cast on *BGS*, season 1, Kim had successfully reestablished himself as a famous entertainer. He was seen as a mentor who deeply sympathized with participants' struggles, and audiences were touched by his sincere comments on each participant's performance (Ha 2011).

Interest in Kim—and also in the contestants he mentored—reached its peak during the mentor school period of the show (episodes 8–13). Although the other mentors' selection process of their four mentees was dramatized for entertainment, Kim's was presented as especially dramatic because it went against expectations (episode 12). All four of Kim's mentees—Cheonggang Baek, Taegon Lee, Jinyoung Son, and Jeongmo Yang—were contestants who had not been chosen by other judges because of their perceived shortcomings to advance to the next round. Kim's mentees lacked typical markers of cultural capital such as attractiveness, a slim body shape, higher education, and stable economic status. In particular, the show emphasized that these contestants had faced discrimination based on their appearance. For instance, Taegon Lee, a mentee of Taewon Kim who ultimately ranked in the top two, said that he had been rejected numerous times at auditions because of his grim face. Jinyoung Son, who ranked in the top four, had been told that he was hard featured and loutish.

Despite these disadvantages, however, Kim took a risk and chose these contestants for his mentor school. His choice was popular: three of his four mentees—Baek, Lee, and Son—eventually ranked among the top four. Audiences wanted to see these contestants overcome social barriers such as discrimination based on appearance because these barriers were so firmly based in reality, outside the world constructed by reality TV. The audiences were able to project fantasies of a fair Korean society onto these participants and feel empowered by actively participating in the show's voting system. Both Kim and his mentees were a perfect fit for the purpose of the show, making a "great birth." This perhaps does not merely refer to a great birth of a new star within the format of a survival audition program; it may also imply a "great (re)birth" of Korea, the nation itself. For example, the hero narrative combined with the mentor school system deeply touched audiences—especially young audiences—in their yearning for a (new) Korea where individuals can achieve their dreams, despite the hardships they are born with, through "fair" competition and the help of "true" mentors, a fantasy that audiences wish to make a reality.

Locating Korea on the Global Cultural Map

The hero narrative combined with the mentor school system mobilized the myth of success under the Korean Dream, which in turn constructs a particular image of Korea's place on the global cultural map. Through the Korean Dream, Korea is imagined as a dynamic space where people can create their own success stories. This particular image of Korea as promising (economic) success is not limited to Korean audiences but shared globally. In particular, Baek's "Korean Dream come true" story migrated back to the Korean Chinese community in China, reinforcing the myth of the Korean Dream there. Baek's first-place win on a Korean audition program inspired Korean Chinese living in Korea, Korean Chinese communities in China, and other immigrants. Baek's courageous triumph in Korea was reported as a feature news item in the Korean Chinese media in China, and every time Baek moved on to the next round of the competition, Korean Chinese society celebrated a small victory (Hur 2011; Jin 2011; H. Kim 2011).

When Baek visited his hometown after his win, many fans from the Korean Chinese community gathered at the airport to meet him in person and celebrated his arrival. The passionate welcome for Baek among Korean Chinese in China projected the hope that the Korean Dream would be possible for them, too. Likewise, Korean Chinese living in Korea made it a community event to cheer on Baek every Friday night as *BGS* aired (Hur 2011). In short, Baek's win on one of the most popular audition programs in Korean television was a symbolic event for Korean Chinese communities in both China and Korea.

Baek's passion for K-pop and his embrace of Korean culture bolstered his popularity among Korean audiences as well. In an interview on the show, he said that when he first watched H.O.T. (the "grand ancestor" of contemporary K-pop groups in Korea and the group that initiated the first stage of the Korean Wave in China in the late 1990s) perform the song "We Are the Future" on Chinese television as an early adolescent, he was amazed and wanted to be like them. Then, in episode 24 of *BGS*, when the contestants were tasked with performing the most important song in their life, Baek chose to sing H.O.T.'s "We Are the Future," recalling and performing his childhood dreams for the audience. This moment represented the global consumption of Korean culture through the eyes of a Korean Chinese boy's fascination with K-pop. Baek's comment that he was inspired by K-pop indicated the success of the Korean Wave in East Asia, and this statement was repeated by the Korean media to increase Korean audiences' national pride. The Korean Wave is a national project combining the desires of the Korean state, market, and audience (Youna Kim 2013; Chua and Iwabuchi 2008), so this Korean Chinese man's childhood dream of being a singer in Korea was pleasing to Korean audiences.

In episode 20, each contestant performed one of the top one hundred international pop songs most popular in Korea. This mission was particularly challenging for Baek, who had never before performed an English pop song on stage. Unlike other participants, who were familiar with these pop songs (David Oh was from the US, Shayne Orok was from Canada, and the Korean contestants had learned English in school), Baek was not familiar with Western pop songs and his English pronunciation was poor. For this reason, the mentors' evaluation was lower for this performance than for his previous performances (he was ranked fifth out of ten in this round), but he survived and was able to move to the next round.

Though Baek struggled to sing Western pop songs in English, he was much better at Korean pop songs—particularly older songs from the 1970s through the 1990s.[7] The mentors appreciated his ability to interpret these songs and said that his voice reached Koreans' hearts. The relative difficulty he had singing Western pop songs compared to the ease of singing Korean songs was viewed positively by Korean audiences. It made Baek appear to be a sincere fan of Korean popular culture. Though Western pop has a much larger market and audience base, Baek's narrative suggested that in some places, K-pop may be received with greater appreciation than Western pop, stimulating Koreans' pride in the Korean Wave and intensifying the fantasy that Korea is becoming a pseudo-cultural empire in the region.

However, this pseudo-imperialistic desire hidden behind Baek's popularity does highlight a rupture in the Korean Dream narrative that the show employs. *BGS*'s season 1 reproduced the myth of the Korean Dream by producing the first Korean Chinese winner of a Korean survival audition program, but it also indicated the impossibility of the Korean Dream. Just before the final round of season 1, an anonymous person made the accusation online that Baek had belittled Korea on his personal web page[8] in 2009. The anonymous post copied the following short passage, alleged to have been written by Baek: "What's good about Korea? They ignore us [Korean Chinese]. When I become a singer in Korea, I will trample them down." Baek immediately denied having ever written the post, and the scandal turned out to be a hoax. Yet the general public's immediate reaction to this controversy was hostility toward him, and he received malicious comments from Koreans. This hoax provided a forum for many Koreans to express their negative feelings about the increasing number of Asian immigrants and Korean Chinese living in Korea and dissatisfaction with governmental multicultural policies.

Baek's personal web page scandal indicates the impossibility (or discomfort) of the Korean Dream, constituting cultural sites where social antagonism between Koreans and internal racial/ethnic others, including Korean Chinese and Asian immigrants, was enacted. For Koreans, the moments revealed immigrants' potential to betray Korea. For Korean Chinese and other immigrants, the moments reminded them that the Korean Dream is elusive and reinforced the understanding that they are allowed in the country only as low-wage labor. Furthermore, the moments informed these immigrants that they are not allowed to be critical of Korea but instead obligated to *love* Korea to avoid suspicion based on their ethnic difference. Immigrants who are unfaithful to or critical of Korea will find themselves the target of hatred, as in Baek's case. Though many

K-pop audition programs suture this type of rupture to produce an ideological fantasy of a multiethnic/global Korea where immigrants can achieve success and the Korean Dream, the impossibility of the dream is made visible through moments of rupture and racial/ethnic antagonism.

Conclusion

This chapter examined how *BGS*, season 1, localized its format and produced a narrative that reimagined a global Korea. I contextualized the show within the globalization of the reality TV genre and Korean media and popular culture. By producing the first foreign national winner, the show drew upon Cheonggang Baek's ethnic and socioeconomic background both to demonstrate the global popularity of the Korean Wave and to describe a triumphant narrative where a marginalized figure is able to attain his goals through the participation of a Korean audience. I argued that the show successfully dramatizes the success of an ordinary Korean Chinese man and projects the fantasy of the Korean Dream for multicultural subjects by showcasing Korea as an open and fair society to all, regardless of racial/ethnic background. Furthermore, the show also projects Korea's desire to be a cultural pseudo-empire in the global cultural imagination by appropriating participants' diverse ethnic background and their passion for K-pop.

Despite the numerous K-pop audition programs aired up until today, Baek still remains the first and only foreign national winner in the history of K-pop auditioning programs in Korea. This means that Baek's success story was produced as a media event at a particular moment in Korean society when his (supposedly less desirable) ethnic difference was consumed as a tool for mobilizing the Korean Dream narrative in its articulation with audition programs that were seeking individual drama and success. In other words, Baek's first-place win was possible as long as his "dream come true story" sustained and propelled the Korean Dream for both Koreans and immigrants. For immigrants, this Korean Dream narrative constructs Korea as a desirable place to be while for (native) Koreans, the image of Korea is also elevated in the global community, placing them in a superior position than those who migrated to Korea to seek a better life and opportunities (Oh and Oh 2016).

Hence, it is not so surprising that Baek's popularity has never exceeded the level that he reached during his performance in *BGS*. Instead, his image as an achiever of the Korean Dream quickly faded away, and his image as an emblematic Korean Chinese media figure was easily consumed as a visual vehicle for some Korean internet users to mock Korean Chinese individuals. Particularly, the online users of *Ilbe*, one of the largest online communities known for its extreme expressions of racism and misogyny, have appropriated his image to belittle Korean Chinese as intrinsically barbaric, circulating racist prejudice and rumors that Korean Chinese eat human flesh. It is ironic that, once produced as the "great birth" of a K-pop star, Baek has become a (national) target of racist hate. Perhaps this moment of irony precisely reveals that his televised Korean Dream has never come true.

NOTES

1. Brad Moore was the band's American drummer; it won second place in *Super Star K*, season 3. Though the media attention primarily focused on the group's front man Beom June Jang, Moore was conspicuous as one of the few foreigners who received national media attention on an audition program.

2. Like Baek, Longguo Jin (in Korean: 김용국) is Korean Chinese from Yanbian Korean Autonomous Prefecture in northeastern China. He gained popularity by surviving multiple rounds of the competition in the second season of *Produce 101*, though he eventually placed 21st among the 101 participants. Baek and Jin, then, share the distinction of being recent rare examples of Korean Chinese K-pop singers who emerged from K-pop audition programs.

3. Because many participants, regardless of their nationality, sing pop songs in English for their auditions on *Super Star K* and *K-Pop Star*, audience comments consistently remark that it is very doubtful these shows are really producing Korean pop stars since many participants sing in English more than in Korean.

4. The twenty teams from abroad included two from Japan, eight from America, three from Thailand, four from China, two from Canada, and one from France.

5. Hong et al. (2013) studied how Korean Chinese contested identity negotiation as they migrated from China to Korea in pursuit of the Korean Dream through in-depth interviews and found that more than half of their interviewees (twelve out of twenty-two) identified more as Chinese than Korean due to the harsh discrimination and everyday racism they encountered in Korea.

6. Each of the five mentors embodied different characteristics and teaching styles to add interest to the program. For instance, Sihyuk Bang, a professional composer and producer, paid keen attention to participants' marketability (commodifiability), whereas Seonghoon Shin, a popular male solo singer, emphasized participants' unique vocal qualities. Yuna Kim, a vocalist and leader of the band Jawoorim, cared more about participants' unique characteristics and free spirit because her band began as an underground indie band. Each mentor's character/persona is an important factor driving the show (see Ha 2011).

7. Baek received high ratings when the mission was to sing a Korean pop masterpiece from the 1980s and 1990s (episode 19), and he chose to reinterpret songs from

Yongphil Cho, Koreans' all-time favorite singer, nicknamed the King of Singing (episode 22).

8. This post was alleged to have come from Baek's personal home page on Cyworld, the most popular website in Korea for blogging and social networking prior to the popularization of Facebook.

REFERENCES

Ahn, Ji-Hyun. 2018. *Mixed-Race Politics and Neoliberal Multiculturalism in South Korean Media*. Cham: Palgrave Macmillan.

Ahn, Ji-Hyun, and Tien-wen Lin. 2019. "The Politics of Apology: The 'Tzuyu Scandal' and Transnational Dynamics of K-Pop." *International Communication Gazette* 81 (2): 158–75.

Bochanty-Aguero, Erica Jean. 2012. "We Are the World: *American Idol*'s Global Self-Posturing." In *Global Television Formats: Understanding Television across Borders*, edited by Tasha G. Oren and Sharon Shahaf, 260–82. New York: Routledge.

Choi, Eunkyoung, and Seung-Hyun Kim. 2010. "The Two Faces of Reality TV: Construction and Deconstruction of Ideological Discourse of Love and Marriage on Reality Program 'Gold Miss Is Coming.'" *Korean Journal of Broadcasting* 24 (3): 175–219.

Choi, So-Mang, and Seung-Mook Kang. 2012. "Analysis on Narrative Structure of TV Audition Reality Show: Focusing on the 'Star Audition: The Great Birth' and 'Superstar K2.'" *Journal of Korea Contents Association* 12 (6): 120–31.

Chua, Beng Huat, and Koichi Iwabuchi, eds. 2008. *East Asian Pop Culture: Analyzing the Korean Wave*. Hong Kong: Hong Kong University Press.

Corner, John. 2002. "Performing the Real: Documentary Diversions." *Television & New Media* 3 (3): 255–69. https://doi.org/10.1177/152747640200300302

De Bruin, Joost. 2012. "*NZ Idol*: Nation Building through Format Adaptation." In *Global Television Formats: Understanding Television across Borders*, edited by Tasha G. Oren and Sharon Shahaf, 223–41. New York: Routledge.

Drew, Emily. 2011. "Pretending to Be 'Postracial': The Spectacularization of Race in Reality TV's Survivor." *Television & New Media* 12 (4): 326–46. https://doi.org/10.1177/1527476410385474

Dubrofsky, Rachele. 2006. "The Bachelor: Whiteness in the Harem." *Critical Studies in Media Communication* 23 (1): 39–56. https://doi.org/10.1080/07393180600570733

Ha, Jae Geun. 2011. "Kim Tae-Won in *The Great Birth*, a Touching Humanity." *MediaUS*. Accessed May 25, 2012. http://www.mediaus.co.kr/news/articleView.html?idxno=16288

Hasinoff, Amy Adele. 2008. "Fashioning Race for the Free Market on *America's Next Top Model*." *Critical Studies in Media Communication* 25 (3): 324–43.

Hill, Annette. 2005. *Reality TV: Audiences and Popular Factual Television*. London: Routledge.

Hill, Annette. 2007. *Restyling Factual TV: Audiences and News, Documentary and Reality Genres*. London: Routledge.

Hong, Jimin, and Eunjoo Lee. 2010. "Why Is There a 'Multinational Trend' in Entertainment Industry?" *Seoul Newspaper*, July 28, 22. Accessed December 5, 2012. http://www.seoul.co.kr/news/newsView.php?id=20100728022007

Hong, Yihua, Changzoo Song, and Julie Park. 2013. "Korean, Chinese, or What? Identity Transformations of Chosŏnjok (Korean Chinese) Migrant Brides in South Korea." *Asian Ethnicity* 14 (1): 29–51. https://doi.org/10.1080/14631369.2012.703074

Huang, Shuling. 2011. "Nation-Branding and Transnational Consumption: Japan-Mania and the Korean Wave in Taiwan." *Media, Culture & Society* 33 (1): 3–18.

Hur, Jae Hyun. 2011. "A Korean-Chinese Baek Chung-Kang's Great Challenge." *Hankyoreh*, April 29. http://www.hani.co.kr/arti/society/society_general/475548.html

Jin, Hyang Hee. 2011. "Korean-Chinese Newspapers Are Eager to Praise Cheonggang Baek as a Hero." *Daily Economy* (Seoul), May 30. https://www.mk.co.kr/news/culture/view/2011/05/344170/

Kilborn, Richard. 1994. "'How Real Can You Get?': Recent Developments in 'Reality' Television." *European Journal of Communication* 9 (4): 421–39. https://doi.org/10.1177/0267323194009004003

Kilborn, Richard. 2003. *Staging the Real: Factual TV Programming in the Age of Big Brother*. Manchester: Manchester University Press.

Kim, Chohee, and Doh Yeon Kim. 2018. "Immigrants and Foreigners in Korean Multicultural TV Programs: Differences by Genre and Changes over Time." *Korean Journal of Journalism & Communication Studies* 62 (3): 309–41. In Korean.

Kim, Hyung Gyu. 2011. "The 'Great Change' That Cheonggang Back Has Made." *Kyunghyang Newspaper*, May 19, 11.

Kim, Nam Seok. 2014. "A Study of Korean-Chinese in *The Yellow Sea*." *Journal of Multicultural Society* 7 (2): 107–36.

Kim, Se Ryoung. 2012. "A Study on the Reproduction of Korean-Chinese Immigrants in Korean Novels since 2000s." *Studies of Korean Literature* 37:425–64.

Kim, Su Mi, and Sun Hyong Jeong. 2011. "Cheonggang Back—The Korean-Chinese Star—Is Standing on the Finish Line to 'Korean Dream.'" *Segye Ilbo*, May 25, 2.

Kim, Sujeong. 2010. "The Cultural Politics of Self-Government in Global Reality Game Shows: In the Case of 'Project Runway' and 'America's Next Top Model.'" *Korean Journal of Broadcasting* 24 (6): 7–44.

Kim, Yeran, and Joo-Yeun Park. 2006. "A Study on Theories and Practices of Reality Programs." *Korean Journal of Broadcasting* 20 (3): 7–48.

Kim, Yoon Mi. 2011. "Audition Programs Captivate Korea." *Korea Herald*, July 22. Accessed June 3, 2014. http://www.koreaherald.com/view.php?ud=20110722000833

Kim, Youna, ed. 2013. *The Korean Wave: Korean Media Go Global*. New York: Routledge.

Kim, Young-Chan. 2005. "Reality Program, Foreign Series and Reshaping Korean Television Programs." *Program/Text* 13:79–93.

KOSIS. 2020. "Status of Foreign Residents by Nationality and Age." *KOSIS: Korean Statistical Information Service*. https://kosis.kr/statHtml/statHtml.do?orgId=111&tblId=DT_1B040A6&conn_path=I2

Kraidy, Marwan, and Katherine Sender, eds. 2011. *The Politics of Reality Television: Global Perspectives*. New York: Routledge.

Kraszewski, John 2009. "Country Hicks and Urban Cliques: Mediating Race, Reality, and Liberalism MTV's *The Real World*." In *Reality TV: Remaking Television Culture*, edited by Susan Murray and Laurie Ouellette, 205–22. New York: New York University Press.

Kwon, June Hee. 2015. "The Work of Waiting: Love and Money in Korean Chinese Transnational Migration." *Cultural Anthropology* 30 (3): 477–500. https://doi.org/10.14506/ca30.3.06

Lim, Joanne. 2008. "Reinventing Nationalism: The Politics of *Malaysian Idol* on Culture and Identity in Postcolonial Malaysia." In *Media Consumption and Everyday Life in Asia*, edited by Youna Kim, 70–82. New York: Routledge.

McMurria, John. 2009. "Global TV Realities: International Markets, Geopolitics, and the Transcultural Contexts of Reality TV." In *Reality TV: Remaking Television Culture*, edited by Susan Murray and Laurie Ouellette, 179–202. New York: New York University Press.

MOGEF. 2013. *A Study on the National Survey of Multicultural Families 2012*. Seoul: Ministry of Gender Equality and Family.

Moon, Katharine. 2000. "Strangers in the Midst of Globalization." In *Korea's Globalization*, edited by Samuel Kim, 147–69. Oxford: Cambridge University Press.

Moran, Albert, ed. 2009. *TV Formats Worldwide: Localizing Global Programs*. Chicago: Intellect.

Murray, Susan, and Laurie Ouellette, eds. 2009. *Reality TV: Remaking Television Culture*. 2nd ed. New York: New York University Press.

Nichols, Bill. 1994. *Blurred Boundaries: Questions of Meaning in Contemporary Culture*. Bloomington: Indiana University Press.

Oh, David C., and Chuyun Oh. 2016. "'Until You Are Able': South Korean Multiculturalism and Hierarchy in *My Little Hero*." *Communication, Culture & Critique* 9 (2): 250–65. https://doi.org/10.1111/cccr.12104

Orbe, Mark P. 2008. "Representations of Race in Reality TV: Watch and Discuss." *Critical Studies in Media Communication* 25 (4): 345–52.

Oren, Tasha G., and Sharon Shahaf, eds. 2012. *Global Television Formats: Understanding Television across Borders*. New York: Routledge.

Park, Gun Wook. 2012. "I Will Be a Civil Diplomat Who Connects Korean-Chinese and Korea." *Herald Economy*, May 1. http://news.heraldcorp.com/view.php?ud=2012050 1000211&md=20120617064636_AP

Park, Hyun Ok. 2011. "For the Rights of 'Colonial Returnees': Korean Chinese, Decolonization, and Neoliberal Democracy in South Korea." In *New Millennium South Korea: Neoliberal Capitalism and Transnational Movements*, edited by Jesook Song, 115–29. New York: Routledge.

Sen, Biswarup. 2012. "*Idol* Worship: Ethnicity and Difference in Global Television." In *Global Television Formats: Understanding Television across Borders*, edited by Tasha G. Oren and Sharon Shahaf, 203–22. New York: Routledge.

Seol, Dong-Hoon, and Jungmin Seo. 2014. "Dynamics of Ethnic Nationalism and Hierarchical Nationhood: Korean Nation and Its Otherness since the Late 1980s." *Korea Journal* 54 (2): 5–33.

Tay, Jinna. 2011. "The Search for an Asian Idol: The Performance of Regional Identity in Reality Television." *International Journal of Cultural Studies* 14 (3): 323–38. https://doi.org/10.1177/1367877910391870

Yoon, In-Jin. 2010. "Multicultural Minority Groups and Multicultural Coexistence in Korean Society." *Korea Observer* 41 (4): 517–57.

4

Narratives of Marginalized Otherness in Migrant Women

The South Korean films *Rosa* and *Thuy*

Eunbi Lee and Colby Y. Miyose

> "We are Vietnamese. Koreans don't listen to us."
> —*Thuy*

> "You are so naïve. Do you think we can go back home? We are manipulated by Koreans."
> —*Rosa*

The Korean films *Thuy* and *Rosa* show migrant women from different races (Asian and White) and nationalities (Vietnamese and Uzbek) who share similar feelings toward Korean people. In their conversations, the women depict Koreans as ruthless, manipulative, and relentless. From the lived experiences of Eunbi Lee, a Korean woman and one of the authors of this chapter, seeing young Vietnamese women working in the farms and holding hands with older local men on the streets was common. Witnessing Uzbek women working at adult entertainment bars was a frequent sight as well. It is not unusual to see media that depict these migrant women as "others" who take up the gendered positions (i.e., female farmworker, sex worker, and housewife in the countryside) that Korean women are reluctant to hold. The migrant women are made into the quintessential objectified and sexualized "other," whose purpose is to restore the population and fulfill underprivileged men's sexual desires. Though these are prevalent portrayals, media accounts do not always show dominant discourses. Particularly, independent films that are relatively free from Hollywood's grasp become a space where creators might produce more complex discourses that show diverse layers of others' lives (Park, Lee, and Wagner 2016, 2). In doing so, the independent movies *Rosa* and *Thuy* can be possible texts that re(de)construct existing discourses of the lives of migrant women in Korea.

Rosa (2012) is based on the true story of a talented eighteen-year-old Uzbek ballerina who migrates to South Korea to earn her tuition for the Bolshoi Ballet Academy in her pursuit of the "Korean Dream." Although she was promised that she could go back to her homeland and school after building her dance career in Korea, she is trafficked and degraded as an exotic dancer and sex worker under the surveillance and coercion of a criminal employer. The movie showcases how she negotiates between her dream of becoming a ballerina and her brutal reality of being forced into dancing and giving sexual services to Korean men without payment. The film premiered in commercial and independent movie theaters across South Korea. In the narrative of the protagonist Rosa, domestic film critics applauded the film for bringing light to the complexity between the forced labor that migrant women face and how they confront these challenges through the embodiment of their lived experiences (Cho 2014).

Thuy (2013) shows the life of a Vietnamese migrant woman who migrates to a rural area in South Korea through a mail-order marriage. The movie highlights Thuy's story of struggling to find the mysterious cause of her husband's death amid threats by her male neighbors. All the while, she continually attempts to assimilate into Korean culture and customs by taking care of her parents-in-law. Thuy is also a loyal and caring friend. She constantly helps her compatriot from being beaten by her Korean husband. The film premiered at the 2013 Busan International Film Festival and was screened at other film festivals such as the Dubai Film Festival, the Los Angeles Pacific Film Festival, the Hawaii International Film Festival, and the Eurasia International Film Festival. The Vietnamese media and film industry also paid attention to the movie because it was the first Korean movie in which a Vietnamese actress, Ninh Duong Lan Ngoc, had starred as the protagonist, portraying the reality of Vietnamese brides' lives (Yong 2014).

In this chapter, we utilize textual analysis to delve into the ways the films describe the lives of migrant women from different races, nationalities, and occupations who are positioned to imply their otherness in Korean society. Before doing so, we present the theoretical lens and methodology that inform the analysis.

Third World Feminism and Cultural Discourses of Migrant Women in South Korea

Racial, ethnic, and national diversity in Korea has rapidly increased since the 1988 Seoul Olympics. In 2016, About 2.36 million international migrants have resided in Korea for various reasons, such as employment, education, general training, and marriage. Of this total, 1.10 million are migrant women mostly from relatively developing countries in East Asia, Southeast Asia, and Central Asia (Heo-oh 2016, 1).

The stream of migrant women into Korea has been heavily influenced by state policies enforced to meet the country's standards of globalization while maintaining Korean social and cultural orders. In other words, the Korean government tries to integrate the neoliberal logic of globalization into their economic market through the flow of economic migrant labor and mobile global capital (Watson 2010, 337). Another reason for the influx of migrant women is that the Korean government aims at emphasizing reproduction to increase the fertility rate in Korea, which will inherently increase the Korean population. During this process, the state foregrounds the importance of upholding traditional family values (H. Kim 2007, 101).

As a result, the Korean government established gendered state policies under the discourses of multiculturalism. For instance, the government offers various types of visas to migrant women. The E-9 (nonprofessional employment) and the E-6 (entertainer) are the most prevalent visas for migrant women from developing countries. With these visas, they end up working in factories, farms, and adult entertainment establishments. Another type of visa, F-6 (foreign spouse), is offered for marriage migrant women, most of whom live with middle-aged and elderly Korean men in rural areas (Ministry of Justice in Korea 2019).

Migrant women from different races, ethnicities, and nationalities tend to be structured into particular professions in Korea for a variety of complicated reasons (Choe 2007, 141). For example, women mostly from the Philippines, Central Asia, and Thailand are easily trapped into working in the sex industry. Filipinos, who are able to speak English, tend to work at brothels and bars to serve US military personnel stationed in Korea. White women from Central Asia and Thai women do sex work for Korean men (Kim and Song 2017, 66–68). In contrast, women who have low-skilled working visas and marriage visas, mostly from East Asia and Southeast Asia, are relocated to rural areas to work in farms and support Korean families.

These patterns of the lives of migrant women in Korea display what Mohanty (1997) terms "Third World women's work," where particular privileges are dependent on race, ethnicity, and class (5). She argues that Third World women tend to be monolithically represented as underdeveloped, traditional, illiterate, and poor, resulting in limited jobs within the frames of racial, gendered, class, and cultural hierarchies (Mohanty 1991, 6). For example, farmworkers, nannies, maids, wives for elderly low-income men, and sex workers are the only positions afforded to these women because affluent domestic women are not willing to perform these roles (Ehreinch and Hoschild 2002, 23). Migrant women from underdeveloped or developing countries are limited to work and live under the hegemonic ideological construction of jobs and tasks linked to hyperfemininity, domesticity, (hetero)sexuality, and racial and cultural stereotypes in the global-local contexts (Mohanty 1997, 6).

Though Third World women tend to live under the racial and patriarchal systems, they are still able to think for themselves, feel emotions, and move toward positioning themselves for better lives. Fine and Speer (1992) argue that one's life develops not only by shared societies and cultures but also by the possibility of speaking of oneself in a specific time and space (10). That is, identities do not remain in the dominant system but move around by subjects who speak up and embody their identity themselves. This account of identity allows us to see emotions, feelings, voices, actions, and powers in our lives. Utilizing this idea, we want to consider Third World women not just as objects but also as subjects. Migrant women, who work for certain jobs and tasks, deal with their emotions and feelings in everyday life. These women embrace the struggles and uneasiness of living in particular categories, as well as reveal a sense of ourselves that fits in their subjectivities. This explanation allows us to see different stages for the representation and exploration of the lives of marginalized migrant women.

With an understanding of the complexity of the representation of Third World women, this study analyzes the ways in which the lives of migrant women in South Korean independent films are re(de)constructing the representation of underserved women in global-local contexts. Several scholars have examined the media representation of migrant women. For instance, White women from Russia and Central Asia are depicted as "white dolls" who cater to the sexual pleasures of rich Korean men (Kim and Fu 2008, 493). Meanwhile, marriage migrant women from developing countries in East Asia and Southeast Asia are described as obedient bodies who conform to Korean patriarchal norms (Cha, Lee, and

Park 2016, 1484). Sumi Kim (2009) analyzed two South Korean films, *Failan* (2001) and *Wedding Campaigns* (2005), that depict the lives of Korean Chinese migrant women (*Joseon-jok*) and Uzbek-Korean women (*Golyeoin*), respectively. She argues that these two movies imply (1) ideological discourses of patriarchy, as female characters preserve their femininity as a bride and a potential mother for children, and (2) the myth of Korean homogeneity, by showing the women trying to assimilate into its culture (222–23). The aforementioned studies display how mass media reinforces stereotypes of these women as being sexual, subservient, and docile objects to Korean patriarchy.

Given the contributions of preliminary research, this study extends on mediated representations of migrant women by examining the two independent films *Rosa* and *Thuy*. These films present two migrant women from different races and nationalities (Caucasian Uzbek and Asian Vietnamese) but from the same classes (both underprivileged) who live in different social and cultural conditions (sex worker and marriage migrant woman). Using a post-structural textual analysis of these characters, this study investigates the ways in which the lives of migrant women are represented in the global-local context of South Korea.

Post-Structural Textual Analysis

Bryman (2004) states that textual analysis is probably the most prevalent approach to the qualitative research of artifacts (32). It is a methodology for those who want to understand the ways in which members of various cultures and subcultures make sense of who they are and how they fit into the world in which they live (Selzer 2003, 289). We interpret texts to try to understand the way people, in particular cultures at particular times, make sense of the world around them.

In a post-structural-inspired approach (instead of a realist or structuralist approach), however, we do not make claims about whether texts are "accurate" or "truthful" or "show reality." Instead, the methodology that we are describing seeks to understand the ways in which these forms of representation take place, the assumptions behind them, and the kinds of sensemaking about the world that they reveal (Stam 1991, 263). Different texts can present the same event in different ways, and all of them can be equally truthful and accurate, hence Stam's argument of polyphony and others' argument of polysemy (257). Some might ask, "Can anybody make any claim that would be acceptable?" This is a valid criticism that we would like to address. Yes, some may have radical readings of texts, but a post-structural textual analysis does not insist that any representation is as acceptable as any other or that any interpretation makes as much sense as any other. In fact, we think the opposite seems to be the case. The reason we analyze texts is to find out what were and what are the reasonable sensemaking practices of cultures, rather than just repeating our own interpretation and calling it reality (260). A variety of perspectives exist, but a finite number of sensemaking positions are available within a given culture at a given time—the keys being intrinsic and extrinsic context, intertextuality, and paratextuality. In short, context matters. Adopting a post-structural approach allows us to analyze the complexities of Thuy's and Rosa's negotiated identities, not just subscribing to the polarized positions of oppressed versus privileged.

Based on this method, we focus on the following questions: (1) In what ways is the sexual and domestic objectification of the female characters deployed within racialized/ethnicized hierarchies? (2) How do agency and subjectivity of the female characters play into the two texts? (3) In what ways do the lives of migrant women imply their otherness in the context of South Korea?

Descriptions of the Films

Rosa begins with the story of an eighteen-year-old Uzbek girl, Diana (Dayana Ruzmetova), who moved to South Korea to earn tuition for her ballet academy. Once she arrives in Korea, she changes her name to Rosa and is degraded to being an exotic dancer. On top of that, her criminal employer, Mr. Cho (Haseok Cho), holds her passport and extends her visa without asking her. Along with Rosa, other White women from Uzbekistan and Russia are forced to work in the sex industry. Their existence is confined to a single house, and they receive no free time unless given permission. The movie depicts how Rosa has a hard time negotiating her life given her situation as a dancer in the adult bar while still holding onto her dream of dancing ballet at the theater. Finally, she defies Mr. Cho by dancing ballet on the stage of the adult bar. Cognizant of this, Mr. Cho forces her to stop dancing at the club and makes her become a karaoke hostess. She cavorts and sings tunes with businessmen, followed by sleeping with them in hotel rooms. One night at work she meets Hamid (Nicholas

Sonku), an Uzbek customer and migrant worker, and falls in love with him. However, Mr. Cho violently threatens Hamid and Rosa not to see each other, ending their relationship.

Thuy is about a Vietnamese migrant woman, Thuy (Ninh Doung Lan Ngoc), who moves to a rural town in Korea to marry an underprivileged (disabled, low-income-class, mentally fragile) man, Jeongsoo. She puts a lot of effort into adapting to Korea's culture, learning its language, and taking care of her in-laws (her mother-in-law is diagnosed with Alzheimer's disease, and her father-in-law worships traditional totemism). She spends her free time with her compatriot friend, Ungwan (Nguyen Thi Binh), who is also a migrant marriage woman in the same village. Unlike Thuy, who is loved by her parents-in-law, Ungwan suffers domestic violence from her husband. She continues to live with him despite repeated beatings, but in the end, she kills her husband after no longer being able to endure his beatings.

One day, Thuy's husband dies in a motorbike accident, but her suspicions are aroused because her husband was physically incapable of riding a motorcycle. When she starts probing into the details of his death, she is confronted with threats by her male neighbors. Meanwhile, a new police officer, Sangho (Seungho Cha), is expelled from Seoul and sent to the rural town due to his crime of illegal gambling, and he begins to investigate the death of Thuy's husband. Thuy and Sangho are persistent in investigating the death, and many of the middle-aged male residents and Sangho's colleagues threaten them to be silent. Sangho nonetheless attempts to help Thuy find clues surrounding her husband's death and even saves her from danger. At the end of the movie, Thuy finds a videotape recorded by her husband showing Sangho and other male neighbors illegally gambling together. In the video, Sangho is yelling at Jeongsoo once he realizes that Jeongsoo is recording them. At that moment, Thuy realizes that Sangho and Jeongsoo had known each other, leading her to suspect that Sangho is Jeongsoo's murderer. Sangho and the other male neighbors are afraid that their gambling operation will be revealed if Thuy pieces together the evidence in the recording. Once Thuy finds out the truth, Sangho kills her and disguises her death as a suicide.

Through analyzing these indie films, we found that they showed two dominant discourses about the othering of Third World migrant women: (1) the othering of migrant women as sexualized and domesticated objects and (2) the othering of migrant women as restricted independent subjects under the patriarchy and state power.

Migrant Women as Other: Sexualized and Domesticated Objects

The female characters in both films represent similar but different sexual and domesticated objectification of migrant women by their races (White/Asian) and nationalities (Uzbek/Vietnamese). For *Rosa*, the opening scene shows Diana standing up in the vast grassland in Uzbekistan. Her face and body are camouflaged in nature, and she is made less visible to the camera due to a wider lens frame. However, when she is made into Rosa, she is shown to be not just visible but the main attraction. She steps onto the stage and starts dancing at the adult bar in the industrial city of Ansan in Korea. Close-up camera shots show particular parts of her and other White women's bodies, such as hips and breasts. These camera angles resemble the way middle-aged Korean male customers view their bodies. This cutting up shows the male gaze that objectifies and desires women's bodies for their sexual pleasure (Mulvey 1990, 62). Though Rosa is visible, she is not fully visible, and only specific parts of her become the center of attention, insinuating that she is seen not as a whole person but merely as objectified parts.

On top of that, Rosa wears a long blond wig that accentuates her white skin color, making her a personified Barbie doll. She represents a Caucasian sex worker from Eastern Russia and Central Asia who meets the demands of Korean men. According to Kim and Fu (2008), the abstract images of a "White woman" symbolize the universal norms of beauty and modernity that trigger a false sense of pride among Asian men, who wish to overcome racial and ethnic conflictual differences built through the history of neocolonial domination by the West (493). When the men have sexual intercourse with White women, whose race is superior to their Asian race, they tend to put their overt masculinity on full display. The influx of White women in the sex industry coalesces with restoring masculinity to Korean heterosexual men and their authority over White women. The combination of her white skin tone and blond wig further exemplifies her desirability as an exotic commodity. The Korean men long to become Westernized and fulfill their desires by drinking whiskey and showing "White fetish" at the adult entertainment bar.

On the other hand, in the film *Thuy*, the young Vietnamese woman Thuy moves to a rural village to marry an older man. In her everyday life, she is able to pass as Korean until she starts to speak Korean. In other words, she is from Vietnam but has an East Asian appearance that seems to resemble Korean society. She does not have the typical look of a dark-skinned Southeast Asian woman. Other migrant marriage women characters in the movie are also more East Asian than Southeast Asian in appearance. Even though they are Vietnamese women who epitomize low-class foreign brides from Southeast Asia, they physically resemble Korean people. By effacing diversities of skin color in the Asian race, these marriage migrant women become vehicles that do not disrupt but maintain ethnic homogeneity—they perform Korean passability (S. Kim 2009, 214).

Moreover, Thuy, as a wife and daughter-in-law, carries out all domestic work for her family, such as doing laundry, cooking, catching shellfish with female neighbors, and performing hospice work for her ill mother-in-law. She also studies Korean intensely, eats local food, and follows traditional rituals such as performing ancestral rites. Although she goes through hardships such as losing her husband and nursing her sick mother-in-law, she shows full respect for her parents-in-law. Also, when her compatriot female friends suggest that she work as a hostess in karaoke, she rejects the idea and shows her devotion and obedience to her deceased husband and to traditions and values. As such, she represents traditional femininity within the family sphere—pure, caring, and respectful to her husband and his family. Thuy becomes an epitomized migrant woman, who studies Korean intensely to communicate with her in-laws as well as to assimilate into the country's traditional culture, preserving the patriarchal structures. This meets the Korean government's goal of marriage migrants reproducing its population and continuing its homogenous culture.

Rosa's White Uzbek female protagonist and *Thuy*'s East Asian–looking Vietnamese female protagonist show differing paths due to race. The patriarchy in Korea requires that White women are shown as hyper-eroticized objects for temporary or nonmarital sexual intercourse to local men. On the other hand, Asian women from similar or passing races and ethnicities become brides who can carry traditional customs of the patriarchal system (Kempadoo 1998, 10). For Rosa, highlighting her race and assimilating into the culture are unnecessary and undesirable, despite that she has to assimilate into the culture to survive. On the other hand, Thuy, because she is of the same race, is considered a sympathetic protagonist who is expected to assimilate into the patriarchal system.

These representations of the two migrant women also interestingly show the ways in which the lives of migrant women are constructed by global/local and colonial/neocolonial discourses. In the White, colonial, and US contexts, White women tend to be constructed as innocent and reproductive figures in the White American national imagination, whereas

Asian women signify excessive sexuality, especially Southeast Asian women, such as Vietnamese, Filipina, and Thai, who are represented as sexually lascivious and debased (Shimizu 2007, 32). However, in Asian, postcolonial, and Korea contexts, Rosa, a White figure, is converted into a sexual object but is presented as an innocent figure before being trafficked in Korea. Moreover, her original name, Diana, implies divine privilege, but her pseudonym, Rosa, refers to a rose, suggesting that she becomes degraded to a temporally beautiful object. It shows that her origin was angelic but that she is forced to be licentious by horrendous circumstances in the sex trade. Meanwhile, the image of Thuy, a Southeast Asian woman, remains as an innocent and subservient wife and daughter-in-law.

We also observe that the women's different races as White and Asian are eliminated and their "Third World-ness" renders both women as mere commodities (Kempadoo 2001, 10). Rosa's body becomes a product for which men pay money to enjoy temporal sexual gratification, whereas Thuy's body is commodified through international marriage brokers with the expectation that she obey traditional femininity and domesticity. Through investigating these two characters, Uzbek and Vietnamese women's low economic statuses offset their presumed racial superiority (White) and equality (Asian). In turn, they become the sexualized and domesticated others who are subordinate to Korean men and families in the patriarchal structure.

Migrant Women as Other: The Korean Dream and the Demise of Migrant Women

On a sunny afternoon, Rosa dreams of her past when she danced *Swan Lake* for the audition at the ballet school and decided to move to Korea for tuition. When Mr. Cho picked her up in her village in Uzbekistan, Diana wore a long skirt, a cardigan, and no makeup. She sat in front of him in the van and said "Hello" (안녕하세요, *Annyeonghaseyo*) with a smile, while the van drove through the grassland. This scene is juxtaposed with the next one, in which Rosa wears a short dress and thick makeup and holds a cigarette while sitting in front of Mr. Cho in the van. She glances at him, speechless, while the van they are in drives along the clubs, bars, karaokes, and hotels at which she works. At the end of the movie, she slowly walks past neon signs of her workplaces on the street as the sun goes down.

Diana's dream of becoming a ballerina is ruined when she starts to live in Korea to support her dream as Rosa. She is the girl who has her own idealized femininity, youthful innocence, and beauty. However, she has to hide herself by wearing a blond wig and a party dress, a costume that symbolizes the commodification of Western White women in the sex industry. Her Korean Dream eventually turns into a nightmare as she becomes a voiceless human commodity. At the same time, her dream is revealed through the glitz of her appearance, which hides the vileness of patriarchal life and violence against migrant women. Showing her dream in this way reveals how little society values migrant women's dreams, built by the delusionary imagination of the nation. When the sun goes down, her Korean Dream that appeared with the daylight comes to an end, and when the neon signs of the bars turn on, she becomes a silent migrant woman on the street.

On the other hand, Thuy rushes into the police department at night and finds her friend, Ungwan, sitting on the ground behind bars, her face bleeding and severely bruised. Ungwan says: "I am so numb as I've been beaten up so long and hard. . . . I thought that I had to leave him, but he could not live without me. So . . ." The previous night, Thuy goes through the keepsakes of Joengsoo, her deceased husband, and finds the videotapes that he had recorded. One of the videotapes shows her wedding ceremony, at which she wore a traditional wedding gown. Another videotape shows Sangho, a police officer who helps her and rescues her when she is in danger, gambling with her husband the night he died. Thuy tells Sangho, a suspect in her husband's murder, what she saw on the video, and he suffocates her, disguising her death as a suicide.

Thuy, who portrays an idealized and desirable femininity as a faithful wife and daughter-in-law, is tragically murdered by Sangho. Because Sangho is a police officer who is supposed to maintain order and safety for the people but is instead a criminal and murderer, Thuy's action in seeking the truth of her husband's death, which is linked to illegal and criminal power, is ironically suffocated by state power. Her demise implies that state power does not accept a migrant woman who tries to divulge corruption and illegality and enforces her voiceless objectification in the Korean ethnic and patriarchal system. On the other hand, Sangho's actions, whether criminal or professional, are validated through state power. Everyone questions Thuy and her motives, but Sangho's privilege as a member of the patriarchal state apparatus builds a sense of ethos for him. His position makes it seem nearly impossible that he could have murdered Joengsoo and Thuy. Thuy's position makes it highly believable that she committed suicide.

Ungwan's justifiable homicide of her husband shows another demise of migrant women. Domestic violence is not just a private incident limited to interpersonal relationships but also a systemic issue associated with racial, ethnic, gendered, and political hegemonies (Franke 2002, 320–21). Third World migrant women, whose lives are inseparable from racial, ethnic, class, and gendered hierarchies and who have to rely on their spouses for their legal status, are more vulnerable to gendered violence. The character of Ungwan perfectly illustrates how a migrant marriage woman becomes the victim of gendered violence under the racial, ethnic, and patriarchal system. She suffers from domestic violence but is contained in a prison cell, symbolizing state power after the police failed to care of her. It shows how the state power that established an immigrant marriage policy entices women to believe in the Korean Dream but how these aspirations are quickly ruined, as seen through the literal ending of their lives. Through the representation of the two migrant marriage women in *Thuy*, the underlining moral of the film is that love across different ethnicities paradoxically functions to maintain the social norms of a homogenous ethnicity and tradition. Korean society is not willing to accept the migrant women's love unless they observe the patriarchal order with silence.

There are some glimpses in the films where Rosa and Thuy attain their own agency and subjectivity, but they are short-lived. When Rosa returns home from work, she continuously dreams of going back to her ballet school in Russia. She reminisces of her life in Russia, where she was able to freely stroll on the street and dance ballet anytime. She also occasionally wears her ballet dress and looks at herself in the mirror, smiling as she reminisces of happier times. As a sign of resistance, after seeing a colleague hospitalized due to their violent employers, she does not perform an exotic dance on the stage but instead dances a ballet piece from *Swan Lake*.

For Rosa, ballet is her way of embodying her subjectivity. She traveled to Korea to support her dream of becoming a ballerina; however, her pursuit is ruined, as she is trapped in the sex industry. Nevertheless, she does not stop dreaming of going back to the stage on which she becomes a "white swan" in *Swan Lake*. Dancing *Swan Lake* is a way of showing her subjectivity, but at the same time it becomes another instrument for highlighting her femininity. Desmond (2001) explains that dancing through specific bodies shows "specific material and ideological conditions and possibilities" (13). As such, dancers, whose bodies mark race, gender, ethnicity, and sexuality, embody cultural ideologies but also show the possibilities of subverting sociocultural norms. Rosa's performance of *Swan Lake* in full ballet regalia represents her idealized femininity, which is beautiful, innocent, pure, and naive. However, when she performs the ballet wearing a blond wig and party clothes at the bar, she subverts sociocultural norms by resisting sexual commodification and violence as a White woman from a developing country. This performance also reveals her naive and innocent purity as a youthful woman dreaming of becoming a ballerina, blurring the lines between hegemonic and subversive.

After her performance, her employer, Mr. Cho, drags her offstage, slaps her face, and never brings her to the dance stage again. Instead, she is forced to work as a karaoke hostess, as well as to sleep with customers every night. While she endures working in the sex industry, she sometimes spends time with Uzbek migrant workers who come to the karaoke bar to share their sorrow, loneliness, and homesickness. Among them, Hamid asks Rosa to be with him in the hotel room. Instead of wanting sex, he brings traditional Uzbek food, listens to her story, and comforts her. Afterward, they fall in love.

While going through these ordeals, Rosa creates a diaspora in the karaoke room. Her coworkers and male migrant workers talk and sing in Uzbek together to express the hardship, sadness, and loneliness stemming from Korean racism, ethnocentrism, sexism, and capitalism. The hotel room in which Rosa and other migrant women have to perform unwanted intercourse with customers and are sometimes raped by their employers creates a miserable space. This horrifying place is then transformed into another diasporic space in which Rosa and her Uzbek boyfriend can share their stories, food, and feelings with each other. In a sense, the karaoke bar and hotel room where Rosa is suffocated by racial and gendered violence transform into safe havens where she temporarily feels companionship, comfort, and love through revealing her subjectivity.

Thuy, in comparison, enjoys a relatively happy life doing domestic work, taking care of her parents-in-law, and being loved by them. After her husband dies from a suspicious cause, she is devastated. Nevertheless, she does not stop taking care of her parents-in-law and tries to probe the real cause of her husband's death. Even though the male neighbors and police officers try to disguise what happened and discourage her by saying, "You are a Vietnamese woman, be quiet," she persistently pursues the truth.

Thuy finds her happiness while preserving traditional femininity as a faithful daughter-in-law and devoted wife. Meeting the expectations of what a patriarchal culture requires of migrant marriage women, she is treated very well by her family and neighbors. In contrast with Rosa, who experiences hard times because she is desired for who she is not, Thuy does not need to deal with discordance between her desire and the social and cultural norms until her husband dies. After she faces the mystery of her husband's demise, she reveals her subjectivity by pursuing the truth of his death, standing up to the male neighbors and police officers who try to hide the truth.

Also, Thuy supports and takes care of her friend, Ungwan, who suffers domestic violence by her husband and unavoidably commits a justifiable homicide. Thuy's concern for Ungwan creates a diaspora for Vietnamese marriage women in ethnocentric and patriarchal Korean society. Thuy's action amplifies the love and caring of women, which does not limit women's stories to the context of victimization in domestic violence but shows a powerful force that enables women to challenge the violent and inhumane domination of the patriarchy (hooks 1989, 26). As such, Thuy simultaneously builds her multiple identities that are mingled with her subjectivity. She finds happiness by amplifying her femininity, which meets the expectations of migrant marriage women, but resists against patriarchal and traditional family structures.

These migrant women perform their subjectivities by showing different actions in their lives. Rosa, Thuy, and Ungwan epitomize the stereotypical roles of Third World migrant women. However, not only are they viewed as "other," but they also endure the struggles and uneasiness of living in the racial, ethnocentric, and patriarchal system to reveal glimpses of themselves from their agencies and subjectivities beyond the system in which they are desired. They live, manage, and defy their lives at every moment. Nonetheless, the films show the tragic consequences of revealing their own voices and feelings to the Korean patriarchal system.

In this chapter, we position the movies *Rosa* and *Thuy* together to show Korea as a place of displaced opportunity—of migrant women whose Korean Dream turns into a nightmare. Both films point to the central cause of their miserable lives, which is a rotten and violent patriarchal system that makes them less human. At the same time, this system causes representational violence to migrant women from the Third World, fitting them into stereotypical victim representations. White women are idealized as innocent beauties, and Vietnamese women are idealized as faithful wives (for poor men). Even though the two women in the movies perform their subjectivities to seek happiness beyond the ethnic and patriarchal system, both are symbolically destroyed for the sake of maintaining the system. In doing so, the two movies show the consequences of attempting to resist the hypermasculine and patriarchal corruption in the delusionary imagination of the Korean Dream—total objectification or even death.

Conclusion

Both *Rosa* and *Thuy* belong to the art house/indie genre, which categorizes itself as being anti-mainstream and in opposition to corporate media and the ideology they support (Hesmondhalgh 1999, 38). As Newman (2009) contends about the independent film, "It calls for questioning or challenging the cultural status quo.... It is a voice of the dispossessed.... In cinema, indie has been the most visible forum for diverse voices and viewpoints" (23). Though this may be the case for Western independent films, we argue that in *Rosa* and *Thuy* there is some semblance of the goals of independent films in displaying a form of agency in the characters but that a limited sense of agency dwelling in the Korean Dream is represented as an unconscious device to quell resistance against a system of power. In the cases of Thuy and Rosa, though we do see glimpses of them negotiating their reality, their resistance to the oppressive patriarchy concludes with their objectification or death.

A major concern is the underlying dominant ideological meanings produced through representations of marginalized groups in Korea and their connection to the Korean economy as an up-and-coming global force. The political economy of the independent film sector has been grossly impacted by larger corporations, with many independent film agencies being integrated into larger media companies (Park, Lee, and Wagner 2016, 14). With such assimilation, independent filmmakers then incorporate a mixed identity of being pseudo-independent, with some agency, while also being influenced by Korean neoliberalism. This hybrid identity can also be viewed in both films, though most of the representation of migrant women, through the narratives of Rosa and Thuy, is mainly stereotypically hegemonic and heteropatriarchal.

Negative depictions can be harmful to minorities, as Enteman (2011) contends: "Stereotypes impose a rigid mold on the subject and encourage repeat use without revision.... Stereotypes are ultimately used to stigmatize" (20). Stereotyping converts real persons into artificial persons. Such stereotypes that appear in film and television may contribute to the discrimination of migrant women. In typecasting groups, people treat others different from themselves with fixed proxies.

Hall (1997a) explains that the representation of an "other" is established by a process in which the context of meaning is found not only in one image but also in how one image is read against or in connection with other images (42). The repetition of images creates textuality, accumulating meaning by playing them off each other (Hall 1997b, 11). In this particular chapter, the two films' textual coherence of the othering of migrant women is sustained. Stereotyping is often fixed by those in a position of power as a way to differentiate between what the dominant group regards as normal according to their own views and what might be excluded as the other (12). Stereotypes may also be developed by what is ignored in, trivialized through, or left out of the mass media, a theoretical approach labeled "symbolic annihilation" (Tuchman 1978, 21).

Yet another consequence of negative portrayals of representation in media is that people learn social, gender, race, and class roles that aid them in defining their own personal identity (Riffe 2009, 4). By comparing themselves with characters in media content and modeling mediated behaviors and attitudes, individuals learn to become who they want to be, as well as what is deemed acceptable by society. For Colby Y. Miyose, coauthor of this chapter and a queer male American-born Japanese, Korean, and Native Hawaiian who has never traveled to Korea, mediated forms of Koreans in film and television helped to inform his own identity while growing up. The media culture has emerged to assist people in producing what constitutes their everyday lives. This shapes their political views and social behavior, as well as provides them with the materials to forge their own identity (Strelitz 2008, 55). Hence, media creates a dialectical relationship between culture as a lived experience and culture as a representation (Strelitz 2008, 58).

It is through the work of post-structural textual analyses such as this study that a deeper and more critical appraisal of such representations can be provided, within specific intrinsic and extrinsic contexts. This analysis also showcases the difficulty of minorities to gain agency and privilege from the systems of oppression in which they live, revealing that the negotiation between privilege and oppression provides potential but limited agency. Though this textual analysis examines only two films, we hope this chapter serves as a vessel in which the complexities of migrant women in Korea can be viewed and lends some voice to an otherwise silenced population.

REFERENCES

Bryman, Alan. 2008. *Social Research Methods*. Oxford: Oxford University Press.
Cha, Nayoung, Claire S. Lee, and Jihoon Park. 2016. "Construction of Obedient Foreign Bodies as Exotic Others: How Production Practices Construct the Images of Marriage Migrant Women on Korean Television." *International Journal of Communication* 10:1470–88.

Cho, Hojin. 2014. "Ballerina kkumkkudeon 'rosa', nuga cheochamhage jitbalbanna." *Ohmynews*, May 27. http://star.ohmynews.com/NWS_Web/OhmyStar/at_pg.aspx?CNTN_CD=A0001996395

Choe, Un Seon. 2007. "Gugje-gyeol-hon i-ju-yeo-seong-ui sa-hoe-mun-hwa jeog-eung-e gwan-han yeon-gu" [A study on social-cultural adaptation of foreign wives in Korea]. *Asia yeoseong yeongu* 46:141–81.

Enteman, Willard. 2011. "Stereotypes, the Media, and Photojournalism." In *Images That Injure: Pictorial Stereotypes in the Media*, edited by Willard Enteman, 20–30. Westport, CT: Praeger.

Fine, Elizabeth, and Speer Haskell Jean. 1992. *Performance, Culture, and Identity*. Westport, CT: Praeger.

Franke, Katherine. 2002. "Putting Sex to Work." In *Left Legalism/Left Critique*, edited by Wendy Brown and Janet Halle, 290–336. Durham: Duke University Press.

Hall, Stuart. 1997a. "The Work of Representation." In *Representation: Cultural Representations and Signifying Practices*, vol. 2, edited by Stuart Hall, 13–74. Thousand Oaks, CA: Sage.

Hall, Stuart. 1997b. "The Spectacle of 'the Other.'" In *Representation: Cultural Representations and Signifying Practices*, vol. 2, edited by Stuart Hall, 230–90. Thousand Oaks, CA: Sage.

Heo-oh, Young Sook. 2016. "International Migration Statistics." Korean Women Migrant Human Right Center. Accessed November 6, 2019. http://www.wmigrant.org/wp/wp-content/uploads/2017/02/2016%EB%85%8412%EC%9B%94-%EC%99%B8%EA%B5%AD%EC%9D%B8-%EC%9D%B4%EC%A3%BC%EB%AF%BC-%EC%84%B1%EB%B3%84-%ED%98%84%ED%99%A9.pdf

Hesmondhalgh, David. 1999. "Indie: The Institutional Politics and Aesthetics of a Popular Music Genre." *Cultural Studies* 13 (1): 34–61.

hooks, bell. 1989. *Talking Back: Thinking Feminist, Thinking Black*. Boston: South End Press.

Hulme, Peter. 1995. "Including America." *ARIEL: A Review of International English Literature* 26 (1): 117–23.

Kempadoo, Kalama. 1998. "Globalizing Sex Workers' Rights." In *Global Sex Workers: Rights, Resistance, and Redefinition*, edited by Kamala Kempadoo and Jo Doezma, 1–28. New York: Routledge.

Kempadoo, Kalama. 2001. "Women of Color and the Global Sex Trade: Transnational Feminist Perspectives." *Meridians: Feminism, Race, Transnationalism* 1 (2): 28–51.

Kim, Hee-kang, and Hyung-joo Song. 2017. "Seong yu-heung-san-eob-eu-lo yu-ib-doe-neun yeo-seong" [Women international migration to the sex/entertaining industries: Focusing on the international division of reproductive labor]. *Jendeowa munhwa* 10:45–81.

Kim, Hyun Mee. 2007. "The State and Migrant Women: Diverging Hopes in the Making of Multicultural Families in Contemporary Korea." *Korea Journal* 47 (4): 100–122.

Kim, Joon K, and Fu May. 2008. "International Women in South Korea's Sex Industry: A New Commodity Frontier." *Asian Survey* 48 (3): 492–513.

Kim, Sumi. 2009. "Politics of Representation in the Era of Globalization: Discourse about Marriage Migrant Women in Two South Korean Films." *Asian Journal of Communication* 19 (2): 210–26.

McCann, Carole, and Seung-Kyung Kim. 2017. "Introduction: Feminist Theory, Local and Global Perspectives." In *Feminist Local and Global Theory Perspectives Reader*, edited by Carole McCann and Seung-Kyung Kim, 1–8. New York: Routledge.

Ministry of Justice in Korea. 2019. "Procedures for Report of Marriage Between a National of the Republic of Korea and a Foreigner." Korean Ministry of Government Legislation. Accessed February 15, 2020. http://www.easylaw.go.kr/CSM/CsmOvPopup.laf?csmSeq=1015&ccfNo=1&cciNo=2&cnpClsNo=1

Mohanty, Chandra Talpade. 1991. "Cartographies of Struggles: Third World Women and the Politics of Feminism." In *Third World Women and the Politics of Feminism*, edited by Chandra Talpade Mohanty, Ann Russo, and Lourdes Torres. Indianapolis: Indiana University Press.

Mohanty, Chandra Talpade. 1997. "Women Workers and Capitalist Scripts: Ideologies of Domination, Common Interests, and the Politics of Solidarity." In *Feminist Genealogies, Colonial Legacies, Democratic Futures*, edited by M. J. Alexander and Chandra T. Mohanty, 3–29. New York: Routledge.

Mulvey, Laura. 1990. "Visual Pleasure and Narrative Cinema." In *Issues in Feminist Film Criticism*, edited by Patricia Erens, 57–68. Bloomington: Indiana University Press.

Newman, Michael Z. 2009. "Indie Culture: In Pursuit of the Authentic Autonomous Alternative." *Cinema Journal* 48 (3): 16–34.

Oh, David C., and Chuyun Oh. 2016. "Until You Are Able: South Korean Multiculturalism and Hierarchy in My Little Hero." *Communication, Culture & Critique* 9 (June): 250–65.

Park, Young-A., Do-hoon Lee, and Keith Wagner. 2016. "Changing Representations of the Urban Poor in Korean Independent Cinema: Minjung Heroes, Atomized Paupers, and New Possibilities." *Quarterly Review of Film and Video* 34 (4): 361–78.

Riffe, Daniel. 2009. "Identity." *Journalism and Mass Communication Quarterly* 86 (1): 2–4.

Selzer, Jack. 2003. "Rhetorical Analysis: Understanding How Texts Persuade Readers." In *What Writing Does and How It Does It*, edited by Charles Bazerman and Paul Prior, 285–314. New York: Routledge.

Shimizu, Celine P. 2007. *The Hypersexuality of Race: Performing Asian/American Women on Screen and Scene*. Durham: Duke University Press.

Stam, Robert. 1991. "Bakhtin, Polyphony, and Ethnic/Racial Representation." In *Unspeakable Images: Ethnicity and the American Cinema*, edited by Lester D. Friedman, 251–76. Champaign: University of Illinois Press.

Strelitz, Larry. 2008. "Biography, Media Consumption, and Identity Formation." *Qualitative Sociology Review* 4 (2): 24–62.

Tuchman, Gaye. 2000. "The Symbolic Annihilation of Women by the Mass Media." In *Culture and Politics*, edited by Lane Crothers and Charles Lockhart, 150–74. New York: Palgrave Macmillan.

Watson, Ian. 2010. "Multiculturalism in South Korea: A Critical Assessment." *Journal of Contemporary Asia* 40 (2): 337–46.

Yong, Wonjoong. 2014. "Segyega meonjeo jumokan dongnibyeonghwa 'mot' 'annyeong, tui.'" *Sports Q*, November 28. http://www.sportsq.co.kr/news/articleView.html?idxno=25868

5

Two Sides of the "Other"

Fear and Loving of Japanese Characters in Contemporary South Korean Cinema

Russell Edwards

The Japanese "other" remains an underexplored aspect of the racialized and nationalistic terrain of recent South Korean film. A number of commercial and often popular films produced in South Korea during the presidency of Park Geun-hye have both directly and indirectly addressed the Japanese colonial era as well as associated issues such as forced labor and sexual slavery, and, by extension, the contemporary relationship of Japan to South Korea. Belonging to what I call the Rising Sun cycle, these films, including well-known titles like *The Age of Shadows* (밀정, *Miljung*, Kim Jee-woon, 2016) and *Assassination* (암살, *Amsal*, Choi Dong-hoon, 2015), frequently use negative images of Japan and the Japanese, while also creating room to explore portrayals of those whose Koreanness becomes questionable due to their relationships with Japan(ese-ness). I have chosen the somewhat provocative term "Rising Sun" precisely because, in most cases, films in the cycle arouse anxieties rather than allay them. In contrast to other scholars addressing South Korean films that deal with Japan[1] and as evidenced by my inclusion of a contemporary horror film in this chapter, I do not believe a film has to be set in Korea's colonial era or has to overtly utilize 旭日旗 (*Kyokujitsu*) Rising Sun images to be counted as part of such a cycle. Regardless of the genre—thriller, horror, or any other—I consider it sufficient that a film portrays Korean anxieties about Japan to be included in the 2014–17 Rising Sun cycle. I also emphasize that in contrast to most of the earlier South Korean films dealing with Japan, the films released during this period were prominent at the domestic box office, adding to the cycle's noteworthiness.

Mindful of the colonial experience, I will examine two films from the cycle that are distinctive in their representations of Japanese and their relationship with Koreans. This includes, though is not confined to, the policy known in Japanese as 内鮮一体 and in Korean as 내선 일체 (*naisen ittai/ naeseon ilche*), which translates as "Japan and Korea as One Body" (Yecies and Shim 2011, 68). The first half of this chapter addresses *The Wailing* (곡성, *Gokseong*, Na Hong-Jin, 2016), a contemporary-set horror film featuring a symbiotic relationship between a Japanese intruder and a Korean shaman. Using textual analysis, I will demonstrate how this film fits alongside other recent films that deal directly with the colonial era. Next, I consider the biopic/romantic comedy *Anarchist from Colony* (박열, *Park Yeol*, Lee Joon-Ik, 2017) for its affectionate presentation of the romance between Korean poet Park Yeol and his lover, Kaneko Fumiko, a Japanese anarchist. These films both dramatize—one metaphorically, one literally—attempts to force the melding of Korean identity with Japanese identity during the colonial experience. More than mere reinterpretations of colonialism's legacy, these films also echo contemporary South Korea's nationalism and the national cinema's ongoing tendency to portray otherness in Japanese or Koreans associated with Japan. I argue that postcolonial themes in these films testify to Japanese colonialism's continued legacy and that the images are more complex and ambivalent than the binary construction of Japanese = bad / Korean = good would superficially suggest.

The Outsider: Fisherman or Bait?

In the recent Rising Sun cycle of South Korean films, there is no shortage of negative depictions of Japanese. Examples abound, such as the brutal commanders of the Hashima mines in *The Battleship Island* (군함도, *Gunhamdo*, Ryu Seung-wan, 2017) or the ruthless real-life politician Mizuno Rentaro depicted in *Anarchist from Colony*. Both of these (and many others in the cycle) are, of course, period films. While, arguably, the Japan depicted in Rising Sun films is the Japan of the past, it is generally accepted that historical films from any country tend to reflect more about the contemporary state of the nation. As an indicator of how the legacy of the past can persist into the present, I will first address Na Hong-Jin's contemporary horror film *The Wailing*, which ostensibly has no relation to the events of the colonial era.

Among South Korean films dealing with the Japanese other, *The Wailing* would be the most distinctive. First, it is a film set in the contemporary era. This is in contrast to the majority of Rising Sun films, which are typically set during some stage of the colonial period. Even in comparison to relatively contemporary films such as *I Can Speak* (아이 캔 스피크, Kim Hyun-Seok, 2017) and *Herstory* (허스토리, Min Kyu-Dong, 2018), which deal with the colonial era through the prism of events taking place in the 1990s and 2000s, *The Wailing* is—on the surface at least—apolitical in that there are no overt references to Japanese occupation or even the contemporary Japanese government. *The Wailing* is also different from most of the films in the Rising Sun cycle in that it belongs to the horror genre. Finally, unlike most Korean films dealing with any aspect of Japan, *The Wailing* prominently features an internationally known Japanese actor, Kunimura Jun, whose global credits include *Kill Bill* (Quentin Tarantino, 2003), *Hard-Boiled* (辣手神探, *Lat Sau San Taam*, John Woo, 1992), and *Black Rain* (Ridley Scott, 1989).

The Wailing is a puzzling and often self-contradictory film with red herrings that often obscure intended meanings to the point of frustrating confusion. Regardless of how muddled or successful the film's narrative may be, *The Wailing* is clearly a work concerned with the relationship between South Korea and Japan and how present perceptions are distorted by the lens of the past. The story unfolds in the remote South Korean village of Gokseong, which is visited by a Japanese tourist (billed as "The Outsider" and played by Kunimura Jun). The arrival of this Japanese visitor coincides with a series of grisly murders. At the film's center is a bumbling policeman, Jong-Goo (Kwak Do-Won), who at first plays down the local citizens' mystical superstitions about the Japanese visitor. However, Jong-Goo is increasingly disturbed when his young daughter, Hyo-Jin (Kim Hwan-Hee), displays unorthodox behaviors that come to be construed by several characters, including Jong-Goo, as an indication of spiritual possession. Jong-Goo's concerns increase with the revelation that The Outsider often takes photographs of the murder victims. At the insistence of his mother-in-law, Jong-Goo employs a Korean shaman known as Il-Gwang (Hwang Jung-Min) to exorcise Hyo-Jin. I will return to the significance of the Korean shaman and his contribution to the film's subtext soon, but first it is necessary to proceed to the film's final images of The Outsider.

Near the film's end, an unordained deacon (Kim Do-Yoon) assisting Jong-Goo with his investigations enters a cave to confront The Outsider and demands for the Japanese visitor to "show his true form." After retorting to the priest that the Korean man had already decided that he was a manifestation of the devil, The Outsider slowly metamorphizes into a demon-like creature complete with horns, goat-like vertical pupils, red eyes, and scaly skin. With his transformation complete, The Outsider plays on the deacon's fears by citing a biblical quotation referencing Jesus Christ's revealing of himself to his disciples after the Resurrection.[2] If this representation of a Japanese man as the devil is not obvious enough—and this in itself would recall for Korean audiences the racial slur *jjokbari* (쪽발이), which refers to Japanese people as cloven-foot creatures because of the Japanese fashion of 足袋 (*tabi*) "socks" and 下駄 (*geta*) sandals—the film drives home the connection with the demonized Outsider presenting a Himatic S Minolta camera. Minolta is, of course, a prominent Japanese brand.

Cameras are an obvious and long-recurring symbol of Japaneseness in cinema. This clichéd use of a camera is often supposed to be humorous, such as in *Dr. Strangelove Or: How I Learned to Stop Worrying and Love the Bomb* (Stanley Kubrick, 1964), where Group Captain Lionel Mandrake (Peter Sellers) observes of his World War II Japanese torture experiences: "I don't think they wanted me to talk really. I don't think they wanted me to say anything. It was just their way of having a bit of fun, the swines. Strange thing is they make such bloody good cameras." Less effective is the appearance of Japanese tourists enthusiastically taking photos as warring skinheads slash each other with knives at the flat-footed climax of *Romper Stomper* (Geoffrey Wright, 1992). So commonplace is the image that, in *The Spanish Prisoner* (David Mamet, 1999), an FBI agent remarks about an assassination conducted by a camera-carrying Japanese woman: "Nobody looks at a Japanese tourist."

The Wailing's camera moment is where director Na mischievously hints that this horror film is a pointed depiction of Koreans' clichéd perceptions and phobias about Japanese. The film is concerned not so much with the other as with who is doing the othering. Though his role as a villain is not in doubt, The Outsider in *The Wailing* is a case where the othering, the literal demonizing of the Japanese man, is only part of the story. As I will demonstrate, it is The Outsider's relationship with Il-Gwang, the Korean shaman hired by Jong-Goo, that is truly the film's central focus. Furthermore, I will indicate how Il-Gwang's association with Japaneseness diminishes his Koreanness.

The Shaman: Driver or Doppelgänger?

To emphasize the way in which exposure to Japaneseness alters Koreanness, it is necessary to explore the film's coda in some depth before exploring the character of the Korean shaman, Il-Gwang. This coda, which takes place only two minutes after the deacon's solo encounter with the demonized Japanese outsider, begins with Il-Gwang arriving at Jong-Goo's house by car. Walking through the property's archway toward the house, Il-Gwang can see the twitching body of the young girl Hyo-Jin sitting on the front stoop of the house, which is desecrated with refuse, debris, and blood. Offering the girl only a cursory glance, Il-Gwang enters another doorway to the house and there finds the corpse of Jong-Goo's wife (Jang So-Yeon) and a distraught and uncomprehending Jong-Goo. Il-Gwang squats in front of Jong-Goo's wife and pulls out an identical Minolta camera to that used by The Outsider. Il-Gwang then takes a photograph of Jong-Goo, who is too traumatized and wounded to rise from his fallen position. Helpless and physically resembling a bloated baby, the rotund Jong-Goo is devoid of the authority he is supposed to embody as either a policeman or a father. Arguably, he is a reversal of the remasculinization theory of Korean cinema put forward by Kyung Hyun Kim (2004). Such infantilized Korean men are emasculated and powerless over Japanese invaders or even over the Korean men who betray fellow Koreans, such as Il-Gwang. As Il-Gwang exits the house, the red light of the camera's recharging flash battery not only underlines the two mystics' shared use of a camera but also recalls the red eyes of the demonized Outsider. Finally, Il-Gwang returns to his car. In the process of his rummaging through items—including props for his shamanistic rituals—stored in the vehicle's hatchback, a box falls to the ground. The box's contents are revealed to be the multiple photographs of the murder victims seen earlier in the film as evidence of the Japanese Outsider's malicious intentions.

Whatever the plausibility (or otherwise) of the film's narrative, it is clear that *The Wailing*, with its double employment of a particular camera brand, establishes a formal connection between the two characters. Similarly, whatever the nature of that connection (i.e., Who is the most dominant? What is their modus operandi? Are they truly "one body"?), the events of *The Wailing* are clearly the product of a collaboration in which the pair work separately for the same result. Before outlining "the result" and any political relevance it may have, let me briefly show how the collaboration is disguised throughout the film and the manner in which it is fleetingly alluded to.

Before Il-Gwang first appears on-screen, substantial time has elapsed in *The Wailing*'s 156-minute duration. Both Jong-Goo and his police partner (who blames The Outsider for all the events to this point) are at a low ebb in terms of their investigation into the murders. Jong-Goo, in addition to having a sick daughter, is himself suffering from nightmares. At the

76-minute mark, *The Wailing* cuts to a high altitude shot of an SUV driving up a paved road on a Korean mountainside. This God's-eye view (or Devil's-eye view as the case may be) is in keeping with the film's genre ancestry, as it recalls the opening shots of *The Shining* (Stanley Kubrick, 1980). The music on the soundtrack is bold and powerful as the film cuts again to a close-up of Il-Gwang at the wheel of the vehicle. This combination of the strong music and the vivid close-up suggests that, after an hour of menace (from the Japanese Outsider) and incompetent police work (from Jong-Goo and his associates), the film's hero has finally arrived. The casting of South Korean actor Hwang Jung-Min, a major box office star, reinforces this sense of a hero's arrival. While Il-Gwang acts in a mysterious manner (he sniffs sand, he whistles menacingly), he is commanding (his first words are "Shut the damn door!"), creating a sense of order in the same way that the arrival of Max von Sydow does in *The Exorcist* (William Friedkin, 1973), another genre precursor to Na's film. Emitting a low-pitch whistle as he scopes the area outside Jong-Goo's house, Il-Gwang leads Jong-Goo's family, their curious neighbors, and the police to a large earthenware soy sauce jar (장독, *jangdok*) that sits with other similar jars on a hill at the back of the property. Il-Gwang commands Jong-Goo to bring the *jangdok* over. When Jong-Goo hesitates, Il-Gwang demonstrates his authority over the policeman by scolding him: "What, are you deaf?" When the *jangdok* is placed in front of him, Il-Gwang picks up a solid wooden pole and smashes it to reveal that a dead crow has been fermenting in the soy sauce. Il-Gwang pronounces, "It's a real wicked spirit we've got here." All onlookers, including the film audience, are supposed to be awed by Il-Gwang's powers of supernatural detection, and this continues after a shamanic examination of Hyo-Jin when he asks questions about who Jong-Goo has recently disturbed. When Jong-Goo answers (at his mother-in-law's prompting) that he had disturbed a Japanese man, Il-Gwang, after a long-knowing sigh, says, "I knew it. That's no man. That's a ghost." In retrospect, it is clear that Il-Gwang can easily make all these predictions because he already knows the answers to his questions.

The end revelation of collaboration does not emerge out of nothingness. Earlier, *The Wailing* makes a visual link between Il-Gwang and The Outsider as the shaman and Jong-Goo have their first private conversation. After Il-Gwang orders Jong-Goo to change his diet and pay a $10,000 exorcism fee, the film shows the shaman disrobing from his traditional Korean clothes while continuing to talk to the policeman and characterizing the Japanese outsider as a "demon." Before donning a tracksuit with a Nike swoosh emblem over one side of his chest and a shield-like emblem of a red flower over the other, Il-Gwang can be seen wearing a traditional form of Japanese underwear known as a *fundoshi*, a garment associated with Japaneseness. Less than five minutes later, The Outsider can be seen wearing the identical traditional Japanese underwear as he chants and moves his joined hands in a prayerlike form while standing under a waterfall.

More visual links between the Korean shaman and Japan come during the extended exorcism of Hyo-Jin. During a preliminary shamanistic ritual, Il-Gwang wears a silky black robe with sleeves adorned with vibrant rings of yellow, blue, pink, green, and orange, in the Joseon tradition of royalty. For the second exorcism, Il-Gwang wears a white robe that is reminiscent of the traditional Korean clothing worn by the peasant class of the Joseon era. In addition to the widely accepted idea that whiteness is symbolic of "good," the color of Il-Gwang's outfit identifies him as archetypically Korean, as whiteness has repeatedly been associated with Korean identity from artworks to the convenience of raw silk and cotton to the March First Independence Movement of 1919 (Lee 2010, 71–72). However, in the midst of his second shamanistic frenzy, Il-Gwang submerges his face in a bowl of chicken blood. When he withdraws his face and continues his frenzied dance, his visage is like a red disc above the white clothing, echoing not just the sprouting red-flowered emblem on his tracksuit but the red sun disc of the Japanese *Hinomaru* flag.

During this second exorcism scene, the film crosscuts between Il-Gwang performing his Korean shamanistic ritual and The Outsider in his mountainside hut banging a drum. Visually they are linked by images of fire from The Outsider's brightly burning candles and the shaman's larger ritualistic pyres. At this point the film's crosscutting deceptively suggests that both men are involved in a spiritual battle for possession of Hyo-Jin. With knowledge of their collaboration as borne out by the film's finale, this suggestion is clearly untrue. As Hyo-Jin writhes in pain, Jong-Goo is increasingly shocked by his daughter's discomfort and the results of his trusting this Korean shaman. The film escalates the pace of its cutting between the hammering of nails into a Korean icon by Il-Gwang, the depicted flinches of Hyo-Jin, and the exhaustion of the Japanese outsider at the mountaintop shack. Such manipulative cutting obscures the possibility that the two entities are working together. When Il-Gwang prematurely finishes his shamanistic activities in response to Jong-Goo's protest, The Outsider suddenly revives. As The Outsider crawls into a blanketed bed, he sees the mysterious young woman named Moo-Myeong (Chun Woo-Hee) emerge from the shadows outside. By *The Wailing*'s end, Moo-

Myeong is revealed to possess considerable mystical knowledge. Although not accentuated, it is clear Moo-Myeong has been observing The Outsider throughout his ritual. The following close-up of the frightened Outsider indicates that it is not the Korean shaman he has been in mystical contest with but the otherworldly Moo-Myeong. Subdued music continues from this scene of the terrified outsider to the cut to Hyo-Jin with her mother in the back seat of the family car as Jong-Goo drives to the hospital. There is a subsequent cut back to the lone shaman as the electronic hum continues, which also suggests that Il-Gwang has been defeated by Jong-Goo's interference. But the question remains (given the final revelation); what objective of the Korean shaman has been thwarted? Significantly, when the film switches to the safety of the hospital where Hyo-Jin receives treatment, the hum on the electronic soundtrack stops.

One of the enduring points of contention between the nations of Korea and Japan is the so-called comfort women issue. The story of forcibly recruited sex slaves for the Japanese army is not only a historical fact but the dramatic impetus for many of the films in the Rising Sun cycle, including *Spirits' Homecoming* (귀향, *Gwihyang*, Cho Jung-rae, 2016), *The Battleship Island*, and *I Can Speak*. I argue that it is beyond coincidence that the battleground for *The Wailing* is the body of the young girl, Hyo-Jin. After the first in the series of murders has been investigated, Jong-Goo is embarrassed to learn that his daughter, Hyo-Jin, has witnessed him having sex with her mother in the back of the family car. While trying to establish the extent of her loss of innocence, Jong-Goo talks to Hyo-Jin on a hillside overlooking the river. While Hyo-Jin is more interested in the gifts her father has bought her and while Jong-Goo wearily concludes that the young girl has seen her parents' sexual rituals in their entirety, the film cuts to Jong-Goo's point of view, which extends out across the river to the opposite banks, where The Outsider was first seen conducting his fishing expeditions. The Outsider is not visible, but the emphasis suggests that the threat of the Japanese fisherman is there—or imagined to be there—somewhere.

The Wailing opens with the aforementioned biblical epigraph and then shows The Outsider baiting a fishing hook. This establishes an early link between The Outsider and Christianity, which has long used the ichthus emblem both for the word's Greek acronym that abbreviates "Jesus Christ, Son of God, savior" and for the apt metaphor it embodies of the disciples being "fishers of men" as well as actual fisherman (Jowett and O'Donnell 2012, 64). The later demonization of The Outsider and his mocking use of the opening biblical quotation to taunt the deacon establish the Japanese visitor as an anti-Christ figure. More relevant to the connection between The Outsider and Il-Gwang is Jong-Goo's first conversation with Il-Gwang, during which the Korean shaman heightens an awareness of The Outsider as a fisherman. Il-Gwang says, "If you go fishing, do you know what you'll catch?" and "He's just fishing. Not even he knows what he'll catch." Soon after, he concludes, "That's all it was."

While Il-Gwang's "it's not personal" explanation may justify events in a random universe, the concerns of Gokseong's citizens and their speculation about the tourist's purpose for visiting their town are very focused on the visitor's Japaneseness. While neither the occupation nor the comfort women issue is mentioned during *The Wailing*, their aura is palpable. Much of the international campaign for a Japanese apology to the comfort women emphasizes the fact that these now aging women were once young. The use of a young girl's figure as the Statue of Peace, or *Sonyeosang* (literally "statue of girl"), places the age of young Korean females as no obstacle to sexualization or indeed sexual slavery. While Hyo-Jin ideally is too young to be regarded sexually, part of her trauma (and her father's) is her evident knowledge of sex and sexual violence, as documented in her notebooks, that is far in excess of that considered appropriate for her age.

Chungmoo Choi writes of the complicity of some Koreans in the facilitation of Japan's comfort women program and its erasure from South Korean history until 1991, when three comfort women took matters into their own hands by taking the Japanese government to court (Choi 1998, 13). While the negative imagery allocated to many Japanese representations in Rising Sun films may address historical conflict, the films also have folded within them the suggestion that some Korean people (with an emphasis on Korean men) cannot find themselves without consequences, responsibility, or guilt. As Hyunah Yang observes: "By looking outward to Japan, Koreans evade questions regarding the responsibility that we have for our own military history" (1998, 127).

While none of the adults—neither her parents nor the grandmother—are able to protect Hyo-Jin from harm, the film's connection between the Japanese and Korean shamans is not in doubt. The contradictory intricacies of *The Wailing* prevent a full explanation of Na Hong-Jin's auteurist intentions; however, the film's ambiguous approach to the villagers' fears about The Outsider and the final emphasis on Il-Gwang imply that it is not the Japanese who are driving the narrative of fear. Rather, the situation is being manipulated and worsened by the same Korean "hero" who was called in to protect Hyo-Jin from Japanese assault. While the film's initial emphasis seems to be on the Japanese outsider, *The Wailing* chooses to end with the Korean shaman rather than the Japanese shaman, thereby placing the emphasis on the hidden, unpunished traitors within rather than the malevolent Japanese forces from outside.

Kaneko Fumiko: Desirable Shadow or Korean Projection?

Using The Outsider's Japaneseness as bait, *The Wailing* hooks a Korean audience into considering the traitors within South Korean society. The narrative trick works because exceptions to a procession of negative Japanese stereotypes in South Korean cinema have been rare. They do exist, however. For instance, while discussing representations of Korean masculinity, Kate Taylor-Jones (2017) highlights *The Sea Knows* (현해탄은 알고 있다 *Hyeonhaetaneun Algo Itda*, Kim Ki-young, 1961), which portrays the arduous experiences of Aro-Un (Kim Wun-Ha), a Korean military recruit in the Japanese army, who later marries Hideko (Gong Midori), a Japanese woman. Taylor-Jones rightly describes the love of a Japanese wife for a Korean man as speaking to a "post-colonial desire to reclaim a masculinity lost in the colonial moment" (2017, 140). However, in doing so, Taylor-Jones also rushes past the fact that Aro-Un first receives friendship from Nakamura (Kim Jin-Gyu), a Japanese military colleague and the brother of Hideko. While Aro-Un does face the objections of his wife's mother and the brutal bullying of his Japanese military superiors, it is notable that the film's hero expresses a rare warmth toward (some) Japanese characters in the cinema of pre-democratic South Korea.

A comparable reconciliation of Japan-Korea conflict was also apparent in the significant casting of Japanese star Joe Odagiri in the more recent war epic *My Way* (마이웨이, *Mai Wei*, Kang Je-Gyu, 2010), with its story of a rivalry that becomes a friendship between a Korean soldier and a Japanese soldier. Notably, Kang's film was a major flop at the domestic box office.[3] The director explained the film's lack of success as a result of misplaced faith in an unpopular idea: "Blockbusters are centered on themes that appeal to the public and a friendship between a Korean and a Japanese man during colonial rule probably appeals to a handful of people" (Sunwoo 2012).

The scarcity and unpopularity of such positive representations highlight the significance of *Anarchist from Colony*. This film not only presents an affirmative representation of a Japanese woman but is also more nuanced than most Japanese characterizations in South Korean cinema. Significantly, and in contrast to *My Way*, *Anarchist from Colony* was popular enough with the public to reach the number one position at the South Korean box office.[4] If, as cultural theorist Jeff Lewis observes, "the meanings of texts cannot be treated as independent of the broader flows and operations of the culture in which the text exists" (2008, 32), then the high profile of this film cannot be separated from the circumstances and conditions of its production and consumption. Observations of depictions that vary from the norm can be said to be aberrations, but undoubtedly popular aberrations can be regarded as culturally significant.

The biopic *Anarchist from Colony* features Korean actress Choi Hee-Seo as Kaneko Fumiko, the live-in lover of the film's titular character, Park Yeol.[5] Both of these characters were real-life figures imprisoned for their political beliefs by the Japanese government. Like other South Korean films set during the colonial era, *Anarchist from Colony* also has negative representations of Japanese. Most prominent is Kim In-woo's portrayal of the era's Japanese minister of the interior, Mizuno Rentaro, who notoriously provoked the mass murder of Koreans in Tokyo by falsely accusing them of poisoning the city's wells after the 1923 Kanto earthquake. In many ways, the film represents a battleground between the two Japanese extremes of racist zealot (Mizuno) and Korean sympathizer (Kaneko).

What also makes the female character of Kaneko of particular interest is that rather than portrayed as a Japanese other to be feared and loathed, she is depicted as trustworthy, desirable, and admirable. Furthermore, notwithstanding the serious subject matter, multiple sequences in *Anarchist from Colony* portray the interracial couple's relationship like a romantic comedy. Genre hybridity is common across South Korean cinema (Choi J. 2011, 84), and more prudently than some genre mixes, *Anarchist from Colony* takes care to balance this romantic comedy flavor so that it never undermines the seriousness of the political situation or trivializes Park and Kaneko's love affair.

Park Yeol (Lee Je-Hoon) is the first character the audience sees in *Anarchist from Colony*. As a romantic ballad plays on the soundtrack, the opening image of the film is the back of Park's head as he runs through a Tokyo street, pulling a rickshaw. However, the first character the audience *hears* is Kaneko. When the film cuts to a wide shot to reveal Park, his rickshaw, and his Japanese passenger in profile, Kaneko's voiceover is heard as she reads Park's poem, *Damn Dog*. It is a strong and cinematic metaphor for the equality of the pair's partnership-to-be. Typically film analysis emphasizes the visual first, with sound being relegated to a secondary place on the hierarchy of cinema's elements. In contrast, Chion (2000, 112) emphasizes the idea that sound, rather than being subordinate, adds value to the image. In turn, Beck and Grajeda argue that "sound makes an equal—and perhaps occasionally—larger contribution to a film's meaning" (2008, 18). Men and women, like sound and vision, are different entities, but the opening of *Anarchist from Colony* alludes to the idea that the combination of the two can be more impactful than either individually. The adding of sound to vision, woman to man, and indeed Japanese to Korean in this film demonstrates the process of value being added on multiple levels. In developing this romantic union, the film presents a 内鮮一体 / 내선 일체 (*naisen ittai* / *naeson ilche*) of a very different kind to that envisaged by the Japanese empire.

When the future couple first meet, Kaneko, like Hideko in *The Sea Knows*, instigates the romance. In a mixture of Korean and Japanese dialogue, Kaneko directly inquires about Park's relationship status. While it is not a formulaic meet-cute of romantic comedy purists (McDonald 2007), this meeting is played for audience amusement. When Park admits that he is single, Kaneko's expression does not seek to hide her pleasure, and she quickly blurts out: "Let's live together." While Park ponders Kaneko's pronouncement, the soundtrack gives its answer by starting up the opening romantic song again, suggesting the affair is already beginning. Challenged by this forthright woman, Park asks his friend Hong, "Is she Japanese or Korean?" Hong's answer describes Kaneko as "Something in between." Witnessing the way this unusual woman has puzzled Park, Hong asks of his friend: "Do you have hard feelings against Japanese?" In counterpoint to the preceding romantic comedy–style banter between the lovers-to-be, Park gravely replies: "I'm against Japanese authorities, not the Japanese people." This suggests that Park as a representation of Korea is prepared to accept other forms of Japaneseness beyond the colonial antagonists depicted in *Anarchist from Colony*.

Unlike most South Korean films dealing with Japan, *Anarchist from Colony* is wholly set within Japan. Consequently, the film's setting allows for the primacy of the Japanese language in a way that is likely to be acceptable to contemporary Korean audiences. It would be less acceptable if a similar scenario was presented in a Korea-set, colonial-era film, as that would signal subservience to imperial rule. In contrast to the Japanese language forced on Koreans, Kaneko reads, writes, and speaks Korean of her own free will. She is not "typically" Japanese, and this is clearly part of why Park responds to Kaneko. It follows that Korean audiences are equally encouraged to respond favorably to her.

While the film's Korean title is *Park Yeol*, Hwang Sung-Goo's script allocates equal representation and characterization to each half of the couple. This ensures that Kaneko is more than a stereotypical object of desire. Kaneko not only drives *Anarchist from Colony*'s romantic narrative but is also politically active throughout the film, demonstrating her ideals of freedom, equality, and personal responsibility. It is Kaneko who writes (in Hangeul) the manifesto by which the couple share their lives, and it is she who monitors the rules of their de facto relationship.

When Park transgresses their cohabitation agreement by keeping a secret from her, Kaneko promptly slaps Park's face. Depictions of Korean characters as the recipient of a violent action from a Japanese character are common. Unprecedented, however, are acts of Japanese violence against Koreans that the film's primary audience are expected to endorse. Such an unusual exchange is structured into the film carefully. From the film's beginning, Park's attraction to Kaneko gives the audience tacit permission to admire Kaneko. It is unlikely that Korean audiences would approve of such a violent action if they were not encouraged to love Kaneko as much as Park does. Similarly, Kaneko's aforementioned embrace of Korean culture is also endearing. Furthermore, while the ferocity of her slap is obvious, director Lee manipulates the moment to make the confrontation more palatable for Korean audiences. Lee does this by emphasizing Park as actor Lee Je-Hoon delivers a "that hurt" slow-burn reaction, thus bringing a comical tone back to the narrative and making Kaneko's violent action easier to accept. That the role is played by a Korean actress makes this easier for Korean audiences again as it erases Kaneko's Japaneseness. While a Japanese actress cast in the Kaneko role and performing the same action may make for a more accurate representation of the Japanese other, the cultural obstacles for a Korean audience to witness, accept, and endorse such a scenario would be considerable.

Later, when Kaneko and Park are jailed for subversion, they are kept in separate jail cells. This individual confinement grants Kaneko several solo scenes in which she speaks to her lawyer about her affinity for Korea. In these interviews Kaneko discusses being abandoned by her Japanese family during her childhood in Korea; describes her identification with the uprising of March 1, 1919; and offers rationales for assassinating members of the Japanese royal family. Finally, when Park and Kaneko's shared trial comes to an end, Park offers a rebellious joke as his parting words. In contrast, and in testimony to her greater (Japanese) eloquence, Kaneko makes an elaborate speech proclaiming eternal and equal love. Kaneko's speech brings Park to tears before the couple, in a trope lifted from the TV series *The Many Loves of Dobie Gillis* (1959–63), share for the last time an exchange of squints that they have repeatedly used to communicate their mutual affection.⁶ Again, Kaneko receives Park's approval for being attuned to justice. Their admiration is equal and mutual. From the film's beginning, Kaneko not only endorses Park but, in her unflagging adoration of the poet, endorses Koreanness in everyone—herself and the film's primary audience included. This accentuating and full acceptance of Koreanness may be the requirement for positive representation of Japaneseness in South Korean cinema.

Another requirement for acceptance may be the death of favorably regarded Japanese characters. Whether it be accident, suicide, or murder, as Lee Joon-Ik's film suggests, Kaneko's premature death remains a historical fact. But in terms of narrative detail, this death is duplicated in the treatment of other positive representations in Rising Sun films where Japanese characters act in the interests of Koreans, for example, the soldier Tanaka, who is executed by his colleagues after he provides an escape map to several comfort women in *Spirits' Homecoming*, and the ill-fated Japanese Kimura, who dies while aiding the Korean resistance movement in *Assassination*.

Such deaths are comparable to the transitional representation of gay characters in mainstream English-language cinema, where a character such as Simon Callow's Gareth in *Four Weddings and a Funeral* (Mike Newell, 1994), Tom Hanks's Andrew Beckett in *Philadelphia* (Jonathan Demme, 1993), or Jake Gyllenhaal's Jack in *Brokeback Mountain* (Ang Lee, 2005) are identified as affirmative representations for gay men but the narrative requires that one partner in the couple dies. Thomas Piontek concludes: "A gay man can lose his mark of difference and become an ordinary person who is typical of all human beings only on the condition that his downfall and extreme sorrow are a forgone conclusion" (2012, 129). Whether these Japanese representations in South Korean cinema are transitional in the same sense as these gay representations in Western cinema remains an open question. Recent heightened tensions between South Korea and Japan (Stangarone 2020) would suggest that *Anarchist from Colony*'s delightfully affirmative representation of a Japanese woman may prove to be more milestone than turning point. Certainly, the favorable portrait of Kaneko does not dilute the transgressions of colonialism or cancel out the depiction of the ruthless politician Mizuno in the same film. However, in terms of cross-cultural representation during a wider cycle of films that frequently offered images of Japanese people designed to create negative impressions, the existence of a film that devotes almost half of its running time to a positive Japanese representation such as Kaneko is unusual.

Conclusion

Beginning with *The Wailing* and continuing with *Anarchist from Colony*, I have presented contrasting examples of the Japanese and the Japanized "other" in South Korean cinema. In different ways, both of these films are contrary to the standard assumption that Rising Sun films would primarily present Japanese people through a negative lens and Koreans would only be viewed affirmatively. Part of this is attributable to the films belonging to identifiably distinct genres. A horror film—including one with a sublimated political agenda—inevitably deals with the othering of a creature or person as a stand-in for an unmentionable idea. In *The Wailing*'s case, the other is the Japanese fisherman, but to achieve the lingering sense of unease that the horror genre demands, the desired lack of closure is obtained by implicating the film's supposed savior as a collaborator. Finally, while history demands that the biopic *Anarchist from Colony* detail Kaneko Fumiko's death, the film's repeated nods to the romantic comedy genre also require a form of closure that honors the film's love affair. Thus, the film repeats the opening romantic ballad once more and highlights the Japanese anarchist's burial in a Korean cemetery and her symbolic reunion with Park Yeol upon his death in 1974. In this melancholy way, not only is the romantic comedy's happy ending trope fulfilled, but Kaneko's otherness as Japanese is almost completely erased. It may be unsurprising that dissimilar genres such as horror and romantic comedy require different types of conclusions. However, as films with distinct genres operating within a film cycle that engaged with numerous genres, *The Wailing* and *Anarchist from Colony* are indicative of the Rising Sun cycle's broad reexamination and renegotiation of South Korea's relationship with the Japanese other. The difference in genre and their resultant differences in representation in these films also suggest that South Korea's audiences are willing to negotiate with their own perceptions of that other, even if their conclusions are sometimes contradictory. It is possible that the greater box office success of *The Wailing* when compared to the more ephemeral popularity of *Anarchist from Colony* may be attributed to audiences' genre preferences rather than an expression of preconceived views of each film's representations of Japanese. Regardless, the intermingling of Korean and Japanese identities in these Rising Sun films cinematically expresses the continuing negotiation of responsibility for Korea's past and demonstrates an ambivalence about the Japanese other as narratives grapple with the acceptance (or not) of colonialism's legacy.

NOTES

1. Frances Gateward (2007), Kyung Hyun Kim (2011), Kate Taylor-Jones (2017), and most recently Hee-seung Irene Lee (2020) have all written on various South Korean films that deal specifically with the Japanese occupation of Korea and use Japanese images associated with that era.
2. Luke 24:38–39: "Why are you troubled and why do doubts rise in your minds? Look at my hands and feet. It is I myself!" (www.biblehub.com/niv/luke/24.htm).
3. According to KoBiz (2017b), the blockbuster *My Way* opened at number two at the South Korean box office, had 2,142,670 admissions, and took in $13,224,628.
4. According to KoBiz (2017a), *Anarchist from Colony* had 2,359,707 admissions and took in $15,042,744 at the South Korean box office, including one week in the number one position. In contrast, KoBiz (2017c) lists *The Wailing* as having 6,879,989 admissions, earning box office receipts of $49,591,042, and placing in the top ten for seven weeks, including two consecutive weeks at the number one position.
5. *Park Yeol* is the Korean title for *Anarchist From Colony*.
6. The pervasiveness of American culture in South Korean society due to army bases and long-standing media outlets such as the American Forces Korea Network ensured that television shows, including *The Many Loves of Dobie Gillis*, were broadcast in South Korea for the pleasure of American residents, but they were frequently viewed by Korean television viewers as well (Park-Primiano 2016, 123).

REFERENCES

Beck, Jay, and Tony Grajeda. 2008. "Introduction: The Future of Film Sound Studies." In *Lowering the Boom: Critical Studies in Film Sound*, edited by Jay Beck and Tony Grajeda, 1–20. Urbana: University of Illinois Press.

Chion, Michel. 2000. "Projections of Sound on Image." In *Film and Theory: An Anthology*, edited by Robert Stam and Toby Miller, 111–24. Malden, MA: Blackwell.

Choi, Chungmoo. 1998. "Nationalism and Construction of Gender in Korea." In *Dangerous Women: Gender and Korean Nationalism*, edited by Elaine H. Kim and Chungmoo Choi, 9–31. New York: Routledge.

Choi Jin-hee. 2011. *The South Korean Film Renaissance: Local Hitmakers, Global Provocateurs*. Middletown, CT: Wesleyan University Press.

Gateward, Frances. 2007. "Waiting to Exhale: The Colonial Experience and the Trouble with *My Own Breathing*." In *Seoul Searching: Culture and Identity in Contemporary Korean Cinema*, edited by Frances Gateward, 191–218. New York: State University of New York Press.

Jowett, Garth, and Victoria O'Donnell. 2012. *Propaganda and Persuasion*. Thousand Oaks, CA: Sage.

Kim, Elaine H., and Chungmoo Choi. 1998. "Introduction." In *Dangerous Women: Gender and Korean Nationalism*, edited by Elaine H. Kim and Chungmoo Choi, 1–8. New York: Routledge.

Kim, Kyung Hyun. 2004. *The Remasculization of Korean Cinema*. Durham: Duke University Press.

Kim, Kyung Hyun. 2011. *Virtual Hallyu: Korean Cinema of the Global Era*. Durham: Duke University Press.
KoBiz. 2017a. "Film Directory: *Anarchist from Colony* (2017)." KoBiz: Korean Film Biz Zone. http://www.koreanfilm.or.kr/eng/films/index/filmsView.jsp?movieCd=20178982
KoBiz. 2017b. "Film Directory: *My Way* (2011)." KoBiz: Korean Film Biz Zone. http://www.koreanfilm.or.kr/eng/films/index/filmsView.jsp?movieCd=20110295
KoBiz. 2017c. "Film Directory: *The Wailing* (2016)." KoBiz: Korean Film Biz Zone. http://www.koreanfilm.or.kr/eng/films/index/filmsView.jsp?movieCd=20140194
Lee, Hee-seung Irene. 2020. "Remembering to Rest: Representations of the Colonial Era in Recent Korean Films." In *Popular Culture and the Transformation of Japan-Korea Relations*, edited by Stephen Epstein and Rumi Sakamoto, 63–77. London: Routledge.
Lee Ihn-Bum. 2010. "On the Debate about the Colour White." In *Asian Aesthetics*, edited by Ken-ichi Sasaki, 70–74. Singapore: NUS Press and Kyoto University Press.
Lewis, Jeff. 2008. *Cultural Studies: The Basics*. 2nd ed. Los Angeles: Sage.
McDonald, Tamar Jeffers. 2007. *Romantic Comedy: Boy Meets Girl Meets Genre*. New York: Wallflower Press.
Park-Primiano, Sueyoung. 2016. "The American Armed Forces Korean Network: 'Bringing Troops a Touch of Home.'" In *American Militarism on the Small Screen* edited by Anna Froula and Stacy Takacs, 111–27. New York: Routledge, Taylor & Francis.
Piontek, Thomas. 2012. "Tears for Queers: Ang Lee's *Brokeback Mountain*, Hollywood and American Attitudes toward Homosexuality." *Journal of American Culture*, 35 (2): 123–34. https://search.proquest.com/docview/1034642747?pq-origsite=gscholar
Stangarone, Troy. 2020. "Parsing the Economic Damage from the Japan-South Korea Dispute." *The Diplomat*. https://thediplomat.com/2020/01/parsing-the-economic-damage-from-the-japan-south-korea-dispute/
Sunwoo, Carla. 2012. "Director Owns Up to Box Office Flop." *Korea JoongAng Daily*. http://koreajoongangdaily.joins.com/news/article/article.aspx?aid=2960539
Taylor-Jones, Kate. 2017. *Divine Work, Japanese Colonial Cinema and Its Legacy*. New York: Bloomsbury Academic.
Yang, Hyunah. 1998. "Re-membering the Korean Military Comfort Women: Nationalism, Sexuality, and Silencing." In *Dangerous Women: Gender and Korean Nationalism*, edited by Elaine H. Kim and Chungmoo Choi, 123–39. New York: Routledge.
Yecies, Brian, and Shim, Ae-gyung. 2011. *Korea's Occupied Cinemas: 1893–1948*. New York: Routledge.

PART 2
Mediating the Co-ethnic Other

6

"Truth? No One Cares about the Truth"

On Marginalized Identities and Belonging in *The Bacchus Lady*

Myoung-Sun Song

"Not everyone's lives can be made into a movie and not every character within a story can become a main character," says director and writer E J-Yong in a press interview for the 2016 film *The Bacchus Lady* (Min 2016).[1] Tackling important issues such as age, class, gender, sexuality, disability, race, and ethnicity in South Korea (henceforth Korea), the film centers around characters who have been traditionally marginalized and consequently underrepresented in Korean media and popular culture. While the film largely focuses on So-Young, a sixty-five-year-old female sex worker, the audiences are also introduced to her housemates: Tina, the landlady and "legendary" transgender performer; Do-Hoon, a miniature figurine artist with an amputated leg; and Adindou, a young Black woman who works in the neighborhood's National Foods Mart. These characters constitute a chosen family as they live together in a two-story house located in the narrow alleyways of Itaewon.

The Bacchus Lady begins with So-Young visiting a gynecologist to get tested and treated for gonorrhea. As she walks into the entrance of the clinic building, she meets a young boy. She stops to ask, "Why are you here alone? Where is your mom?" The boy does not respond, and So-Young continues her way to the clinic. As she checks her prescription, she hears a great commotion. A woman by the name of Camilla Badua shouts to the doctor, Juhwan, in English: "I don't understand. You never called me for five years. How could you do this to me? Minho is your son. He came here with me." When the doctor refuses to listen and instead calls the security guard, she stabs him with a pair of scissors. The nurse reveals in a later scene that the doctor is actually a married man with three children. Minho was conceived when Juhwan was studying abroad in the Philippines. Minho is a "Kopino," a portmanteau of Korean and Filipino. Kopino children "are often abandoned by their Korean fathers, many of whom are already married with children in Korea" (Pack 2018, 483). Amid this chaos, So-Young takes Minho, the boy she met on her way into the clinic. Had Minho been left alone there, he would have been taken by the police and separated from Camilla while she remains in custody.

The original title of the film is *Jugyeojuneun Yeoja*. The word *yeoja* means woman. The word *jugyeojuneun* has sexual connotations of "being great in bed" or "having a killer body" but in its verb form means "to kill." So-Young, who is known for the sexual services that she provides, becomes a woman who literally "kills" when she gets involved in the deaths of three men. Within the legal framework of Korea, So-Young's actions are punishable. But the realities of her life reveal that perhaps she is the real victim of society. The English title draws from the term "Bacchus grandmother," referring to elder women who solicit male clients in public parks, most notably in Seoul's Jongno district.[2] Bacchus-F is a popular energy drink that takes its name from the Roman god of wine. "Do you want a bottle of Bacchus?" serves as a code for prostitution, which takes place in nearby motels for about "40,000 won, which includes the 10,000 won motel fee" (*The Bacchus Lady*).

In this chapter, I examine the notion of marginalized otherness as manifested in the dimensions of age, class, gender, sexuality, disability, race, and ethnicity. In analyzing *The Bacchus Lady*, this research converses with and extends existing academic work in (1) the representation of marginalized identities in Korean media and popular culture and (2) the emergence and potential of a nontraditional family in Korea. As a female Korean scholar, I inform this study by feminist methods that Jeom Suk Yeon (2009) and Dongok Lee (2011) advocate. By closely interrogating the relationships formed around and by So-Young, the chapter demonstrates the costs at which Korean society has prioritized younger productive heterosexual able-bodied Korean men as desirable and belonging to its nation. Consequently, anyone who is not young, productive, heterosexual, able-bodied, male, and ethnically Korean is deemed non-desirable and non-belonging to the imagination of Korea.

I first examine So-Young's body in two contexts: (1) as an elder sex worker who physically embodies the traumas of modern Korea and (2) as a matriarchal figure who by unconditionally embracing Minho signals the potential for Korean society to recognize racial and ethnic differences. Yet, the potential also presents an irony, as So-Young herself is denied this role in her own biological family. Next, I discuss So-Young and the characters within her chosen family. By analyzing their relationships, I examine a seemingly idyllic space where differences are accepted without questions. Yet, challenges remain even within this space as marginalized characters become further marginalized (1) by not being given a more nuanced character development within the film and (2) by an essentialist thinking among characters that results in racial stereotyping. In the final section of this chapter, I argue that So-Young's *muyeongo* (no surviving family or friends) death ultimately serves as a metaphor for and mirror of Korean society's failure and inability to accept difference.

Embodying Korea's Patriarchal Traumas

Yoon So-Young (née Yang Mi-Sook, June 19, 1950–October 5, 2017) was born just a week prior to the beginning of the Korean War. In the film, So-Young symbolizes "a marker of historicity and the reflection of a dying past" (Taylor-Jones 2017, 280). She is a *sampalttaraji*, a slang term that refers to people who fled North Korea at the outbreak of war. As a war orphan, she had to support herself throughout her life.[3] She worked as a housemaid and labored at factories before making her way to Lena House, a brothel in Dongducheon. Here, she changes her name to So-Young.[4] She has a baby with Steve, an African American soldier who drinks excessively and is physically abusive. Ultimately, she puts their son up for adoption. Calling herself a "bad b****," she says that she will never be forgiven and that she will end up in hell for her actions. For women like So-Young who serviced Black soldiers, they were cast by society as "the lowest of the lowest" (Byun 2014, 299). In a similar vein, multiracial children from these relationships represent those who are "never able to call Korea their home" (J. Park 2016, 242).

Throughout history, the Korean government treated the women of *gijichon* (camp towns) not as its "citizens" but more as a "tool" in leveraging relations with the US military (Youn Jee Kim 2013, 126). The term *yanggongju* (Western princess, Yankee princess) is a highly derogatory word that refers to female sex workers who served the US soldiers in these camp towns. Naming these women *yanggongju* "reveals the silent nod to the existence of society's treatment of these women as low and disgraceful"

(Park and Min 2011, 153). Min Kim and Jiho Tae's (2019) study on the disproportionately high and intentional use of the term *yanggongju* in newspaper reports from 1952 to 1999 confirms this idea. Korean society has persistently tried to erase the presence of these women (Youn Jee Kim 2013, 100) because "the existence of the yanggongju, in fact, denies the town/nation's homogeneity with stories that differ drastically from the shared narrative of the majority" (Park and Suh 2009, 275).[5] Though scholars like Yeonsuk Kim (2003) argue that a paradoxical possibility exists for the *yanggongju* to escape patriarchy through the cracks and ruptures of society (152), it does not remove the sociocultural and economic marginalization that is cast upon her. Consequently, So-Young's body carries the traumas and prejudices that are attached to this history.

Throughout the film, one of the most visually defining aspects of So-Young's body is her fashion. So-Young wears jeans that are historically and socioculturally associated with the youth and the US. She clenches her coat tightly at the waist, which shows her slim figure and contrasts with the long, loose cardigans that the other Bacchus ladies wear. It is noteworthy to add that Youn Yuh-Jung, the actor playing So-Young, is admired by the public as a fashion leader. Topping the best dressed lists, Youn is famous for casually mixing and matching high-end designers like Chanel and Hermès with "younger" choices like jeans and sneakers. Forging a trailblazing career of more than five decades, Youn gained international acclaim for her role in *Minari* (2020), in which she plays Soon-Ja, a Korean grandmother who does not necessarily conform to her Korean American grandson's ideal of a "real grandma." Youn won Best Actress in a Supporting Role at the 93rd Academy Awards in 2021, making her the first Korean actor to win an Oscar. Throughout the entire awards season, her witty and candid interviews and acceptance speeches—delivered eloquently in English without an interpreter—were adored by global audiences. Youn effectively and powerfully utilized these opportunities to not only carefully raise but also confidently address her thoughts on many pertinent issues, including gender, race, aging, single motherhood, diversity, and representation. As Jin-Wol Yoo (2018) argues, Youn in many ways is distant from "the stereotypical elderly female": (1) she maintains her skinny figure, which adheres to the beauty standards of Korean society; (2) she has a modern and sophisticated look; and (3) she is independent in her career choices (291). As such, So-Young's body—through Youn—becomes a "competitive one" (Yoo 2018, 286). Yet, So-Young's body remains highly vulnerable to commodification and exploitation. For example, Joohee Kim (2016) reads So-Young's body within "the politics of belonging; for survival in the Korean prostitution market, [where] women must rely on 'instant mobility' to find better work conditions and repeatedly create a 'fresh' body" (62).

It is important to note that So-Young refers to her own body as a "product." When Tina asks her why she came home so early, So-Young replies, "I couldn't sell anything today because there is a defect in the goods." The "defect" is gonorrhea. Yet, in the act of selling her services, she often romanticizes the process: "Who are you waiting for? Do you want to go on a date with me? Don't you know what dating is? I'll be good to you. I'm not expensive." Once it is known among the other Bacchus ladies that So-Young is a *yanggongju*, she cannot frequent her usual solicitation spot. In search of work, So-Young endlessly wanders across hiking trails of public parks (Yong-Hee Kim 2018, 46). As she wanders, her body remains limited to these specific places, which demonstrates that "she lives a peripheral life strictly excluded from the majority" (Cho 2017, 81).[6]

Throughout the film, the audiences are never shown So-Young's bare body. The only type of nudity displayed is that of the men she services. In fact, the male bodies in the film depict what Yong-Hee Kim (2018) defines as "a body that has exhausted its economic and social function" (51). In one scene, the camera shows the hairy torso of a fully naked man. He forces So-Young to perform fellatio. So-Young, in a black camisole and black boy shorts, runs to the bathroom to wash her mouth out. This is a distinct shift from previous Korean films wherein the faces of female prostitutes are highlighted in scenes involving sex (Jung and Kim 2010, 24). Still, So-Young is forced, which emphasizes how "men's sexual desire become[s] more recognizable and active until the old age, even justif[ying] the commercial sex and sexual violence performed by men" (Dongok Lee 2010, 69).

Mothering Korea's Undesired Children

In a study of twenty films screened in Korea from 2008 to 2011, Dongok Lee (2011) finds that elder women are never seen as those who need care, while their care for elder men is deemed as natural (155). This is well demonstrated in *The Bacchus Lady*, where So-Young is continuously expected to service men in various ways from fulfilling their sexual desires to assisting their death. These expectations come at the sacrifice of So-Young. In a similar vein, Youn Soon Kim (2005) argues that elder women are influenced by Confucian values in that they pride themselves most on being good mothers (139). As such, the most intimate relationships they form is not necessarily with their partners but with their children (Youn Soon Kim 2005, 140). This relationship is, however, not always beneficial for women. In other words, "maternal love-based care can be interpreted as a violent device forcing women's sacrifice in traditional patriarchy" (Lim 2017, 259).

This idea is translated within the film as So-Young's lasting guilt for putting her son up for adoption. If the family constitutes the smallest unit that makes up a nation, it is telling who can claim membership to a family and by extension to that nation.[7] In one scene, as So-Young awaits her order at KFC, she sees a young soldier eating by himself. Although the movie officially credits his name as "Customer #2," the name tag on his uniform reads "Thompson." She approaches him with an almost instinctual interest:

> THOMPSON: [Sees So-Young sitting down next to him] Hi, how are you?
> SO-YOUNG: Hello. [So-Young stares at Thompson]
> THOMPSON: Is something wrong?
> SO-YOUNG: You very handsome.
> THOMPSON: Thank you. Thank you.
> SO-YOUNG: You American, right?
> THOMPSON: Of course, I'm American. American soldier. Uhm . . . *miguk gunin* [American soldier].
> SO-YOUNG: I see.
> THOMPSON: I'm half Black and half Korean. I'm mixed. *Twigi saram* [a debasing term referring to multiracial people].
> SO-YOUNG: Your mom, Korean?
> THOMPSON: Yes.
> SO-YOUNG: Where your mom?
> THOMPSON: I don't know her. I was adopted when I was a baby.
> SO-YOUNG: Really?
> THOMPSON: My father left when I was a baby and my mom, she couldn't take care of me so she put me up for adoption. At least that's what I was told.
>
> [So-Young stares into the space.]
>
> THOMPSON: Why? [So-Young does not respond.] Ma'am, are you okay? [The employee calls out that the jumbo order is ready.] Ma'am, I think your chicken is ready.

As So-Young picks up her jumbo chicken order, the soldier disappears. So-Young rushes out to find that he is inside a cab. As he leaves, he waves goodbye to her. It is clear from this interaction that So-Young has a maternal curiosity that drives her to question whether Thompson is her son. Chances are highly unlikely that he is, but what this scene suggests is that there are more women like So-Young and more children like Thompson. Like the soldier at KFC, Minho reminds So-Young of the son she gave up for adoption. When So-Young brings Minho home, her housemates do not question or critique her choice. So-Young as a matriarchal figure who unconditionally embraces Minho signals the potential for Korean society to recognize and accept racial and ethnic differences. Yet, the situation presents a harsh irony as So-Young herself is denied this role within her own biological family. Nonetheless, Minho's presence brings So-Young and her housemates closer as a "family" as they take turns taking care of him when So-Young has to work.

Since the 1997 Asian financial crisis, a greater number of Koreans have visited the Philippines due to its relatively low cost and convenient proximity (Han 2016, 32). Many Koreans choose the Philippines as a destination to learn English, which serves as an alternative to more costly countries like the US, Canada, and Australia. Korean men, during their temporary stay, often form romantic and/or sexual relations with Filipina women, with some resulting in pregnancy. When the men return to Korea, they cut ties with the women and abandon their children. Consequently, when the Filipina mothers come to Korea in search of recognition and financial support from the fathers, "the abrupt presence of the Kopino children and the existence of their mothers become a very startling situation for Korean society" (Han 2016, 26). In Korean media, Kopino children and their mothers are represented as "passive and pitiful victims who need help" (26). This situates them as "the eternal other," whose presence highlights how "Korea has silently overlooked the actions Korean men have taken outside the geographical boundaries of its nation" (26).

Regarding the question of marginalized identities and belonging, the film posits an intentional comparison and connection between So-Young and Camilla. First, they are ethnically marginalized: So-Young as originally from North Korea and Camilla as Filipina. Second, they are mothers of "undesired children" as defined by the "homogenous" nation of Korea. In essence, "generational gender inequities are seen as transferring away from Korean women who dated and married American GIs towards Filipin[a] women and their Korean/Filipino mixed children" (Taylor-Jones 2017, 282).[8] When So-Young visits Camilla in lockup, there is an immediate unspoken understanding between the two mothers. So-Young assures Camilla in English, "Don't worry. He's with me. I take care of him, okay?" Third, they have committed "crimes" that get publicly reported as "news": So-Young by "killing" men and Camilla by stabbing Juhwan. Do-Hoon tells So-Young that he has recently read on the internet that "a Filipina woman stabbed a doctor with a knife." So-Young corrects him by stating that it was not a knife but scissors. What this demonstrates is that media, as the "official" narrative, manufactures a new "truth" in the name of "news." When Camilla speaks of Juhwan's irresponsible actions, his answer is, "Shut the f***. You crazy." Her truth becomes immediately rejected and silenced.

Like his mother, Minho is rarely heard speaking throughout the film. The first time Minho speaks is when Adindou, a Black woman, asks his name. Minho replies in a full articulate sentence in the Korean language. So-Young, who has repeatedly asked him whether he could speak and why he does not speak, is shocked when he finally does. It is apparent from Minho's picture diary that he has the ability to express himself, although this is not vocalized within the film. In the rare instances when Minho does speak, it is a very brief "Thank you." In the scenes with his mother, he speaks in Tagalog, but again only uses short words. This is not only an indictment of how Kopino children are not given opportunities to properly voice themselves in Korean society but also a reminder of the marginalized positions they hold within.

We Are Family?

In an effort to follow So-Young "honestly" (Jun 2017, 269), *The Bacchus Lady* does not employ any flashbacks. Any information regarding a character's past is only revealed through the conversations between characters. Consequently, other than So-Young, there is very little background information on or development of the other characters within the film. Though So-Young, Tina, Do-Hoon, and Minho do not really need to know of one another's past to become a family,[9] the marginalization of marginalized characters is worth problematizing. This marginalization occurs in two dimensions: (1) by not offering proper character development, the housemates simply function as "accessories" in highlighting the marginalized position of So-Young; and (2) through essentializing and racial stereotyping, instances occur where characters marginalize each other.

So-Young is situated in what Ungsan Kim (2018) calls "the critical social turn of queer Korean cinema . . . [where] alternative kinship ties based on intimacy, interdependency, and absolute hospitality" emerge (110). In looking at this new "family," the film raises the question of whether these opportunities of chosen families and kinships are only allowed within the historically unique spaces of Itaewon. Son-Ho Kim, Sung-Eun Kim, and Seung-Hyun Kim (2014) identify "four distinct historical periods according to which the meanings of Itaewon have been transformed":

(1) space of modernity during the Japanese occupation
(2) space of exteriority since the deployment of the U.S. military troops
(3) space of consumption tailored to the tastes of international visitors and shoppers in the 1980s–1990s
(4) space of multiculturalism since globalization. (342)

As these shifting meanings demonstrate, Itaewon has always been a contested space symbolizing foreignness and/or difference (Song 2011). In what Elisabeth Schober (2014) describes as the "Itaewon suspense," there is "a distinct ambiguity that presently characterizes the area: the uneasy positioning of the neighborhood between allure and repulsion that seems to dominate many people's imaginations" (39). For example, even if Itaewon has notable areas that are predominantly occupied by sexual minorities (Han 2013, 268), "the invisibility of LGBTQ identities on the main street reflects the unquestioned heteronormativity naturalized through this urban space" (Eun Young Lee 2016, 132). One can also allude that living in Itaewon and visiting Itaewon offer two completely different sets of experiences.

Toward the end of the film, So-Young invites Minho, Tina, and Do-Hoon on an excursion.[10] They ride the merry-go-round, visit Imjingak, take group selfies, and eat eel. In other words, they engage in activities that a typical family would do together. Quite significantly, although Adindou lives with them, she is not included in this family excursion. This suggests that although Minho, who is of Asian descent, can be accepted as "family," Adindou, who is Black, cannot be fully integrated as part of Korean society. In this volume, Benjamin Han explores the Korean television industry's adoption of "strategic blackness." While Han's case studies are specific to Black male entertainers on television, the showcasing of their fluency in the Korean language as a marker used to determine their Koreanness can be compared with Adindou in *The Bacchus Lady*. In the scene where So-

Young and Minho visit the National Foods Mart, So-Young asks Adindou, "Do you have Pongpong?" Adindou looks confused and repeats after So-Young, "Pongpong?" So-Young remarks, "Don't you know Pongpong? You know, what you wash dishes with. Pongpong." Pongpong is a dishwashing liquid that was released by Lucky Corporation (currently LG Household & Health Care) in 1972. Because of the item's nationwide popularity, its name became synonymous with dish soap. Unlike the Black entertainers Hyun-Min Han and Sam Okyere that Benjamin Han discussed in chapter 2, whose fluency in the Korean language translates to their perceived value and position, Adindou's lack of knowledge signals her distance and consequently inability to be fully accepted by Korean society.

This inability to integrate is further exemplified in the scene where the characters eat pizza together. Although it is unclear whether she was invited, Adindou is again absent from this gathering. This pizza scene in particular illuminates many issues pertinent to imagining a "multicultural" Korea. Eating pizza together on the rooftop, Do-Hoon and Tina comment on Minho's situation. This scene takes place after So-Young and Minho's visit to Camilla earlier that day where it was revealed that she will be released from the detention center in ten days. The social worker and public defender confirmed that the paternity lawsuit was going well, as they were able to prove Minho's biological relation to Juhwan. Tina buys pizza to celebrate this small but important victory. Do-Hoon comments how they are able to "feast" thanks to Minho. He also adds that there are going to be more cases like Minho in the future. Tina joins the conversation by pointing out that this is a problem not only in the Philippines but also in Vietnam. They seem to be very understanding of the situation. When Do-Hoon offers Tina a slice of Hawaiian pizza, she refuses by saying that she does not like pineapple, which is one of the pizza's main toppings. Do-Hoon then takes the slice and offers it to Minho. He says, "Eat this. People from the Philippines like pineapple, right?" Minho does not say anything but accepts and eats the pizza. So-Young remains silent throughout this scene.

In a typical Korean family configuration, Do-Hoon would be considered the patriarch of the four. This role is exemplified in the scene where So-Young pleads with Do-Hoon to accompany her and Minho on their first visit to the Multicultural Family Support Center. So-Young tells him that "only when she goes with a man, she will not be ignored nor looked down upon." That So-Young does not feel entirely safe or welcome to visit spaces like the Multicultural Family Support Center, which exists in principle to protect women and children, is indicative of the hardships and discrimination that she has faced throughout her life. While Do-Hoon as a heterosexual man asserts more power than So-Young, his physical disability and economically abject state marginalize him in society. At times, he can even be rejected by his own chosen family, symbolically through Tina's rejection of the Hawaiian pizza. As the only father figure of the group, Do-Hoon ends up racially stereotyping Minho, a boy who came to Korea in search of his father, by essentializing that "Filipinos like pineapples." What this scene represents is the difficulty and complexity that rest in envisioning Korea as a multicultural nation. In short, while the father figure tacitly rejects Minho, the mother figure embraces him. This suggests that Korea's multicultural future is only possible through the maternal influence, but as the next section will demonstrate, the matriarch is disciplined and punished when she goes to jail and dies there.

Death as Restoration and Resolution?

So-Young embodies what Myung Sun Park (2002) calls the "feminization of poverty" (240). As "the economic destitution of elderly women" (240), this poverty represents an accumulation of sexist practices that women have endured throughout their lifetime (Choi 1999; Choi 2005). Even so, So-Young strives to live each day to her fullest. This is a direct contrast to the male characters she "services." The film does not dwell on highlighting the sexual aspects of So-Young's daily job. Rather, it concentrates on her relationships with former clients, who define their own existence as meaningless due to their age, illness, and inability to perform sexually. In this way, So-Young helps—directly and indirectly—with the deaths of three men: "Savile Row" Song, Jong-Soo, and Jaewoo.

Savile Row is a nickname for Song, who is remembered by So-Young as "the gentleman who always wore tailored suits." In another reading of the name, Eun Mi Jang and Hee Jeong Han (2017) suspect that it may be spelled "Sébire," drawing from Chantal Sébire, whose controversial death in 2008 raised debates around euthanasia. Song not only was dapper but also received a handsome pension, which he used generously to pay So-Young. Song had been bedridden for more than a year. His grandchildren refuse to hug him because "he stinks." When So-Young visits him at the hospice, he says, "I smell, right? I can't do anything by myself. Even if I want to die, I can't do it by myself." He pleads for So-Young's help. Reluctantly, she buys and feeds him pesticide. In doing this, So-Young experiences unspeakable emotional pain and suffering. When So-Young confesses to Jaewoo that she helped Song die, he takes her to meet his friend Jong-Soo, who is suffering from dementia. Jaewoo asks So-Young for a "favor": to help Jong-Soo end his life. Although resistant at first, she eventually helps Jong-Soo by pushing him off a mountain. When she comes down the mountain, Jaewoo awaits her, and So-Young gives him a resentful look.

Finally, Jaewoo asks So-Young on a "date." He takes her to a hotel (as opposed to a motel), where his true intentions are revealed. His wife had passed away five years ago, and their child was killed in an accident a long time ago. Consequently, Jaewoo had been suffering from depression. He gives a couple of sleeping pills to So-Young and takes a fistful himself. So-Young tries to stop him, but she fails. The next morning, So-Young wakes up, and as she checks Jaewoo, a teardrop rolls down her face. The men who ask her for "favors" demonstrate "extreme selfishness" (Yoo 2018, 290), as they do not care about the consequences that she will face once she "helps." For these men, death ends their own troubles (Han 2020, 174).

After the fateful night with Jaewoo, news reports state that an elder man was found dead inside a hotel room. Having checked the hotel's surveillance cameras, the police suspect that an elder woman "lured and killed" the man for his money. The police are assured that this was the "motive for the murder" when they discover that 1 million won had been withdrawn from the man's bank account the day before. Not knowing that So-Young is involved, Tina condemns the killing of people for money, while Do-Hoon remarks that "grandmothers are scary." So-Young quietly replies, "I'm sure that person has a story to tell. No one can really know what the real circumstances are. Everyone merely assumes and jabbers, judging only by what's on the outside."[11] So-Young never knew about the 1 million won. Similarly, when she goes to a temple to pray the day after Jaewoo's death, she discovers an envelope that he had slipped inside her bag. Inside the envelope, she also finds a gold ring and a handwritten apology note. She only takes 100,000 won and puts everything else into the temple donation box.

It is important to note that So-Young, who makes a living on monetary exchanges for her sexual services, never demands economic compensation for her "services" in killing. Even the 100,000 won is spent on buying toys and clothes for Minho and on paying for the family excursion. As So-Young prays, an artwork can be seen on the building facade behind her. It depicts the Bodhisattva Avalokiteshvara. "The Bodhisattva of Compassion" holds a water jar (associated with purity) in the left hand and a willow branch (associated with healing) in the right hand. A comparison can be drawn between the Bodhisattva of Compassion and So-Young, who "heals" elder men by assisting with their death. A circular shape surrounds the head of the Bodhisattva Avalokiteshvara. As So-Young prays with her hands clasped together, this circular shape is reminiscent of the halo of the Virgin Mary, which So-Young now embodies. She gets arrested the next day.[12]

Within the history of modern Korea, the notion of family becomes increasingly severed. Kyung Hyun Kim (2004) argues that, under these conditions, male characters in Korean films are often alienated and traumatized. Their suffering is symbolically represented through physical, verbal, or mental impairments. As Kim writes, "The male lack [is] located in every field imaginable: of the accoutrements of power in sexual potency, paternal authority, communal function, historical legitimacy, and professional worth" (12). In essence, there is a desire to regain wholeness and to recover from the oppressive conditions of society. But this comes at the sacrifice or destruction of women. In this crisis and the consequent recuperation of masculinity, Kim finds, "the images of women remain prefixed on the rigid, bifurcated convention of whores and mothers" (8). As demonstrated in *The Bacchus Lady*, So-Young—as whore and mother—is disciplined and punished by society even as she wholly sacrifices herself to restore the nation as symbolized through the men's dignity in death.

Jonghyun Lee and Tchi-Wan Park (2017) claim that So-Young exemplifies what they call "unsympathetic empathy." They argue that So-Young is able to help others because she does not try to empathize with them: her deliberate distance allows her to better understand others. Ultimately, even though So-Young sacrifices herself in serving the needs of others, she is put in prison, where she dies as a former prostitute and convicted murderer. As the police car leaves the narrow alleys of Itaewon, So-Young does not show any resistance:

> Can I go to prison when spring comes? I get cold easily. I promise I won't run away. I guess this turned out for the better. I can't afford to go to a retirement home anyways. They give you three meals there, right? I wonder what the *banchan* [small side dishes] is these days. I hope this winter isn't as cold.

Her words turn into a monologue, as the policemen do not pay any attention to her. These are the last words So-Young speaks on-screen. The two years that So-Young spends inside Cheongju Women's Correctional Institution, the only long-term female prison in Korea, are cut from the film.

The deliberate erasure of this time and space shows the status she holds in society. The mental and physical exhaustion she endures is also cut out. Whether she had a fair trial does not seem to matter. Yong-Hee Kim (2018) argues that this symbolizes "an ironic ridicule of state law that judges and rules without knowing the truth and facts of each individual" (58). Whether Tina and Do-Hoon gave her a proper funeral also does not seem to matter. Whether Minho's father acknowledged the boy as his son does not seem to matter either. So-Young's room is now probably occupied by someone equally as marginalized as her.

In the final shot of the film, So-Young's given name is officially introduced: Yang Mi-Sook. Above her name, written in black marker, lies the word *muyeongo*, meaning "no surviving family or friends." Her ashes are placed not in an urn but inside a cheap wooden box. Ungsan Kim (2018) reads this as "an act of fixing and disciplining So-Yeong's wandering path or mobility in the intelligible and recognizable terms of the state" (107).[13] Her cremated ashes remain in between Sang-Moon Lee (August 1945–October 3, 2017) and an unidentified individual whose birthdate is unknown and whose date of death is October 6, 2017. As dictated by law, their ashes will remain there for the next ten years. This haunting image is a stark reminder of how So-Young is deemed unworthy and made invisible to the public's eyes. While So-Young's story may be "a life that can be made into a movie," *The Bacchus Lady* does not show or eradicate any of the underlying problems she faced.[14] Here I am not arguing that films must provide clear solutions or remedies.

Maybe it is not the film but rather So-Young who had been suggesting an answer all along. "Truth? No one cares about the truth," she says firmly. In remembering Yoon So-Young, one remembers Yang Mi-Sook: a North Korean war orphan who, unprotected by the government, had no better option than to become a sex worker. In remembering Yang Mi-Sook, one remembers Yoon So-Young: an independent woman who accepted and aided those who were marginalized by their age, class, gender, sexuality, disability, race, and ethnicity. As the framework for this volume, David C. Oh, in the introduction, proposes the term "anthrocategorism" as "a system of othering that creates a hierarchical and concentric understanding of human difference." In conversation with the visualization of anthrocategorism offered by Oh, I see Yoon So-Young's and Yang Mi-Sook's identities intertwining like the Möbius strip. If one imagines walking the Möbius strip, one realizes that the "inside" and "outside" are connected as one. As the Möbius strip suggests, a single half turn—or a simple interest in the truth—can help to uncover a new possibility in not only understanding marginalized identities but also expanding the notion of belonging in Korea.[15]

NOTES

1. This chapter follows the romanization of Korean provided by the Ministry of Culture, Sports, and Tourism. For the names of people, preferred romanization is used. Quotations from the film and references written in the Korean language have been translated from Korean to English by the author. For the names of the director, actors, and characters in *The Bacchus Lady*, the Korean order of Last name First name is utilized. Any inconsistencies in the spelling or hyphenation of words reflect the efforts to retain the original formatting of the quoted text.

2. E J-Yong did not conduct any interviews with the "Bacchus grandmothers" while writing the script. He was inspired by documentaries and journalistic reports on the subject. He did observe the "Bacchus grandmothers" from afar. At first, he could not tell them apart from the "regular grandmothers," but after a while he claimed that "a light seemed to have disappeared from the faces of the Bacchus grandmothers" (Min 2016).

3. While it is unclear whether So-Young is illiterate, there are three instances within the film where she avoids the act of reading: reading information off a smartphone, reading the menu at KFC, and reading the menu at a restaurant. She simply asks the other characters within the scene to make the decisions for her. These are subtle indications that show the lack of education she has received and/or the lack of education opportunities she has had.

4. As So-Young is soliciting men, she runs into Bok-Hee, who remembers her as Mi-Sook eonni (*eonni* meaning "elder sister"). They worked together at Lena House. In Bok-Hee's enunciation and emphasis of the word "so young," it becomes clear that young(er) bodies are considered more valuable as sexual commodities. It is for this reason I chose the spelling "So-Young" for this chapter as opposed to the alternative "So-Yeong."

5. While the majority of Korean women have left the *gijichon*, these spaces still remain and are now largely occupied by "Philippine juice girls" (Kim 2013, 100). Margo Okazawa-Rey (1997) points to the irony that "the class status of the GIs may not be very different from that of the bar women. Many have joined the military for lack of other alternatives, drawn by the employment opportunities, education, and travel" (97).

6. Cf. Eun Mi Jang and Hee Jeong Han's (2017) study on heterotopias in *The Bacchus Lady* and Jinhee Choi's (2015) work on the "flâneur" as a mode of observation or being in contemporary Korean cinema.

7. Cf. Ji-Hyun Ahn's book (2018) for chapters discussing Hines Ward (Black Korean) and Daniel Henney (White Korean) and the politics of mixed-race identity in Korean society.

8. This is further visualized in the two family photos that are utilized within the film. In Minho's family photo, which becomes key evidence in the paternity lawsuit that is filed against the doctor, Juhwan holds baby Minho. Camilla is smiling next to him as the three stand in front of a carrousel. In a much faded photo, So-Young holds her baby while Steve, whose face is torn out, stands beside her. He wears a military uniform.

9. In the scene at KFC, So-Young first asks for "enough chicken to feed her and a

child" but quickly changes the order to the "largest one." This signals that she wants to feed Tina and Do-Hoon as well. In Korean, *sikgu* (family) literally translates to "those who live together and eat together." Tina calls So-Young "*eonni*" and Do-Hoon calls So-Young "*nunim*," both terms meaning "elder sister."

10. Yong-Hee Kim (2018) compares this excursion to "The Last Supper" (61).

11. The word "*sayeon*" means "circumstance" or "reason." Throughout the film, this word is used, along with "*sajeong*," to show the different stories and realities of each character. Tina and Do-Hoon have a *sajeong* of their own. The word "*jareuda*" (to cut) is used to describe their situations: Tina as a transgender woman and Do-Hoon as an amputee. Tina tells Do-Hoon that had she known of his "defect," she would not have allowed him to rent from her. His disability does not hinder the two from forming a sexual relationship. E J-Yong revealed in an interview that the original script had included the detailed histories of each character but were later cut out from the film. For example, Do-Hoon lost his leg during a motorcycle accident in high school. His friend, who was a passenger, died on the spot. Having lost his leg, Do-Hoon thought of suicide but eventually persevered (Min 2016).

12. One can infer that the date of So-Young's arrest is November 28, 2015. The film includes news reports about Baek Nam-Gi. Baek, a sixty-eight-year-old farmer, came to Seoul to join a protest demanding that farmers be paid a fair price for rice. After being struck by a police water cannon, Baek became "a symbol of what government critics call rising police brutality and the erosion of freedom of assembly" (Choe 2016). Baek never wakes up from his coma and passes away from a brain hemorrhage on September 25, 2016.

13. Cf. Jong Hyun Lee's (2017) analysis for a different reading of these names.

14. In some ways, this resonates with Noh-Hyun Park's (2017) study on the television program *Dear My Friends*, where "the helplessness of old age is largely reduced to the domain of the individual," leaving only a "heartful fantasy that tells us to leave all of the current aversion to aging and the fear of the future aside" (259).

15. This chapter is indebted to David C. Oh for his vision and dedication in spearheading this important project. Much appreciation goes to the anonymous reviewers who generously provided feedback and advice and to the editorial staff at the University of Michigan Press for their assistance and expertise.

REFERENCES

An asterisk in front of the author's last name denotes that the original work was written in the Korean language. Most Korean journal articles provide an official title and abstract in the English language written by their author(s). As such, the references draw from this information.

Ahn, Ji-Hyun, 2018. *Mixed-Race Politics and Neoliberal Multiculturalism in South Korean Media*. London: Palgrave Macmillan.

*Byun, Hwa Yeong. 2014. "Tattoo of Korean War, the Black Mixed-Blood and the Foreigner's Whore." *Journal of Korean Fiction Research* 57:295–320.

*Cho, Heup. 2017. "The Bare Life of *The Bacchus Lady*." *Journal of the Korean Society of Civil Engineers* 65 (2): 80–82.

Choe, Sang-Hun. 2016. "Activist in South Korea Dies of Injuries from Police Water Cannon." *New York Times*, September 25. https://www.nytimes.com/2016/09/26/world/asia/activist-in-south-korea-dies-of-injuries-from-police-water-cannon.html

*Choi, Hee Kyung. 2005. "An Analysis on Poor Elderly Women's Lives and Characteristics." *Korean Journal of Gerontological Social Welfare* 27:147–74.

Choi, Jinhee. 2015. "Seoul Flâneur? Breathless and Café Noir." *Journal of Japanese and Korean Cinema* 7 (1): 57–72.

*Choi, Sun Wha. 1999. "Causes of Poverty among the Elderly Women throughout the Life Cycle." *Korean Journal of Family Welfare* 3:187–211.

*Han, Kyuryang. 2020. "The Life and Death of Suicide Attempter—Focused on Old Age Film." *Journal of Ethics* 128:159–78.

*Han, Seunghee. 2016. "An Exploratory Study of Kopino in the Philippines." *Minjok Yeonku* 65:26–45.

*Han, Yu Seok. 2013. "Appropriation of Space and Community Making by Sexual Minorities—A Case Study on Itaewon Fire Station Street." *Seoul Studies* 14 (1): 253–69.

*Jang, Eun Mi, and Hee Jeong Han. 2017. "Existent, but Non-Existent Spaces for Others: Focusing on Discourse Spaces of a Korean Movie *The Bacchus Lady*." *Korean Journal of Communication & Information* 84:99–123.

*Jun, Jee-Nee. 2017. "Can Minorities Be in Solidarity? The Question That Feminist Films in 2016 Asked—A Reconsideration on *Missing* and *The Bacchus Lady*." *Journal of Popular Narrative* 23 (4): 251–89.

*Jung, Sa-Gahng, and Hoon-Soon Kim. 2010. "A Study on the Representation of Prostitute Women in Korean Movies." *Media, Gender & Culture* 13:5–35.

Kim, Joohee. 2016. "Instant Mobility, Stratified Prostitution Market: The Politics of Belonging of Korean Women Selling Sex in the U.S." *Asian Journal of Women's Studies* 22 (1): 48–64.

Kim, Kyung Hyun. 2004. *The Remasculization of Korean Cinema*. Durham: Duke University Press.

*Kim, Min, and Jiho Tae. 2019. "Gendered Images of the Yanggongju through the Lens of Post-Colonial Feminism: An Analysis of the KBS Special Documentary, War and Women: Her Dreams." In *Proceedings of 2019 Bi-Annual Association of Global Cultural Contents Conference*, 73–77. Korea University Sejong Campus.

*Kim, Son-Ho, Sung-Eun Kim, and Seung-Hyun Kim. 2014. "Representing a Liminal Space: A Social Semiotic Analysis of News Discourses on Itaewon." *Semiotic Inquiry* 39:301–42.

Kim, Ungsan. 2018. "The Critical Social Turn of Queer Korean Cinema: Hospitality and the Temporal Economy of Queer Kinship in *The Bacchus Lady* (2016)." *Korea Journal* 58 (2): 88–112.

*Kim, Yeonsuk. 2003. "Women's Body and Sexuality Represented by Yang-gong-ju." *Issues in Feminism* 3:121–56.

*Kim, Yong-Hee. 2018. "The Ritual Meaning of 'Taboo Violation' and 'Border Dismantling' in *The Bacchus Lady*." *Asian Cinema Studies* 10 (2): 41–67.

*Kim, Youn Jee. 2013. "Instrumentalized Other, Korean Military Prostitutes, and Korea Cinema: Movies about Korean Military Prostitutes after the Korean War." *Journal of Korean Cinema Education* 15:99–133.

*Kim, Youn Soon. 2005. "Korean Old Women's Sexuality through the Method of Life History." *Korean Journal of Women's Health* 6 (2): 121–46.

*Lee, Dongok. 2010. "Feminist Study on the Sexual Discourse of the Elderly in Korean Society." *Journal of Women's Studies* 26 (2): 41–69.

*Lee, Dongok. 2011. "Sexuality and Love of Old Women Represented in Movies." *Media, Gender & Culture* 20:137–71.

Lee, Eun Young. 2016. "Looking Forward: Decentering and Reorienting Communication Studies in the Spatial Turn." *Women's Studies in Communication* 39 (2): 132–36.

*Lee, Jong Hyun. 2017. "The Representation of Trans-Identity through Facial Aesthetics: Focused on the Character of *The Bacchus Lady*." *Film Studies* 72:237–64.

*Lee, Jonghyun, and Tchi-Wan Park. 2017. "The Koreans' Cultural Genes and the Restoration of Community Spirit: Focused on the Film *The Bacchus Lady*." *Humanities Contents* 45:149–72.

*Lim, Eun-hee. 2017. "A Study on the Multicultural Thinking and Otherness of 'Yanggongju' Motif in Modern Novels." *Journal of Korean Literary Criticism* 54:241–67.

*Min, Yongjun. 2016. "Interview with *The Bacchus Lady*'s E J-Yong." *HuffPost*, November 11. https://www.huffingtonpost.kr/yongjun-min/story_b_12859224.html

Okazawa-Rey, Margo. 1997. "Amerasian Children of GI Town: A Legacy of U.S. Militarism in South Korea." *Asian Journal of Women's Studies* 3 (1): 71–102.

Pack, Sam. 2018. "'F^@king Koreans!': Sexual Relations and Immigration in the Philippines." *Journal of Asia Pacific Studies* 4 (4): 469–91.

*Park, Jong Hyun. 2016. "Silent Diaspora: The Representations of Women in Military Camp Town and Children of Mixed Blood." *Bulletin of Korean Society of Basic Design & Art* 17 (1): 231–43.

*Park, Jong Hyun, and Byung Wook Min. 2011. "Scapegoats of Divided Korea—Korea Photos View of Women in the Military Camp Town." *Bulletin of Korean Society of Basic Design & Art* 12 (4): 151–59.

Park, Joohyun, and Jungkyu Suh. 2009. "The Subaltern Speaks: *Silver Stallion* as the Rhetorical Space for Yanggonju." *Comparative Literature* 49:261–80.

*Park, Myung Sun. 2002. "Labor and Poverty of the Elderly Women: Focused on Jeonbuk Area." *Korean Journal of Sociology* 36 (2): 175–204.

*Park, Noh-Hyun. 2017. "Poetic Elderly, Translated Old Age and Romantic Aging: Based on the tvN Mini-Series of 'Dear My Friends.'" *Korean Language and Literature* 72:239–62.

Schober, Elisabeth. 2014. "Itaewon's Suspense: Masculinities, Place-Making and the US Armed Forces in a Seoul Entertainment District." *Social Anthropology* 22 (1): 36–51.

*Song, Do Young. 2011. "Formation and Communication Strategies for an Urban Multicultural District of Korea: A Case Study of Itaewon, Seoul." *Discourse 201* 14 (4): 5–39.

Taylor-Jones, Kate. 2017. "Handbags, Sex, and Death: Prostitution in Contemporary East Asian Cinematic Urban Space." In *Prostitution and Sex Work in Global Cinema: New Takes on Fallen Women*, edited by Danielle Hipkins and Kate Taylor-Jones, 265–86. London: Palgrave Macmillan.

*Yeon, Jeom Suk. 2009. "Feminism and Ageism: Older Women as the Other within/outside Feminism." *Feminist Studies in English Literature* 17 (1): 109–27.

*Yoo, Jin-Wol. 2018. "The Representation of Elderly Women as Sexual Subjects." *Studies of Korean Literature* 59:267–95.

7

Staging North Korean Defections

Uncharted Borders, Ideological Disorientation, and Diasporic Conditions

Miseong Woo

As Korea is rapidly transitioning from a traditional ethnocentric country of kinship to a globalized multicultural society of citizenship, Koreans' collective desire to understand their nation's history and restructure its racial, national, and cultural identity is exploding in its post-authoritarian era like never before. As an alternative medium, theater provides its audience with direct engaging moments of communication on the stage, and the collective interpersonal experience of theatergoers can catalyze revelatory intellectual change and, ideally, festive social revolution. This chapter offers a comparative perspective on how two theater productions dramatize North Korean defectors' border-crossing experience and perform mediated constructions of the notion of kinship and otherness for both South Korean and global audiences, assessing what is at stake in this abrupt diasporic displacement. Eun-sung Kim's *Sister Mok-rahn*, featuring as protagonist a female *Bukhanitaljoomin*—North Korean defector settler in South Korea—premiered in 2012 in Seoul and was introduced to New York audiences as part of the PEN World Voices International Play Festival on May 7, 2017. Mia Chung's *You for Me for You* premiered at Woolly Mammoth Theatre Company in Washington, DC, on November 5, 2012, and the play's Korean translation met audiences in Seoul between June 30 and July 16, 2017, as a part of the Korean Diaspora session organized by the National Theater Company of Korea. Given that *You for Me for You* tells the story of two North Korean sisters separated at the North Korean border, one landing in New York and the other falling behind at the border, and that the two productions simultaneously crossed transpacific borders, snaring the attention of audiences in the US and Korea, the North Korean defector narrative has clearly emerged as a transnational issue and a new current in theater.

Sister Mok-rahn: North Korean Defectors in Social and Ideological Limbo

Sister Mok-rahn is the first South Korean theater production to introduce a North Korean defector as a protagonist. This might at first seem quite surprising, given that this dramatic and traumatic separation of a country has been in place for over seven decades. However, any topics related to North Korea had been considered taboo issues until the Kim Dae-jung government's Sunshine Policy toward North Korea in 1998, when the imaginary space of the world's most isolated country entered South Korean popular culture with the resounding commercial success of *Shiri* (1999), the first film to portray North Korean spies in South Korea. Not only is *Sister Mok-rahn* the first major South Korean theater production to deal with the struggle of North Korean defectors who try to settle in South Korea, but it raises the issue of the defectors' attempts to return home to North Korea, highlighting complicated realities and paradoxes surrounding the defectors' identity.[1]

During the 1960s and through the 1980s, only a small number of North Koreans crossed the border to the South, and those defectors were called *guisoonyongsa*—"returned heroes." The term's underlying connotation reflects the pervasive attitude of liberal countries toward communist societies, indicating the South Korean government's strategy of putting the defectors to propagandistic use. After the end of the Cold War in 1991 with the fall of the Berlin Wall and the dissolution of the Soviet Union, and the North Korean famine between 1995 and 1999, the number of defectors increased, and the South Korean government referred to them as *saeteomin*—"people of new land"—until 1997 (Kim and Park 2016, 172), emphasizing the government's assimilation policy toward and social affinity for the defectors, although the term still carried the South's triumphalist insinuations with respect to the economic imbalance between South and North Korea. North Korean defections to South Korea indeed proliferated, reaching 2,000–3,000 annually from 2003 to 2011. From 2012, however, with the onset of Kim Jong-un's regime, the number of North

Korean defectors plummeted almost 50 percent, and since then, North Korean defection has continued to decline to an average of 1,300 per year. The total number of defectors in 2019 was 1,047, and approximately 30,000 North Korean defectors currently reside in South Korea as of 2020 (Ministry of Unification 2020). It is worth noting that in 2012, when *Sister Mok-rahn* premiered, Kim Jong-un took power as chairman of the Workers' Party of Korea following his father Kim Jong-il's death in December 2011, after which he intensified a politics of fear and securitization near the border. This political change in the North Korean regime was accompanied by a drop in defections to South Korea, and *Sister Mok-rahn* boldly reflects the Kim Jong-un generation of North Korean defector issues, which are much more complex than those in previous decades.

Sister Mok-rahn opens with an intentionally chaotic montage in which a man draws a huge portrait of North Korean founder and leader (1948–94) Kim Il-sung on the left side of the stage as a propaganda song blares, while a depressed young South Korean man, Tae-san, aimlessly faces the audience on the opposite side of the stage. Audience members must shift their gaze quickly to follow the spotlights switching frequently between the two divided island stages indicating the two Koreas that are so close yet vastly different. In his stage description, the playwright Kim explains that this first scene symbolizes the "Korean peninsula in chaos" (*Nanjangpan Chosunpaldo*) (E. Kim 2015, 10). The visual juxtaposition of the South and the North side by side on the same stage challenges the notion of ideological difference as an insubstantial and eminently crossable divide, while at the same time highlighting the ethnic kinship and the linguistic foundation shared by the two Koreas. This theatrical juxtaposition creates opportunities for qualitative analysis that are not as readily apparent when other media contrast separate otherizing images.

A former member of the Pyongyang elite, protagonist Cho Mok-rahn, who has been frustrated with her life in South Korea since defecting several months ago, now wants to go back to North Korea, driven by her concern about her sick mother in her hometown. Mok-rahn's decision to cross back to North Korea from the very beginning of the narrative sets the tone for her perception and the production's entire portrayal of the distorted reality of South Korea. Intent on saving 50 million won to pay a broker for help her return to the North, she seeks a job as an accordion player at a brothel, which is disguised as a nightclub, and later becomes a domestic caretaker for Tae-san, the eldest son of Jo Dae-jah, who owns and runs the brothel. The darkly humorous depiction of the family matriarch Jo Dae-jah not only provides comic relief and a stark portrayal of the illicit sex business operating in South Korea but lays bare how the family's current reality has been based on a rickety superficial notion of material success. Dae-jah's family as a microcosm of South Korean society reveals an ironic portrait of three young people once driven by material success and fierce social competition yet lacking the philosophical grounding and fundamental ethics needed to make their envisaged rise in society. Dae-jah's eldest son, Huh Tae-san, is an unemployed Korean history scholar who suffers from long-term depression over the breakup with his girlfriend. Dae-jah's second son, Huh Tae-gang, is a philosophy professor, but his university is about to close his department, and he feels defeated when his frustrated students demand action, his cynicism plunging him into constant drinking. Tae-san and Tae-gang's younger sister, Huh Tae-yang, is a novelist-turned-scriptwriter who struggles to come up with a successful scenario for a blockbuster film while grappling to maintain her creativity and romantic relationship with an elderly male writer. Metaphorically, the bitter, depressed Tae-san denotes the sense of national historical amnesia, and the struggle of Dae-jah's family reveals the collective discontents of the South Korean people, who have seesawed from the drastically compressed development that continued into the 1990s to the economic stagnation that began in the 2000s.

The narrative positions Mok-rahn at the opposite end of the spectrum from South Koreans, where she serves as an illuminating catalyst for all three siblings and a prism through which the South's moral defects are uncovered, as the two sons develop a crush on her and Tae-yang capitalizes on Mok-rahn's grandmother's story as a key source for her new film scenario. Emotionally grounded and possessed of a more developed sense of morality equipped with wisdom, experience, dignity, and strength, Mok-rahn provides the three siblings with the consolation, courage, and inspiration they need. However, the potential romance and union between the North Korean female protagonist and the South Korean men turns out to be elusive, and the narrative reveals the withheld truth that Mok-rahn's affective labor toward South Koreans has been prompted by her desperate attempt to set up a financial resource to cross back to the North as soon as she can. When Dae-jah's illegal brothel is shut down and Dae-jah has to flee from a police raid, Mok-rahn explodes in frustration and threatens to kill Tae-yang, demanding the payment Dae-jah promised her. Eventually, Tae-gang, the second son, hands the 50 million won to Mok-rahn under the condition that she starts a new life with him in a foreign country, which Mok-rahn takes as his intention of buying her off as a permanent caretaker, not as a gesture of mutually respectful affection. While the emotionally immature and dependent Korean men's courtship of Mok-rahn evokes the possibility of union between a South Korean man and a North Korean woman and, by extension, between the two Koreas, the scenes between Mok-rahn and Tae-san or Tae-gang lack the fundamental trust that would be needed to bring these bonds about, paralleling the unstable state-level relations between North and South Korea; rather, the scenes serve to warn of the danger of coercive acts of sexual harassment. The lingering sexualized undertones of the representations of the female characters as entertainers and as a personal caretaker, and Mok-rahn's singing and dancing, including a rendition of "Bangapseupnida" (meaning "nice to meet you"), the North Korean song most well known among South Koreans, risk allowing traditional gendered power dynamics to overshadow the potentially harmonious rhetoric of national kinship, thus not provoking a more critical vibe but losing the nuance of the play's Brechtian techniques.

The production stages the border-crossing between the two Koreas not as a perilous escape from the demilitarized zone but rather as a capitalist matter of voluntary exchange, accumulation of wealth and operation for profit. What connects the extremely capitalistic and morally decayed South Korea and the militant, oppressive, one-man-worshiping North Korea is indeed capital. Mok-rahn's departure from North Korea was intricately arrived at in conspiracy with a broker who declares himself to be named Kim Jong-un rather than initiated by her strong desire to escape. In the last scene, the audience can all too easily espy that the ultimate winner of all these machinations surrounding the money will be the broker who runs off with it. Mok-rahn, unable to return to North Korea, is compelled to enter China, where she seductively sings in Chinese at a small nightclub somewhere near the North Korean border, hoping to make another big sum that can get her back home. This ironic and poignant reality reveals the sickening underground market in human trafficking developed across and around the borderline of North and South Korea.

The North Korean defector who once struggled to survive in South Korea and ends up outside the border of the Korean Peninsula altogether serves as the most powerful social commentary in the playwright's critique against the two vastly different societies' inability to handle basic human rights issues and humanitarian needs. Wandering through a third country, without the ability to return to her hometown, Mok-rahn ultimately falls into the status of a diasporic being in limbo. In other words, the Korean Peninsula fails to embrace its ethnic Koreans. From Mok-rahn's perspective, the division between the two Koreas cannot be narrowed. Seen through the eyes of North Korean defectors, South Korea is a place where political division comes to be overridden by capital—money is all it takes to enter or leave. The North Korean defector/broker who adopts the nickname "Kim Jong-un," the most formidable and deceptive character in the play, is equally contemptuous of the depressing communist system in North Korea and the materialistic capitalism in South Korea and is able to move between and operate simultaneously within the two different Koreas with equanimity.

The play exposes the ugly faces of the two Koreas' distorted modern history and loss of innocence, with the extreme ideological brainwash in one country and the blinded catch-up drive for economic survival in the other. There is no escaping the irony in the fact that the South Korean matriarch, Dae-jah, has underwritten her three children's high-minded careers in Korean history, philosophy, and writing by running a deeply disreputable illegal brothel. The morally contradictory Dae-jah is a South Korean version of Brecht's character Mother Courage, a survivor who has done everything she can to see her three children succeed. Her cherished family treasure is the hammer that her husband used in Saudi Arabia as a Korean migrant worker in the 1970s to earn oil money for his family living in the poor motherland, South Korea. Her husband's father also used it to fight against Japanese colonizers and North Korean communists. The hammer thus serves as a strong visual symbol of the violence and crude nature of human relationships pervasive in modern Korean history, its humble sturdiness serving as a foil to the Jo family's problematic morality and cheap snobbish values. When the broker asks Mok-rahn why she wants to go back to North Korea, she responds: "I want to live with my mother"; when the broker asks again, "What's the real reason?" Mok-rahn cynically answers, "I do not want to spend another day in this shit" (E. Kim 2015, 25). Mok-rahn is witness to the remnants of the compressed modernity South Korea has gone through for the last seven decades. Coined by South Korean sociologist Chang Kyung-sup (1999, 2010), "compressed modernity" describes extremely rapid economic, political, social, and cultural changes occurring in a condensed time and space. When used as a theoretical tool to understand postwar South Korean society, compressed modernity is revealing: the forced, top-down nature of the country's fast modernization and economic development explains the underlying vulnerability and collective discontent arising from the hypnotic effect of this rapid industrialization. The character Dae-jah's ruthless mentality and survival tactics represent the South Korean postwar baby boomer generation's obsessive developmental imperative. When

South Korea's economic growth began to wane following the global financial crisis in 2008, the never-ending competition in the education and job market led the younger generation into collective despair and discontent, as evidenced by Dae-jah's offspring. *Sister Mok-rahn* ends with the juxtaposition of adult Mok-rahn and a ten-year-old North Korean defector girl, Yoo Mok-rahn, nervously looking around the stage about to cross the border, suggesting that there will always be more "Mok-rahns," no matter what. Translated as "nomadic orchid," the name Yoo Mok-rahn signifies the girl's destiny as a floating entertainer who will repeat the life path of her adult namesake. Among the thirty-five thousand North Korean defectors living in South Korea (as of 2020), 72 percent are women, of which 58 percent are in their twenties and thirties (Ministry of Unification 2020). The lingering uneasy feeling that *Sister Mok-rahn* leaves with its audience is even more disturbing when they come to comprehend how gendered experience operates in the defectors' settling-in and survival process.

Mok-rahn's journey reflects the actual historical context of North Korean defection on the Korean Peninsula and in neighboring countries. South Korea's Ministry of Unification reported that it only had records of thirteen double defectors as of 2014, but the actual number is thought to be higher. Double defectors taking a route through third countries such as China, Thailand, or Vietnam sometimes end up staying in the United Kingdom or the US to educate their children and to avoid any immediate political climate change in the Korean Peninsula affecting their safety. The motivation for crossing the North-South border has become much more complicated due to more frequent digital media exposure of North Korean defectors since Kim Jong-un took power. Some defectors are trying to leverage their vulnerable status, or are having it leveraged by the state, for political propaganda between North and South Korea. In early 2017, Ji-hyun Lim, a twenty-five-year-old woman who escaped North Korea in 2014 and became a popular TV personality in South Korea, voluntarily went back to North Korea. Then, she appeared on a North Korean TV program in August 2017 to talk about her troubled life in South Korea. South Korean intelligence officials were investigating whether she had been abducted to Pyongyang. According to an announcement by the North Korean regime, a total of twenty-five North Korean defectors had voluntarily returned to North Korea between 2012 and 2014 (McCurry 2014). Even though North Korean defectors who fail in their attempt to return receive a maximum seven-year prison sentence in South Korea, some of them risk it because of the unbearable pain of missing their family members and because of the North Korean regime's changing attitude toward defectors who return. They are no longer treated as traitors but are instead considered valuable propaganda assets. In other words, the defectors crossing borders between North and South Korea can encounter both the danger and the opportunity of exploitation as political pawns.

The character Mok-rahn represents a prototype of the majority of North Korean refugees who, as stateless subjects—to use Hannah Arendt's term—escaped political oppression in North Korea through a life-threatening epic struggle only to be denied recognition either as South Korean citizens—though designated as such in the South Korean constitution—or as escapees (*t'albukja*) from North Korea, and ended up remaining on the outskirts of China, constantly longing for their motherland. As a critical marker of the Cold War legacy and as a remnant of nineteenth-century nationalism, their predicament and struggles are not things of the past but ongoing threats to their survival. The playwright Eun-sung Kim has expressed in several interviews that South Korea's less than successful national effort to accommodate North Korean defectors in the mid-1990s sparked his interest in exploring the topic in *Sister Mok-rahn*. When South Korean society cannot even handle the small number of North Korean defectors as part of "us," how can the nation dream of reunification? The prospect of reunifying the two Koreas remains an ongoing topic of intense political and cultural debate. Theater provides an affective platform for exposing potentially sensitive social issues to generate discussions and negotiations for enlarging boundaries and potentials.

You for Me for You: Juche Ideology Dismantled

The Korean American playwright Mia Chung started writing *You for Me for You* as her master of fine arts graduation project at Brown University in 2010, and the play premiered at Woolly Mammoth Theatre in Washington, DC, in 2012.[2] In an interview, Chung phrased her primary question when it came to North Korea as "Why hasn't the country fallen apart?" and "How soon until the social system falls apart?" (Styles 2012). Closely following the case of Laura Ling and Euna Lee, two female American journalists who were detained in North Korea in 2009 for filming defections, and many documentary films about North Korea, Chung was particularly inspired by a BBC documentary focused on two North Korean sisters. One of them paid a smuggler to help her flee to South Korea and paid the same smuggler to get her younger sister out.

In the same year, 2009, Chung encountered the news story of Jaycee

Dugard, the woman in northern California who had been kidnapped for eighteen years from the age of eleven. She even had two children with her kidnapper and did not want to testify against him to the police and courts. Her Stockholm syndrome, which refers to groomed sympathy held by the hostage for the person who controls them, gave the playwright a paradigm for understanding North Korean society. Chung insightfully points out: "I feel like the government has kidnapped its people. It's not an island, there's something else that's keeping people from leaving" (Williams 2015). In communist North Korea, the most isolated country in the world today, citizens do not have access to the internet or to media content from other countries, and the government strictly prohibits its citizens from traveling to the outside world. The regime's compulsively riveting propaganda, systematized for the last seven decades, has left its citizens stuck almost at the level of the emotionally infantilized victims of Stockholm syndrome. *You for Me for You* draws an evocative psychological sketch of the mindscape that the North Korean regime has created inside the two sisters, articulating how their emotional experience manifests ideological confusion and disorientation during their dramatic journey crossing borders and settling in a new host country.

Chung's *You for Me for You* works like a prequel to *Sister Mok-rahn* in terms of portraying how severe poverty and extreme famine lead some young North Koreans to leave their family members behind to find an alternative livelihood outside North Korea. Two North Korean sisters attempt to escape from the most forbidding, oppressive, and secretive regime in the world, only to be separated at the border. Minhee, an exemplary citizen who has internalized loyalty to, and guilt arising from, the North Korean government's political ideology, fails to escape from "the best nation in the world" (Chung 2015, 11) and falls into an imaginary well where she converses with various inanimate objects, while her younger sister, Junhee, ends up in New York, the iconic space of "the West . . . full of immoral imperialists" (Styles 2012). North Korean authorities control their citizens through mandatory confession and self-criticism sessions that have been part of students' and ordinary citizens' weekly routine for many years. Initially, writing about North Korea felt impossible to the playwright because information about everyday routines in North Korea is scant, and thus visualizing the totalitarian, forbidden country onstage seemed challenging, but Chung decided to stage "their imagination, their psychology" rather than a realistic setting. The play, therefore, allows for a minimalist set design, a bare space inviting the audience's willing suspension of disbelief. With dim lighting signifying an imaginary limbo space accompanied by timed sound effects such as drops of water, echoes, and the croak of frogs, it turns into a well, a forest, and a state border. Similar to *Sister Mok-rahn*, the set of *You for Me for You* designates the North Korean region through two framed portraits of Kim Il-sung and Kim Jong-il, which remind the audience that the regime operates under the tight control of a premodern lineage of a single "royal" family.

Encompassing several different geographical spaces, the play juxtaposes Junhee's scene in New York and Minhee's space in North Korea, thus effectively highlighting each character's epic ventures on the same open stage. Minhee and Junhee are Alices in Wonderland who have fallen into the labyrinth of the twenty-first-century totalitarian state of North Korea and the center of neoliberal capitalism, respectively. Both worlds are equally heart-wrenching and amplify the sisters' feelings of isolation. The voice of the well represents Minhee's remorseful subconscious: "You've let your younger sister throw herself to the wolves. You failed to protect each member of your family. For one so faithless and incompetent, this private fate is too kind. Eternal humiliation will be yours now!" (Chung 2015, 28). This moment of magic realism turns Minhee's struggle from more than a physical one into psychological torment. To stage Minhee's fall into the well, director Park Hae-sung in the 2017 production let hundreds of green and blue swimming pool balls drop onto the stage to visualize the surge of water inside the well. Torn between the fear of punishment and guilt at betraying her state, Minhee tries to maintain conversation with a frog and a man in a bear suit holding an accordion. These fairy-tale-like or folkloric characters symbolize Minhee's psychological regression toward the good old days when she and the world around her were young and innocent of politics or state authority. Other characters she encounters, including "Farm Hand" and "Disembodied Voice," constantly remind her of her civilian duty toward the state and its leader. At the same time, Minhee cannot free herself from the sense of family obligation and the traumatic void of losing her son and husband to the state's violence. Minhee's flashback reveals that her son, Jin, was taken to a reeducation camp after he was caught watching South Korean videos, and her husband, Youngsup, was publicly executed after enduring strenuous labor until his back was bent and broken.

The scene of the dark gloomy portrayal of North Korea quickly switches to a brightly lit animated space of a hospital in New York City. Wearing scrubs and a fine-particulate filter mask, Junhee works as a nurse and takes care of her patient, Liz. Interestingly, a further three characters—a hospital administrator, Junhee's coworker, and a psychotherapist—are all named Liz and are played by a single performer who speaks fragmented broken languages, which effectively represent the bewildered and disoriented Junhee's understanding of English and American society. Junhee is surrounded by a cartoon-like world of incomprehensible words, attitudes, and rules that parallel her level of understanding of her unfamiliar harsh environment. Liz's fragmented English speech and her puppet-like movement alienate the audience as well from the stage action and dialogue, thus temporarily forcing them to experience Junhee's disenfranchised linguistic and social positions and ensuring that they vicariously partake of her experience of racial discrimination. As Junhee gradually improves her grasp of English and the American way of life, the speech of the characters Liz becomes clearer. Junhee also embarks on a relationship with Wade, an African American man from the South, and gradually comes to grips with her new life as a New Yorker. Only when she feels close enough to Wade does she throw a series of questions at him regarding sports culture, marketing strategy, and the American worldview including capitalism: "Why is it called the World Series when they're really only American teams? . . . Can you take me to the Stock Exchange? . . . I really want to go to Walmart . . . I also want to do jury duty. And meet a paparazzi. . . . Also . . . do you understand the '100% money-back satisfaction guarantee'?" (Chung 2015, 64–65).

As Junhee's life in New York finally reaches the silver lining point of happiness, she cannot help but think of her sister left behind in North Korea, and she pays a smuggler to take Minhee out to the North Korean–Chinese border. In the midst of a military whistle blowing and gunshots at the border, it is Junhee this time who sacrifices herself for her sister, Minhee: "I believe you. I'll believe you're ready to go. I'll believe you've left home forever. I'll believe you won't change your mind. If you leave first" (98). With a gunshot, Junhee "crumples to the ground" (98), and she even hands Minhee her handbag and American passport, which symbolize the freedom and material success she briefly tasted in New York City. The next scene features Minhee on her release after an orientation at Hanawon Resettlement Center for North Korean defectors in Seoul, the capital of South Korea. After a subway ride, Minhee arrives at her small apartment with entirely bare walls, a table, and two chairs. After the long ritualistic preparation of a bowl of rice, a plate of kimchi, a pot of tea, and pieces of dried fish, Minhee, for the first time throughout the entire production, having been so eager to feed her family members, finally picks up a spoonful of rice and eats. Food is, as Roland Barthes put it, "a system of communication, a body of images, a protocol of usages, situations, and behavior" (2008, 29) and reveals identity negotiations and an act of private yet political decision. Her constant act of yielding food to others and her final act of eating signal the shifted relationship between food and the sine qua non of social values, the loss of her North Korean self and her determination to focus on her temporality in the neoliberal capitalist social condition in South Korea, and ultimately her commemoration of her sister Junhee's sacrifice.

The imaginary well represents the world's most guarded society, North Korea, and how the state-level ideology operates within the mind of an individual. As the eldest sibling and a model citizen, Minhee has internalized a strong sense of responsibility that parallels North Korea's Juche ideology. When the Korean Peninsula suffered political instability after independence from Japanese colonization in 1945 and the armistice immediately after the Korean War in 1953, North Korea was in a tough situation. It was located near the world's two largest socialist states, the Soviet Union and China, with Stalinist ideology and Maoism becoming their respective backbones. The term "Juche" was first mentioned officially in a speech given by Kim Il-sung at a "Propaganda and Agitation" Congress of the Workers' Party of Korea on December 28, 1955, entitled "On Establishing Self-Reliance and Eradicating Dogmatism and Formalism in Ideology Projects" (Beauchamp 2018). Juche in Korean means "self-reliance," and the North Korean government has always justified the people's isolated state as political and economic independence. To procure legitimacy and validation as a newly emerging small government, the initial Juche ideal of "self-reliance" centered on ideological autonomy, economic self-sufficiency, and military independence from imperial influence (Beauchamp 2018). In reality, however, North Korea's economy depended heavily on the Soviet Union during the post–Korean War period and, later, on China. By emphasizing autonomy as the primary ideology, North Korea could claim to be fully aligned with traditional Korean nationalism, thus attempting to render the state more legitimate compared to South Korea, whose postwar recovery period was associated with the US's military occupation.

Juche also means "principal agent" or "subject," and it has theoretically justified the one-man rule under Kim Il-sung's family. At an ontological level, the ideology has been associated with traditional Confucianism, thus co-opting filial piety into the service of the state. Juche, therefore, expands on this family-like structure of society, in which the leader is portrayed as a father and the ruling party as the mother of all citizens (Kurbanov 2019). The highest ruler is *suryoung*, "father" or "parents" who ultimately take care of all citizens' well-being, and in the domestic sphere the responsibility of taking care of the family unit falls on the shoulders of a father, a husband, and an eldest sibling. The North Korean political, social, and educational system revolves around the Juche ideology, which was created and enforced by the dictator-founder of North Korea, Kim Il-sung, and his successor and son, Kim Jung-il. Brainwashing North Koreans, Juche ideology has operated at all levels of civilian life, from unbelievable mythical stories about the leaders that North Korean children learn at school through to the celebration of the two leaders' birthdays as the biggest national holidays, let alone the constant surveillance, fear of punishment, and isolated confinement. Despite the extremely harsh and poor conditions, what sustains North Korean society is this quasi-religious Juche belief that the Kim Il-sung dynastic legacy and leadership is their only and ultimate savior.

The North Korean "Others" and the Korean Diaspora

Sister Mok-rahn and *You for Me for You* provide a paradigm with which to look at current crucial issues surrounding North Korean defector narratives. In the changing multicultural landscape of South Korea, North Korean defectors' position is unique in that they share the same ethnicity with South Koreans as *hanminjok*. After sharing the same historical lineage rooted in the same Dangun myth, the same blood, and the same language for the past several thousand years, the North and South Koreas have developed a vastly different ideological orientation and civic acculturation over the last seven decades, yet ironically the immediate postwar division and drastic difference in economic development have caused the inter-Korean relationship to drift further apart. To North Korean defectors completely isolated from the world, the multiculturalism and social diversity that have been quickly changing South Korean social demographics are yet another global phenomenon to which they find it difficult to adjust. The majority of the North Korean defectors are "opposed to being categorized or treated as one of [a number of] multicultural minority groups, because they tend to believe 'ethnicity' is the core of their identity," and "they wanted to be recognized as 'the Korean people just like native-born South Koreans'" (Kim and Yoon 2015, 325).

Many North Koreans have been starting to get a taste for capitalism through an emerging market economy ever since the relatively younger leader Kim Jong-un took power. The growth of markets is the single most significant socioeconomic development in North Korea over the last two decades, although the economy is still centrally controlled and state planned. In particular, the priority of the *jangmadang*—"open market"— generation of North Koreans is not loyalty and respect toward the country's leadership but economic stability and survival. After all, it was not the military that defeated communism in the Cold War but capitalism and the free market system. Many North Korean defectors testify that people's lives revolve around the market now and "no one expects the government to provide things anymore" and "everyone has to find their own way to survive" (Lockie 2017). According to micro-surveys of residents in provinces across North Korea, 100 percent of respondents felt the government's public distribution system does not provide them with what they want for a good life, and 72 percent received almost all of their household income from markets, while 83 percent found outside goods and information to be of greater impact on their lives than decisions by the North Korean government (Cha and Collins 2018, 3). These statistics and many defectors' testimonies indicate that the ideological difference between communism and capitalism does not cause much difficulty or complication for North Korean defectors in new host countries.

The real obstacle that North Korean defectors face in a noncommunist society is neoliberal individualism. North Koreans have strengthened their identity as group members through organizational life. The political ideology of the state has been acquired and internalized through a collective organizational lifestyle constructed by mutual criticism and surveillance. Continuing her self-criticism session, *You for Me for You*'s protagonist Minhee confesses her inability to meet the state's expectations. To her neighbor, who is jotting down a note about Minhee's behavior, Minhee criticizes her own shallow sentiment by saying, "Only the false hearts among us would question such persistent altruism. . . . I would never confuse such unrelenting kindness and overwhelming scrutiny with interference or obstruction or anything unpleasant or suspect" (44). The audience of *You for Me for You* leaves the theater with the haunting image of Minhee, who wanted to become "a faithful warrior in the Eternal Revolution" (46), dwelling in a capitalist neoliberal operational system in South Korea. Would she follow the path of Mok-rahn?

More than any other Asian country, South Korea has wholly embraced the neoliberalism that puts all the onus on the individual, particularly since the 1997 International Monetary Fund crisis and the financial crisis of 2007–8. As the society steers toward a more democratic and Westernized economic model, South Koreans have proudly established a firm social belief in free markets and individual private property, which is liberalism combined with a set of social and economic practices derived from capitalism. Since North Korea has been gradually moving toward a profit-seeking and commodity-trading market system in which each family and individual essentially seeks the accumulation of capital, what alienates the North Korean defectors in South Korea is the extremely competitive neoliberalism. Neoliberalism has justified most of the democratic government's minimal intervention in the modes of production, labor market, and social welfare system, thus making the defectors feel even more vulnerable and backward, lacking any necessary resources for competition and a social safety net. In fact, Mia Chung's play, from its title to each scene, meticulously answers the playwright's own question of why this highly unusual state has not fallen apart despite all the odds. Tightly dependent on one another, just like a web, in a big conformist family-state that is the antithesis of individualism, North Koreans have not had much option other than idiosyncratically sacrificing themselves for the others to survive in the North Korean regime, which is an almost surreal space of premodern horror seething with torture, public execution, kidnapping, and starvation.

Although there are differences in identity, gender, and language between the Korean male playwright Eun-sung Kim and the Korean American female playwright Mia Chung, whose cultural backgrounds definitely affect representational patterns and the diasporic scope of the characters, *Sister Mok-rahn* and *You for Me for You* contribute to mediating North Korean "others" into South Korean mainstream audiences' understanding of the unique aspects of the Korean defectors' diasporic condition. What constitutes the Korean diaspora is the abrupt and traumatic dispersion in space and time within and across state borders and the migrants' political and economic upheaval, which dismantles the diasporic subject's frame of existence. Sandra So Hee Chi Kim argues that diaspora is a phenomenon that "emerges when displaced subjects who experience the loss of an 'origin' (whether literal or symbolic) perpetuate identifications associated with those places of origin in subsequent generations" (2007, 337). Although several representative diaspora scholars such as Gerard Challand and Jean-Pierre Rageau raise questions about the Korean migration's identification as a diaspora in terms of the magnitude of its size and space and its limited destinations, the Korean diaspora population has grown 17 percent during the past ten years, and its community is ever expanding compared to other racial and ethnic groups (Choi 2003, 16). Such diasporic migration is dynamically ongoing, and more and more

North Korean defectors seem to be visible outside the Korean Peninsula. Approximately six hundred, the largest North Korean community in Europe, reside in southwest London in the United Kingdom, and Germany follows as the second largest (Fischer 2015; Yonhap 2018). As the journeys of Mok-rahn and sisters Minhee and Junhee suggest, ever more North Korean defectors tend to, through force or free will, become transnational refugees staying in a third country, thus making the North Korean defectors' settlement and human rights a global concern. As conveyed by the two theater productions' presentation of the firsthand material, emotional, and psychological experience of North Korean defectors, one of the productions' primary attributes is the profound sense of fluctuation between ethnic belonging and ideological and cultural displacement that North Korean defectors encounter in a neoliberal capitalist society. While attempting to assimilate and find like-minded minorities of other ethnicities in their new host country, along with seeking a sense of belonging as new economic migrants in their motherland, North Korean defectors come to realize that there is no such thing as a permanent home or utopia. Unlike other media platforms, theater provides a tangible space and an affective realm in which North Korean defectors' border-crossing experience and struggling subjectivity meet the global audience. These productions will increase public awareness of the diasporic consciousness of North Korean defectors as at once intranational and transnational refugees and will continue to reflect Koreans' burgeoning collective aspiration to reconstruct post-memory as they move toward a globalized society of citizenship.

NOTES

1. *Sister Mok-rahn* opened at the Doosan Arts Center in Seoul, South Korea, in 2012 and 2013, and the production won Eun-Sung Kim, one of the most visible playwrights in South Korea today, several prestigious accolades, including the 2012 Korea Theater Award and the Dong-A Theater Award for Best Play. He founded his own theater company, Dalnara Dongbaekkot, in 2010, and since then his plays have touched on sensitive social and political issues pertaining to groups such as migrant workers of ethnic Korean descent in China and North Korean defectors living in South Korea.

2. My analysis in this chapter is based on the Korean production of *You for Me for You*, translated by Nahm Kee-yoon and directed by Park Hae-sung, which ran from June 30 to July 16, 2017, at Theatre Pan in Seoul, South Korea.

REFERENCES

Barthes, Roland. 2008. "Toward a Psychosociology of Contemporary Food Consumption." In *Food and Culture: A Reader*, edited by Carole Counihan and Penny Van Esterik, 23–30. New York: Routledge.

Beauchamp, Zack. 2018. "Juche, the State Ideology That Makes North Koreans Revere Kim Jong Un, Explained." *Vox*, June 18. https://www.vox.com/world/2018/6/18/17441296/north-korea-propaganda-ideology-juche

Cha, Victor, and Lisa Collins. 2018. "The Markets: Private Economy and Capitalism in North Korea?" *Beyond Parallel*, August 26, 1–7.

Chang, Kyung-sup. 1999. "Compressed Modernity and Its Discontents: South Korean Society in Transition." *Economy and Society* 28 (1): 30–55.

Chang, Kyung-sup. 2010. *South Korea under Compressed Modernity: Familial Political Economy in Transition*. New York: Routledge.

Choe, Sang-Hun. 2017. "North Korean Defector, 'Treated Like Dirt' in South, Fights to Return." *Asia Pacific*, August 5.

Choi, Inbom. 2003. "Korean Diaspora in the Making: Its Current Status and Impact on the Korean Economy." In *The Korean Diaspora in the World Economy*. Washington, DC: Peterson Institute for International Economics. https://www.piie.com/publications/chapters_preview/365/2iie3586.pdf

Chung, Mia. 2015. *You for Me for You*. London: Bloomsbury.

Fischer, Paul. 2015. "The Korean Republic of New Malden: How Surrey Became Home to the 70 Year-Old Conflict." *The Independent*, February 22. https://www.independent.co.uk/news/uk/home-news/the-korean-republic-of-new-malden-how-surrey-became-home-to-the-70-year-old-conflict-10063055.html

Haas, Benjamin. 2018. "'Forever Strangers': The North Korean Defectors Who Want to Go Back." *The Guardian*, April 26.

Jacobs, Harrison. 2019. "North Koreans Understand Their Government Lies, but There's One Thing They Don't Know, According to a Defector." *Business Insider*, February 27.

Kim, Eun-sung. 2015. *Sister Mok-Rahn* [목란언니]. Seoul: Yunkeuk-kwa-Inngan.

Kim, Hyun Jung, and Sun Hwa Park. 2016. "다문화정책 관점에서 본 북한이탈주민 문제" [North Korean refugees from the multicultural perspective]. *Journal of the Humanities for Unification* 66:161–96. http://www.dbpia.co.kr/journal/articleDetail?nodeId=NODE06715338

Kim, Sandra So Hee Chi. 2007. "Redefining Diaspora through a Phenomenology of Postmemory." *Diaspora: A Journal of Transnational Studies* 16 (3): 337–52.

Kim, Yoon-sun, and In-jin Yoon. 2015. "Multiculturalism Is Good, but We Are Not Multicultural: North Korean Defector Students' Perceptions of Multiculturalism." *Korean Educational Review* 21 (2): 325–50.

Kurbanov, Sergei O. 2019. "North Korea's *Juche* Ideology: Indigenous Communism or Traditional Thought?" *Critical Asian Studies* 51 (2): 296–305. https://doi.org/10.1080/14672715.2019.1566750

Lockie, Alex. 2017. "Capitalism Is Already Breaking Down North Korea's Government—and It Could Be the End of Kim Jong Un." *Business Insider*, November 20.

McCurry, Justin. 2014. "The Defector Who Wants to Go Back to North Korea." *The Guardian*, April 22. https://www.theguardian.com/world/2014/apr/22/defector-wants-to-go-back-north-korea

Ministry of Unification, Republic of Korea. 2020. "Policy on North Korean Defectors." June 16. https://www.unikorea.go.kr/eng_unikorea/relations/statistics/defectors/

Styles, Hunter. 2012. "Mia Chung on Writing You for Me for You." *DC Theater Scene*, November 6.

Williams, Holly. 2015. "You for Me for You: New Drama Examines Why Not Every North Korean Wants to Escape the Country's Brutal Dictatorship." *The Independent*, December 6. https://www.independent.co.uk/arts-entertainment/theatre-dance/features/you-for-me-for-you-new-drama-examines-why-not-every-north-korean-wants-to-escape-the-country-s-a6762576.html

Yonhap News Agency. 2018. "820 People from N Korea Obtain Citizenship in EU from 2007 to 2016." *Yonhap News Agency*, April 10. https://en.yna.co.kr/view/AEN20180410003200315

8

Enemy of the State

Cold War Rhetoric and Representation of North Korea/ns in *Hallyu* Films

JongHwa Lee

The Korean Peninsula today remains the only place in the world with an active cold war. After the deaths of 1.2 million soldiers and 3 million civilians, the displacement of 3 million refugees and 2 million children under the age of eighteen, and the separation of 2 million family members, the legacy of the Korean War (1950–53) still lingers (Yuh 2015). To sustain its Cold War status, South Korea (alone) spent about $38 billion on its military budget in 2018 (Ministry of National Defense 2018), with 618,000 standing (plus 2.7 million reserved) military troops in 2017 (Congressional Committee on National Defense 2017).

Yet, despite the real and present condition of the Cold War (truce without peace treaty), interestingly, to identify and articulate North Korea as the "main enemy" (of the state) has been a heated topic of public debate over the last decades, especially whether to include such a notion (the *main enemy*) in the National Defense White Paper or to distinguish "North Koreans" from "North Korean *government and military*" as such enemy. This question often appears as an ideological litmus test at "political inquisitions," for presidential debates as well as congressional appointment hearings for high-ranking government positions ("On 'North Korea as Main Enemy'" 2017). The debate illustrates a thorny problem that South Korea faces in the current historical/political atmosphere—a phenomenon that is, at its heart, a discursive problem: North Korea/ns appears (as articulated, framed, and constituted by respective discourses) as both "the same people" to identify/embrace in a nationalistic sense and "the hostile other" in the armistice status. In other words, while the political leaders of the two countries have historic summit meetings (in 2018 as well as in 2000 and 2007), embracing and hugging in front of the "public screen" (DeLuca and Peeples 2002), the Constitutional Court of South Korea is still deciding (since 1991) whether the lower courts should apply the National Security Law to prosecute people for making positive comments about North Korea or spreading North Korea's propaganda materials (Human Rights Watch 2015; Hyun 2017). Again, South Korea is still under an active Cold War condition, militarily and legally, but the naming of North Koreans as the "main enemy" (at war) remains in contention. This chapter begins with this rather elusive and ambivalent appearance toward the enemy of the state (Who/what is the "main enemy" of the state?), particularly by interrogating its visual representations (What does it look like?).

The ambivalent (or polyvalent) nature of North Korea/ns also appears in the popular media (including films), offering an interesting communicative/discursive space where the identity of North Koreans is contested, negotiated, and deconstructed. The visual representations of North Korean identity are wide-ranging, from the separated families/siblings to poor neighbors and evil communists. Yet, what is noteworthy is that South Korean films today increasingly feature North Koreans in more complex and nuanced ways, starring A-list actors and producing significant viewership and commercial success. Considering the phenomena of *Hallyu* (the "wave" of Korean cultural products appealing to wide, global audiences), the commercial success of these films often means popular appeals not only in South Korea but also overseas (an important rationale for investigating their cultural and political implications)—a thesis famously advanced by cultural studies school (Hall, Evans, and Nixon 2013): we need to take pop culture more seriously because images (of popular/cultural representations) matter as they have real consequences (political, economic, militaristic, etc.) in everyday life.

Stuart Hall (1989) highlights how cinematic/cultural representations of identity are critically implicated in the history of colonialism and postcolonial resistance. Rather than taking identity as natural, eternal, or essential, Hall articulates identity as an example of Derridean *"différance,"* as a "matter of becoming" (70), "always constructed through memory, fantasy, narrative and myth. Cultural identities are . . . unstable points of identification or suture, which are made, within the discourses of history and culture. Not an essence but a *positioning*. Hence, there is always a politics of position" (72). In short, identity is constituted, not outside but within representation; and hence of cinema, not as a second-order mirror held up to reflect what already exists, but as that form of representation which is able to constitute us as new kinds of subjects, and thereby enable us to discover who we are. (80)

Therefore, the contention over representation (North Koreans in popular films, presidential debates, and the National Defense White Paper) is a struggle over meaning; power/politics fixes a meaning "to be the way things are and should be," to give the meaning a naturalized and permanent look. As such, by analyzing the mechanisms of power and representation, we gain important insights to understand how the status quo came "to be" (as naturalized and normatized) and, therefore, acquire clues to "un-do" and "re-do" the way things are. Thus, it is crucial to unravel the politics of representation if we are to navigate complex cultural/political dynamics (again, both domestic and global) and ultimately to challenge "how things are" and to build more peaceful relationships with North Korea/ns.

In short, this chapter analyzes two recent, popular *Hallyu* films that feature North Koreans as main protagonists/antagonists within the main narrative context of the Cold War and that gained significant (domestic and global) market attention (*The Spy Gone North* and *Confidential Assignment*). I focus on the characters and their discursive scenes/contexts through the lens of rhetorical theories (specifically, Burkean dramatism and pentadic cartography) to highlight "sutures" and "ruptures" in the representations of cultural identities and their "positions of enunciations" (Hall 1989, 68). In doing so, this chapter explores the cultural-political implications of Cold War rhetoric and the images of the enemy in *Hallyu* films within the context of current geopolitical dynamics in the Korean Peninsula and Northeast Asia. But, before I come to this analysis, let me briefly discuss the rhetorical implications of "the art of enemy making" and "pentadic cartography," my theoretical approach to analyzing the films.

Faces of the Enemy and Cold War Rhetoric

Critical analysis of "communication and war," more specifically the "representation of the enemy," has a long history within communication studies. In fact, the experience of wartime persuasion over World War I and World War II provided an important foundation for the birth of communication as a modern discipline of social science (Jowett and O'Donnell 2019; Sproule 1997), although the study of "war rhetoric" can be traced back to ancient Greece (Ayotte 2002; Zoido 2007). After all, it takes an extraordinary "reason" (or "mood") to justify or even glorify such sacrifices in personal comfort, safety, or welfare (whether physical, psychological, or financial) and acts that bring death to others (and themselves). Thus, for communication studies, the art of enemy making, and of justifying and glorifying war efforts, has been a critical topic of interest (and concern) (Jowett and O'Donnell 2019).

Keen (1986), for example, traces a pervasive (historically omnipresent) practice of "the art of enemy making" and calls humans "*Homo hostilis*, the hostile species, the enemy-making animal" (10). According to Keen, most nations create their sense of identity (their solidarity and loyalty too) by such an art of enemy making, "dividing the world into a basic antagonism: Us vs. Them; Insiders vs. Outsiders; The Tribe vs. The Enemy . . . Good vs. Evil" (16–17)—a Manichean morality play that "makes killing or dying in war a sacred act performed in the service of some god or immortal ideal" (19). What is particularly significant for this study is Keen's emphasis on not only the "pervasiveness" but also the "constitutive" nature of such rhetoric: "In the beginning we create the enemy. Before the weapon comes the image. . . . Propaganda precedes technology" (10).

Particularly, World War II and Hitler provide a powerful example of devastatingly real consequences of "war rhetoric" and "the art of enemy making." Indeed, for Hobsbawm (1994), the twentieth century is the "Age of Extremes" for its world wars, massacres, rebellions, and revolutions. Here, Burke (1973) underscores the constitutive power of naming a "common enemy" in creating a "unity": "Men who can unite on nothing else can unite on the basis of a foe shared by all, a common enemy, the Prince of Evil himself" (193). Burke also notes that we must not simply dismiss Hitlerism "as a cult of the irrational. . . . Irrational it is, but it is carried on under the *slogan* of 'Reason' . . . developed 'in the name' of humility, love, and peace" (199). Yet, Burke (1984) equally warns of a rhetoric that frames "Us and Them" in what he calls "tragic frames." In such a tragic frame, human motives are interpreted based on their essential and inherent nature (either good or evil), and the frame/logic leaves only one "rational" solution—complete destruction or annihilation of the evil other.

The logic/desire of the "complete destruction of the evil other" continued through the Cold War era. The doctrine (i.e., a principle derived from political or religious beliefs) of "Mutually Assured Destruction," for instance, provides a chilling reminder of the image we had on the enemy (the enemy deserving to be annihilated, even at the expense of everyone, including us). The West, according to the US Cold War rhetoric/imagination, was in *ultimate conflict* with evil communists who threaten "our" system (capitalism, democracy), way of life (religion, family life), and core values (freedom, individualism) (Klumpp 2015). In this rhetoric, as Klumpp points out, "the most important ideograph in opposing Communism was 'freedom,' thus connecting the ideology to a basic American value" (2). Therefore, what was at stake, for the US, was "freedom" that defines us as "who we are" against the evil communists who attempt to "enslave" us and to eliminate our autonomy and individuality. In short, as Medhust (1997) claims, "A Cold War is, by definition, a rhetoric war, a war fought with words, speeches, pamphlets, public information (or disinformation) campaigns, slogans, gestures, symbolic actions, and the like" (xiv). In that sense, a cold war is also a cultural war,

> as not only the "soft power" realm in which superpowers and national regimes alike vied for "hearts and minds" but also as a terrain of lived experiences and practices upon which the often contradictory demands of ideological disciplines, aesthetic ideals, and global cultural influences were negotiated. (Chung and Park 2017, 272)

As such, a cold war enemy is the ultimate other, confronting/confronted in the antagonistic, material, discursive, and existential battle. In confronting a "cold war enemy," unlike a more casual term like "opponent" (in a game or sports), one's victory in such a battle results in the violent erasure of the other, with the loss of physical properties, financial capitals, symbolic integrities, and life/existence.

However, Cold War experiences in East Asia, and Korea in particular, show several unique features. As Chung and Park stress, the Cold War is "a war of ideas that descended into military conflict" (271); "continual outbreaks of hostilities and contention with the ruins of colonialism" (274) were especially true and more unique in East Asia. As Paek (2009) explains, "Although Asian countries experienced a major historical departure, independence from the colonial system, as a temporal-historical stage, they were swamped by the following waves of the Cold War system in the end. The memory and temporality of colonialism were not overcome but merged into the current system, and reproduced into a dual-system" (15). Particularly, the ambivalent nature of race/ethnicity in Japanese colonialism (Korea was colonized by an Asian nation in the region) as well as the Korean War (as both civil/domestic as well as international conflict) further complicated the line between "Us" and "Others/Them." Therefore, for Korea, the dual system (of post/colonial and Cold War) and the dual nature of the Korean War (as civil and international war) fundamentally shaped the cultural psyche of contemporary Korea, including a cultural logic of us/others intersecting with historical struggles of racism, imperialism, colonialism, and nationalism.

For the reasons above, Korean cinema provides a powerful window to understand the cultural Cold War, to investigate how the cultural logic of "us" and "others/them" is re/produced, negotiated, and contested with what ideological, discursive, and material consequences. Specifically, this chapter analyzes two recent Korean films that feature North Koreans as main protagonists/antagonists within the theme/context of Cold War (*The Spy Gone North* and *Confidential Assignment*), by tracing discursive positioning of North Koreans in the films through the lens of pentadic cartography. In advancing Burke's (1969) theory of dramatism and the pentad, Anderson and Prelli (2001) propose "pentadic cartography" as a heuristic lens to "map verbal and visual symbolic terrains" and "a method for charting the ways terminologies . . . open and close the universe of discourse" (73–74). In addition to the three steps of pentadic dramatism, pentadic cartography identifies multiple possibilities of mapping and compares how competing maps manifest different emphasis ("featured") and deemphasis ("slighted"), which offer unique opportunities and limitations (of the vistas and the paths for action, imagination, and reality) (Li and McKerrow 2020). Pentadic cartography highlights the danger of the "closed universe of discourse," because it fosters "one-dimensional rationality" (Marcuse 1964), which renders "all critical thought for qualitative social change incapable of meaningful linguistic expression and thoughtful consideration" (Anderson and Prelli 2001, 74). In short, pentadic cartography is a method to chart/map the symbolic landscape "around dramatic action" (83), to reveal "multiple orientations [motives] toward political and social reality" where the dominant mode of realization (hegemonic linguistic reality) "becomes but one of many successive reality orientations" (78), and in so doing, to identify alternative views "conducive to qualitative social change" (75) and to "open the closed universe of discourse" (74).

Cinematic Representations of North Korea/ns and Cold War

Over the last two decades, Korean films have featured various themes of the Korean War (both the Korean War and the following Cold War), with diverse characterizations of North Koreans (from soldiers to spies to brothers and families) (Byeon 2001; M. Kim 2015; Kim and Kim 2013; Hyeonjin Lee 2013; Hana Lee 2019; Seo 2011; Song and Baek 2014). Historically, there existed a dominant trend of featuring North Koreans with a strong anti-communist theme since the late 1940s until the 1970s (M. Lee 2014). Then, after the quiet period of the 1980s, a new trend of Korean films started to appear in the late 1990s (around the fall of the Eastern Bloc) in which they were more self-reflexive on the Cold War ideology and the division of Koreas, while featuring more "humane" faces of North Koreans (Song 2018). Even since the 1990s, however, "action" has been the most popular genre to capture North Koreans in (hot) war movies and (cold war) spy movies.

The Spy Gone North directly engages with the complexity of identities and the murkiness of ideologies in today's Cold War politics/rhetoric. The movie is ranked in the top 115 in South Korean film box office history (as of August 2020), grossing $36,118,203 with a domestic viewership of 4,974,512 (www.kobis.or.kr). Set in the 1980s and early 1990s, when North Korea was suspected of developing its nuclear capacity after leaving the Treaty on the Non-Proliferation of Nuclear Weapons, the movie follows the experience of a South Korean spy, Park Seok-Young (played by Hwang Jung-Min), who hides his identity as a business person in order to infiltrate the inner circles of North Korea to find out about the status of the nuclear program in the North. After years of secret operations working with his North Korean counterpart, Ri Myung-Woon (played by Lee Sung-Min), Park finally earns enough trust to meet with the Supreme Leader (Kim Jung-Il) to seek his permission for a business project—a Trojan horse for Park's South Korean team to visit and survey the sites under suspicion (for the North's nuclear activity). Here, the spy character, with a Trojan horse project, plays a significant yet consistent trope with the Cold War cultural imagination; what is apparent may not be true—real identity and truth are deferred. What makes the movie particularly interesting is that it is based on a real story of a real spy (known through the code name "Heuk Geum Seong" [Black Venus]) (D. Kim 1998).

A powerful conversation takes place when Park's supervisor (at the South Korean Central Intelligence Agency) tells him to bring a letter to North Korea written by the leaders of the conservative party in South Korea because the party is behind by a few points to the progressive party in the upcoming presidential election. The letter asks North Korea to bring aggressive military action/provocation in order to scare the public and to stir up the general mood to create a more conservative climate to benefit the ruling conservative party in the election, which the movie shows had happened before. Park is immediately resistant to the idea because he believes that the letter might expose his (spy) identity, thus jeopardizing his operation to learn about the North's nuclear capacity, which, for him, is more important. Then, the supervisor tells Park almost exactly the same thing that he himself was told from his superior, the director of the agency: "This is an order. An order comes before an operation." When asked, "Order from whom?" the supervisor says, "It's an order from the country. It is the will of the company. Just follow the company line." When further asked about how the letter is more important than surveying the North's nuclear capacity, the supervisor answers, "The election is in a few weeks. We must stop the progressive candidate from becoming the next president. Do you want to risk handing over our country to such a communist?" While this conversation may suggest a pessimistic picture of "politics as usual," the very presence of power/political struggle also illustrates indeterminacy—the result is open and deferred, without guarantee.

Here, in the narrative, the country/nation, the conservative party, the company/agency, and the director appear interchangeable and share common interests/purpose together (to maintain the status quo), yet through a very confusing logic—to stop a progressive candidate (labeled as "communist") from becoming the next president, "we" must ask for help from the communists in the North. The paradoxical logic appears even more clearly at the end of the movie when Park decides to go against the company line/order to talk to the Supreme Leader himself, asking for his help to not comply with what the South Korean conservative party/incumbent president wants and persuading him that the aggressive military act would jeopardize the joint business project, which can bring more "economic benefits than those 4 million dollars that the South Korean party promised for the provocation." In the end, Kim Jung-Il decides not to give what the South Korean conservative party wants, and the progressive candidate becomes the president of South Korea. The movie ends with the joint project's launch.

Table 8.1 shows the pentadic mappings of the movie's universe of discourses (items in bold indicate the featured elements, and items in capitals and bold indicate the dominant/driving elements). "Scene" first appears to be a prominent element in the movie, which is common in Cold War rhetoric—the material condition as the most powerful root cause to condition/drive/justify human action ("In this cosmic battle against the Evil Prince, we are left with no option but to fight back with every possible

Enemy of the State | 167

TABLE 8.1. Pentadic Mappings of *THE SPY GONE NORTH*

	Hegemonic Cold War rhetoric	North Korean rhetoric	South Korean CIA	Heuk Geum Seong	Ri Myung-Woon
Agent	**Warrior-saint**	Warrior-anti-fascist	Spy	Public servant	Public servant
Agency	By all means	Resistance / by all means	**Secret / illegal collaboration**	**Joint project / Trojan horse**	**Joint business project & secrete collaboration**
Scene	**MANICHEAN MORAL / COSMIC BATTLE**	**IMPERIALISM / FASCISM**	About to lose election	Hypocrisy of Cold War politics	**DIRE & ARDUOUS POVERTY**
Purpose	To defeat the enemy	**Independence / self-defense**	**STATUS QUO / TO STAY IN POWER**	**TO BUILD PEACE PROCESS**	To change
Act	Cold War battle	Cold War battle	Cold War battle	Détente	Détente

means."). For example, the "scene:purpose" and "scene:agency" ratio may apply to explain the North's rhetoric—pursuing its nuclear program for its primal interest in survival, to find an extreme measure out of a desperate situation. Similarly, the lead North Korean character, Ri, is primarily motivated by the dire circumstances in his effort to develop the joint project ("scene:agency" ratio). Even when Ri becomes suspicious of the hidden agenda or purpose ("Trojan horse project") of Park, Lee warns/reminds Park about the importance of the business project as the first of its kind after forty years of confrontation. Later in the movie, when Park asks Ri for his reason to trust Park (and the project), Ri says, "I had no choice. Three million people are dying of hunger and sickness. Kids are sold for $10. A change was needed." On the other hand, Park, the South Korean protagonist, appears to be a believer of denuclearization and economic collaboration ("agency") to promote peaceful Korea beyond the division and the hypocrisy of Cold War politics ("purpose"). For him, the North's "nuclear weapons" would jeopardize the peace in the Korean Peninsula, but "reform and openness" would bring the development that will help the North (and the South). Similarly, "asking for the North's military provocation" for winning the election is also a wrong choice (with respect to his "purpose"), because the joint program (for mutual trust and prosperity) is the right agency to benefit both Koreas. Still, the identification over an "agency," despite differences in "purpose," is significant, to acknowledge the possibility of collaboration, a pragmatic approach to conjoin diverse interests.

On the other hand, the South Korean CIA's rhetoric provides a dangerous picture of the Cold War; preserving their position of power ("purpose") becomes the primal motive, which justifies secret/illegal collaboration with the North. At one point, Park shouts back at his supervisor at the agency, "Why can't you be just honest—that the group you belong to always needs an enemy, and you don't want to lose the power in your hands!" Further, an interesting characterization happens with the Kim Jung-Il role; Kim Jung-Il appears as the most critical key player in the movie, exhibiting full capabilities in choosing his own actions, and he knows it ("The South Korean comrades can't do anything without me. That's why they come to me for every election and ask me for military actions and shooting missiles."). In other words, he is the one who can decide to bring conflict to Korea, as well as peace, and he can make the conservative party in the South win elections and bolster their power—an image far from the incapable/irrelevant "Evil Prince" to be taken out of the scene.

In a way, the narrative setting of the 1980s and 1990s in *The Spy Gone North* may seem more appropriate for the film's overall theme to emphasize the "scenic" element (the predominant power of the Cold War logic and its deterministic factionalism)—perhaps more "coherent" with the popular view of the time. However, the storyline also suggests a departure, moving beyond the "scenic" understanding/determinism over the Cold War politics. By exposing its hypocrisy and deconstructing its rhetoric and moving toward a more "purpose"-centered mapping, the story highlights a contested agenda among powerful groups that are driven primarily by their self-interests, thereby suggesting an alternate constitution from the hegemonic scene of the collective/universal struggle. The other film under discussion, *Confidential Assignment*, is set in today's time, which interestingly demonstrates the prominence of a more contemporary zeitgeist ("agency" rather than "scene") as a main motive to drive its drama, although "agent" appears as a powerful "anti-element" to disrupt the hegemony of "scene" and "agency."

Confidential Assignment (Sung-hoon Kim, 2017) is an action film with a comedic undertone in which a North Korean ex–special forces/special investigator, Lim Cheol-Ryung (played by Hyun Bin), comes to South Korea and teams up with a South Korean investigator, Kang Jin-Tae (played by Yoo Hae-Jin), to retrieve counterfeit plates that were stolen by a North Korean, Cha Gi-Sung (played by Kim Ju-Hyuk), who smuggled them into South Korea and who was also a leader of the special forces that killed Lim's wife. The movie is ranked in the top 41 in South Korean film box office history (as of August 2020), grossing $53,848,557 with a domestic viewership of 7,817,446 (www.kobis.or.kr).

A comedic scene happens when Kang brings Lim to his home, where Kang's wife and sister-in-law are watching TV. As soon as his sister-in-law, Park Min-Young (played by Im Yoon-A), sees Lim's face, she drops the TV remote control out of surprise and admiration. There is something unusual about this (comedic) scene, especially in its gender dynamics. Hyun Bin, an actor known for his talent and handsome looks, is one of the top A-list stars in South Korea today, and Im Yoon-A is also a popular star, known as the "visual" member of the idol group Girls Generation. While Yoo Hae-Jin (Investigator Kang, as Hyun Bin's South Korean partner) is equally well known (especially for his comedic roles in other films), his fame does not come from his "pretty face." In short, the leading North Korean character (Lim) has a number of attractive/personable points for identification; he is driven (determined to bring justice), capable (ex-special forces), loyal (to his team/friends), noble (beyond his personal interest/welfare), romantic (for the love of his wife), and handsome—a "face of the enemy" that was never given in the earlier movies.

Table 8.2 provides pentadic mappings of the movie's universe of discourses (items in bold indicate the featured elements, and items in capitals and bold indicate the dominant/driving elements). "Agency" first appears as a strong dramatic element, driving the storyline for the conflict over the (stolen) counterfeit plates, which substitutes the traditional emphasis in the "scene" of the Cold War rhetoric. As Cha steals the plates, he tells Lim, "With these plates, I can live pompously even without the damn Republic"; in another scene, he tells his group, "After this operation, we will get eternal freedom. I will pay you for the cost of the comrades' blood that the Republic wasted—the Republic that failed to build the nation of the People." For Cha, the plates symbolize the "justified" rewards that he (and his people) was supposed to get from the Republic (in exchange for being a "Republic's faithful dog," as he puts it), yet with the death of his wife, who was sent to a labor camp and died there for the crime Cha had committed, Cha was more determined to claim his own way out (away from the "scenic" determinism). Losing everything (his country and wife), the only thing left for Cha was his primal desire to live on his own terms.

Importantly, for all three main characters (protagonists and antagonists), the primacy of "scene" no longer exists—it no longer determines/

TABLE 8.2. Pentadic Mappings of *CONFIDENTIAL ASSIGNMENT*

	North Korean rhetoric	Cha Gi-Sung	Lim Cheol-Ryung	Kang Jin-Tae
Agent	Secret forces	Criminal/defector	**FAMILY MAN & SPECIAL INVESTIGATOR**	**FAMILY MAN, COP**
Agency	**Counterfeit bills**	Counterfeit plates	Joint assignment	Joint assignment
Scene	**COLD WAR SANCTION**	Failed states & loss of wife	Loss of wife & loss of counterfeit plates	Daily hardship to make earning, through a government job
Purpose	Economic gains	**LIVE POMPOUSLY & FREELY**	**Revenge & justice**	**To support family & justice**
Act	Cold War battle	Survival in the jungle	On a double mission (personal & official)	Work

drives the narrative motive. This is a transition, opening up a closed universe of discourse determined by the power of "scene," such as the "scene:agent" ratio (i.e., "who we are and what we do" is conditioned to the terms of the scene/larger context, as in "Republic:patriot") and the "scene:agency" ratio (i.e., the means are justified to the terms of the scene; a desperate measure is born out of a desperate situation, as in "Cold War/sanction:by all, including illegal, means necessary"). Now, through the transition, the "Republic's faithful dog" is turning against the supremacy of "scene," for its failed promise/telos of the Republic, exiting for a better life of freedom by stealing the plates (constituting the "purpose:agency" ratio). What is lost (for Cha) is a "purpose" set in a "scene": he is no longer able to justify his role (esteemed warrior) and act (noble struggle), rooted in the powerful urgency of a cosmic/just war. What is left is a jungle of competing interests, where everyone is motivated by their self-interests and, eventually and ironically, "purpose" loses its supremacy with its omnipresence. Instrumental efficiency (agency) remains everyone's goal.

Lim, however, is an idealist; "agent" is not confined to the terms of other elements (be it scene or agency); instead, "agent" itself conditions other elements. At the end of the movie, Lim asks his South Korean partner for help to capture Cha in exchange for giving up the plates (to the

South), knowing that the plates were his main mission/order and that he would be punished for not bringing the plates back to the North. When asked, "Why?" Lim replies, "It's not that the Republic is doing the right thing"—a moment when Lim shows a virtue that transcends national/factional duty for a larger/universal moral duty. Lim's partner, Kang, is also an idealist, who similarly demonstrates such a universal/transcendental moral virtue beyond the immediate confinement of his setting/condition. When his superiors order him to return to his station after he acquires the plates, although Lim still wants to catch Cha, who is still at large, Kang refuses and tells his supervisor, "What does South or North matter for a cop to catch a bad guy!" Lim and Kang build a trusting partnership ("brotherhood") and turn the dominant Cold War logic (the supremacy of historical/material condition, with the "scene:agent" ratio) to the "agent:act" ratio that individual moral characters, shown in personal/brotherhood relationship, drive his/her act, while this "act" serves the "purpose" of his sacred quest/mission. This is a very interesting and unique feature of Korean spy films; the national and ideological division is often transferred to (and transcended by) the matter of personal (gendered/romantic) or family (brotherhood of a pseudo family) relationships (M. Kim 2015; Kim and Kim 2013; Hana Lee 2019).

Hana Lee (2019) traces the cultural history of Cold War spy films in the West and East Asia and argues that spy films in the West were born with a desire to demonstrate an Anglo-American cultural hegemony and to serve their national interests, which are equated with the interests of the West. Yet, after the 1990s, Western spy films go through narrative transformations to capture opportunistic capitalists, arms dealers, and terrorist groups as main villains (like the Cha character in the film), replacing the old enemy of the USSR, while spies go through a confusion or redefinition of their identities (Hana Lee 2019). On the other hand, East Asian spy films (after the 2000s) are set typically in the 1920s through 1940s, when national conflicts were at the peak in the region and when the Cold War and the post–Cold War were complicated with postcolonial problems (Hana Lee 2019). As Suzy Kim (2020) argues, "The history of imperialism, colonialism, and neocolonialism in East Asia is deeply unmeshed with the Cold War even before its established beginnings, when the 1920s and 1930s anticolonial, anti-imperialist struggles found an ally in the Soviet Union" (509). In other words, for East Asian spy films, "the front" was between Korea/Japan and China in the Cold War context, but at the same time "the front" also lay in between Korea/China and Japan in the postcolonial and post–Cold War context (Hana Lee 2019).

South Korean spy films, however, show additional unique characteristics different from the spy films of the West and East Asia. South Korean spy films, too, emerged in the 1960s, in combination with strong anti-Communist ideology and the global hit of the "007" series at the time (Kim and Kim 2013). However, what is unique for South Korean spy films is that these films (re)constituted the experience of the Korean War into cultural memories based on a strong theme/value of "family-ism" combined with "anti-communism" (M. Kim 2015). Particularly, after the 2000s, South Korean films show a strong new trend: (1) "family" narrative takes over, replacing the national ideology, as a main motive of spies, to protect their family rather than to serve their nation (i.e., to advance their national ideology or interest); (2) spies show more nuanced characters, rather than "typical" masculine types, to have more "humane" faces; and (3) a strong distrust of the National Intelligence Agency appears, reflecting an anxiety that the "nation/state" would no longer protect and serve the people (Kim and Kim 2013). Further, South Korean spy films today complicate the theme of conflict against communism by (4) twisting and resolving the conflict through the development of romance and bromance between South and North characters (Hana Lee 2019), although (5) there is a consistent underpinning (unchallenged) narrative/ideological structure to represent/idolize the South Korean system as superior to North Korea (Song and Baek 2014).

Confidential Assignment resonates with this "genre" of South Korean spy films, particularly by complicating the Cold War politics with "family-ism" as personalized relationships (romance and bromance) become the key motive to drive the drama. A critical impetus for the villain, Cha, is the death of his wife (who died in a labor camp), and for Lim, it is to get revenge against Cha for killing his wife, who was pregnant at the time of her death. Kang, too, is a "family person." At the final climax of the movie, Cha takes Kang's wife and daughter as hostages in exchange for the plates, which are in Lim's possession. With Kang's cries for help, Lim returns with the plates (against the order of the Supreme Leader) and saves the day—to kill Cha and rescue Kang's family. Then, Lim and Kang together throw the plates into the ocean. This "feel good" moment and the "happy ending" complete the overall storyline/theme of the movie—the main characters, identifiable/personable, go against the "company line" (factionalism embedded in the "scenic" emphasis in the division/Cold War) and also against the instrumental logic ("agency"/consequentialism triumphs other virtues) to find a common virtue (for "family" and "partnership") and a common "humanity" (identification with a virtue, beyond the division/estrangement).

Conclusion

This chapter applies pentadic cartography and analyzes two Korean films (*The Spy Gone North* and *Confidential Assignment*) that feature North Koreans as main protagonists/antagonists within the narrative context of the Cold War. *The Spy Gone North* features a "hidden spy war" over a joint business project between the South and the North, developed in the heightened Cold War confrontation in the 1980s–1990s. Like many spy films of the Cold War, "scene" dominates the main storyline, and the historical/material condition sets the tone/style for the engagement/act; therefore, "agent" and "agency" are spoken to the terms of the preexisting condition of the Cold War. Yet, despite the power of the "scene," closing off the universe of discourse (i.e., "leaving no choice but," due to the dire circumstances), the movie also shows alternate "modes of realization," by opening up a new universe of discourse (collaboration, beyond ideological factionalism) and by disrupting "one-dimensional rationality" of the "scenic" narrative by exposing its hypocrisy and the hollowness/groundlessness of the binary Cold War logic/politics. *Confidential Assignment* follows a joint investigation between a North Korean officer and a South Korean officer to capture a North Korean criminal who has stolen counterfeit plates and smuggled them into South Korea. As such, "agency" (i.e., the plates) appears as a powerful element to drive the drama, as a "key" to "set free" the oppressed "agents" (the criminal) and "scene" (poverty and suffering). However, the idealists (lead characters) from the North and the South overcome the conflict (over factionalism embedded in the "scene" of the Cold War, and the instrumental logic) by finding a "common humanity" over the shared value of family and justice.

From a larger perspective, this chapter was launched with an awareness that "one-dimensional rationality" (of a closed universe of discourse) is dangerous. Remember that when President Trump engaged in a "war of words" with the North Korean leader, Kim Jung-Un, President Trump warned, "They will be met with fire and fury like the world has never seen" (Amaro 2017). Senator Lindsey Graham confirmed this "vision" of President Trump: "If there's going to be a war to stop [Kim Jung-Un], it will be over there. If thousands die, they're going to die over there. They're not going to die here. And he has told me that to my face" (Ortiz and Yamamoto 2017). Whether the estimated casualties for the next war are thousands of, or twenty thousand deaths daily for South Korea alone (Daniels 2017), or simply "catastrophic" and "probably the worst kind of fighting" (Freedman 2017), obviously some political leaders are capable of estimating (or entertaining) such a possibility as an option. Further, before the

2019 Trump-Kim Hanoi Summit, John Bolton (then the national security advisor) attempted to obstruct the summit (to come to "no deal") once he believed that President Trump and the State Department negotiation team were eager to come to an agreement with North Korea (Baek 2020). In his memoir, Bolton recollected that Japanese prime minister Abe insisted that North Korea is an object that the US must press with maximum strength and overwhelming military power, and Abe congratulated Trump for walking out of the summit with "no deal" (Park 2020). Apparently, there are multiple parties, with multiple motives, to "deal" with (or to leave "no deal" for) North Korea/ns. Again, this only shows that the front (dividing "us" and "them," sharing common interests/enemies) is elusive, complicated, and shifting: As Suzy Kim (2020) explains, "Cold War in East Asia is unended since the process of decolonization is far from over, as proven by the continuing struggles to overcome the legacies of Japanese imperialism in the region" (509). Yet, what makes the decolonization process even more complicated is the US Cold War politics, as "the US Cold War strategy in East Asia positioned Japan as a bulwark against communism . . . as a forward base in safeguarding US military dominance in East Asia" (512).

For those who believe in "no deal, except complete victory," their approach is consistent with the Cold War logic (a binary Manichean logic) that closes the universe of discourse—that the other is not a partner with whom to negotiate but an object to be quelled by all means necessary. The fastest way to close the universe of discourse is, simply, to give the other an ultimatum and to not allow anyone to talk. In this "one-dimensional rationality" (of a closed universe of discourse), any alternative imaginations are rendered unthinkable/irrational, and it is precisely for this reason why it is important to explore "new modes of realization" in order to bring any meaningful social change. As this chapter attempted to "recenter" the public that has been neglected/marginalized (in the international geopolitical power relations and the international media flow), by studying the public discourse and the popular imagination in *Hallyu* films, there we find a small possibility to open a closed universe of discourse: the hegemony of the Cold War rhetoric is challenged for its hypocrisy, and the divided people of South and North are able to find a common "humanity" over the shared value of family and justice. According to Park (2017), there lies a potential of films, as a mnemonic storytelling device for historical trauma, playing an important role to reflect and "decompress condensed modernity and to embrace time . . . to finish the incomplete work of mourning" (407). Perhaps, that is where we are—displacing the same old (repeated) "company line" or myths of the Cold War, between the West and the East, the Occident and the Orient, and Good and Evil, of a tragic frame. With such displacing of the myth, there appears more humane faces who are diverse (we/they are not all the same) and fallible (capable of errors and mistakes rather than essential/eternal evil deserving to be annihilated completely)—a "comic frame" (Burke 1984), a humility through reflexivity, a transcendence beyond the division.

REFERENCES

Amaro, Silvia. 2017. "How Did the War of Words between Trump and Kim Kick Off?" *CNBC*, August 11. https://www.cnbc.com/2017/08/11/how-did-the-war-of-words-between-trump-and-kim-kick-off.html

Anderson, Floyd, and Lawrence J. Prelli. 2001. "Pentadic Cartography: Mapping the Universe of Discourse." *Quarterly Journal of Speech* 87 (1): 73–95.

Ayotte, Kevin. 2002. "The Art of War: Aristotle on Rhetoric and Fear." In *The Philosophy of Communication*, vol. 2, edited by Konstantine Boudouris and Takis Poulakos, 45–57. Athens: Ionia.

Baek, Jongmin. 2020. "Boltoneui Jipyohan Hanoi Bukmi Hoedam banghoe 'Gongjak'" [Bolton's persistent "ploy" to obstruct the North-US Hanoi Summit]. *Asia Economy*, June 23. https://www.asiae.co.kr/article/2020062306230322775

Barthes, Roland. 1972. "Myth Today." In *Mythologies*. New York: Hill and Wang.

Brockriede, Wayne, and Robert Scott. 1970. *Moments in the Rhetoric of the Cold War*. New York: Random House.

Burke, Kenneth. 1969. *A Grammar of Motives*. Los Angeles: University of California Press.

Burke, Kenneth. 1973. "The Rhetoric of Hitler's 'Battle.'" In *The Philosophy of Literary Form: Studies in Symbolic Action*, 3rd ed., 191–220. Berkeley: University of California Press.

Burke, Kenneth. 1984. *Attitudes Toward History*. 3rd ed. Berkeley: University of California Press.

Byeon, Jaeran. 2001. "남한영화에 나타난 북한에 대한 이해: '쉬리' '간첩리철진' '공동경비구역 JSA'를 중심으로" [Understanding on North Korea appearing in South Korean films focusing on Swiri, Spy Lee Chul-Jin and Joint Security Area-JSA]. *Yeongwha Yeongu* 16:241–76.

Chung, Steven, and Hyun Seon Park. 2017. "Guest Editor's Introduction." *Journal of Korean Studies* 22 (2): 271–79.

Confidential Assignment. 2017. Directed by Sung-hoon Kim. South Korea: CJ Entertainment.

Congressional Committee on National Defense. 2017. "The Size of Military Troops with Respect to Division and Rank." National Assembly Budget Office. http://stat.nabo.go.kr/fn03-48.jsp

Daniels, Jeff. 2017. "Pentagon Scenario of a New Korean War Estimates 20,000 Deaths Daily in South Korea, Retired General Says." *CNBC*, September 25. https://www.cnbc.com/2017/09/25/korean-war-simulation-by-dod-estimates-20000-deaths-daily-in-south.html

DeLuca, Kevin, and Jennifer Peeples. 2002. "From Public Sphere to Public Screen: Democracy, Activism, and the 'Violence' of Seattle." *Critical Studies in Media Communication* 19:125–51.

Gardner, Lloyd., Arthur Schlesinger Jr., and Hans J. Morgenthau. 1970. *The Origins of the Cold War*. Waltham: Ginn.

Hall, Stuart. 1989. "Cultural Identity and Cinematic Representation." *Framework: The Journal of Cinema and Media* 36:68–81.

Hall, Stuart, Jessie Evans, and Sean Nixon. 2013. *Representation*. 2nd ed. Thousand Oaks, CA: Sage.

Hobsbawm, E. 1994. *The Age of Extremes: A History of the World, 1914–1991*. New York: Vintage Books.

Human Rights Watch. 2015. *South Korea: Cold War Relic Law Criminalizes Criticism*. Human Rights Watch. https://www.hrw.org/news/2015/05/28/south-korea-cold-war-relic-law-criminalizes-criticism

Hyun, Soeun. 2017. "Is It Possible for '8th Try-7th Failure' . . . National Security Law Article 7, Its 8th Time on the Judgment Table for Constitutionality." *Hankyoreh*, August 11. http://www.hani.co.kr/arti/society/society_general/806476.html

Jowett, Garth, and Victoria J. O'Donnell. 2019. *Propaganda and Persuasion*. 7th ed. Thousand Oaks, CA: Sage.

Keen, Sam. 1986. *Faces of the Enemy: Reflections of the Hostile Imagination*. San Francisco: Harper & Row.

Kim, Dang. 1998. "Heukgeumseongkwa Sinroe Gwangye 16 Gewol Chwije Ilgi" [Trusting relationship with Heukgeumseong for 16 months of investigative diary]. *Sisa Journal*, April 2. http://www.sisajournal.com/news/articleView.html?idxno=78390

Kim, Mihyeon. 2015. "한국 반공영화 서사의 기원에 대한 연구" [A study on origin of anticommunist Korean cinema in the 1950s]. *Yeongwha Yeongu* 63:71–98.

Kim, Suzy. 2020. "Cold War Feminisms in East Asia: Introduction." *Positions: Asia Critique* 28 (3): 501–16.

Kim, Youngjun, and Seungkyeong Kim S. 2013. "최근 한국 첩보영화에 대한 연구: 다문화시대의 간첩 인식 변화를 중심으로" [A Study on recent Korean spy films: Focused on the changing perception of spy in the multicultural age]. *Damunwha Contents Yeongu* 15:249–78.

Klumpp, James. 2015. "Rhetoric of the Cold War." Voices of Public Leadership in the 20th Century, University of Maryland. https://terpconnect.umd.edu/~jklumpp/comm461/lectures/cold.html

Lee, Hana. 2017. "북한 '반간첩영화'에 나타난 냉전 이미지와 냉전형 인간" [Cold War human and the Cold War imagery in North Korean "counterespionage films"]. *Hyeondae Bukhan Yeongu* 20 (2): 38–92.

Lee, Hana. 2019. "1990년대 이후 스파이영화의 지역적 계보" [A regional genealogy of post-1990 spy films]. *Daedong Munwha Yeongu* 105:433–70.

Lee, Hyeonjin. 2013. "분단의 표상, 간첩: 2000년대 간첩영화의 간첩 재현 양상" [The representation of division system, Gancheop—A study on representations of Gancheop in 2000s Korean Gancheop films]. *Cine Forum* 17:73–104.

Lee, JongHwa, and Minwha Han. 2011. "Transforming the Image of the Other: Representations of North Korea/ns in Hallyu Cinema." In *Hallyu: Influence of Korean Popular Culture in Asia and Beyond*, edited by Dokyun Kim and Minsun Kim, 155–80. Seoul: Seoul National University Press.

Lee, Myeongja. 2014. "반공영화" [Anticommunist films]. *Encyclopedia of Korean Culture*. http://encykorea.aks.ac.kr/Contents/Index?contents_id=E0074419

Li, Zhou, and Raymie McKerrow. 2020. "Xi Jinping's Keynote in the Belt and Road Forum: A Pentadic Cartography." *Critical Discourse Studies*. https://doi.org/10.1080/17405904.2020.1761411

Medhurst, Martin, Robert Ivie, Philip Wander, and Robert Scott. 1990. *Cold War Rhetoric: Strategy, Metaphor, and Ideology*. New York: Greenwood Press.

Ministry of National Defense. 2018. *The Structure of 2018 National Defense Budget*. Ministry of National Defense. http://www.mnd.go.kr/mbshome/mbs/mnd/subview.jsp?id=mnd_010402010000

"On 'North Korea as Main Enemy,' an Expert's Criticism." 2017. *Huffington Post Korea*, April 20. https://www.huffingtonpost.kr/2017/04/20/story_n_16123234.html

Paek, Wŏndam. 2009. 냉전 아시아의 문화풍경 2 [Cultural landscape of Cold War Asia 2]. Seoul: Hyŏnsil Munhwa.

Park, Hyun Seon. 2017. "Cold War Mnemonics: History, Melancholy, and Landscape in South Korean Films of the 1960s." *Journal of Korean Studies* 22 (2): 389–412.

Park, Jinju. 2020. "Hanbando peonghwaneun andwae . . . Abeeui Iganjil" [Peace in the Korean Peninsula is not allowed . . . Abe's mischief]. *MBC News*, July 1. https://imnews.imbc.com/replay/2020/nwdesk/article/5828514_32524.html

Seo, Insuk. 2011. "한국형 블록버스터에서 분단의 재현방식: 한과 신파의 귀환" [The representation of Korean political division in Korean blockbuster film: The return of Han and Sinpa]. *Munhakkwa Yeongsang* 12 (4): 981–1015.

Song, Chiman, and Il Baek. 2014. "북한을 바라보는 한국 영화의 시선: 간첩의 서사적 역할 분석을 중심으로" [Perspective of Korean movies about North Korea—Focused on narrative role of spy]. *Tongil Inmunhak* 59:263–86.

Song, Kyeongwon. 2018. "How Are North Koreans Portrayed in South Korean Cinema, from the Time of Armistice to 2010s." *Cine21*, June 27. http://www.cine21.com/news/view/?mag_id=90500

Sproule, J. Michael. 1997. *Propaganda and Democracy: The American Experience of Media and Mass Persuasion*. New York: Cambridge University Press.

The Spy Gone North. 2018. Directed by Jong-Bin Yoon. South Korea: CJ E&M.

Yuh, Ji-Yeon. 2015. *Beyond Numbers: The Brutality of the Korean War*. Legacies of the Korean War. http://legaciesofthekoreanwar.org/wp-content/uploads/2015/08/Article-Ji-Yeon-Yuh.pdf

Zoido, Juan. 2007. "The Battle Exhortation in Ancient Rhetoric." *Rhetorica: A Journal of the History of Rhetoric* 25 (2): 141–58.

9
Reframing the Difference of Co-ethnic Other in Japan

An Analysis of Representations and Identifications in the South Korean Documentary Film *Uri-Hakkyo*

Min Wha Han

At the dawn of the new millennium, I visited South Korea (hereafter Korea) for the first time in my life. Around that time, I experienced two drastically significant events in my life. One was that I had become a student at a Japanese college. This seemingly ordinary change for any high school graduate was a big change for me, given that I had spent my twelve years of primary education at Korean schools in Japan. The other event was that I had recently gained South Korean citizenship, dropping the *Joseon* nationality[1] that I had lived with since birth. Although all my grandparents were from southern parts of the Korean Peninsula, it was only in my early twenties that I could see the land where my grandparents were born and raised and that they had to leave during the time of annexation.

Throughout my college years, I was in the middle of an identity crisis. I could not get rid of my disappointment at Japanese students' ignorance toward "us"—Koreans as an old ethnic minority in Japan. At the same time, I made good friends with international students from Korea, and, therefore, I had a strong desire to see the homeland I had never been allowed to visit but was now entitled to enter.[2] Looking back at this time of my life, perhaps I was looking for my cultural belonging, a place/space where I could feel the same Koreanness with Koreans *from* and *in* Korea, something I could not fulfill in my relationships with Japanese friends. This sort of desire for belonging, however, was half-fulfilled and half-betrayed. While I was excited to see and experience Korean culture, the impression I received by interacting with people in Korea was, ironically, similar to the sort I felt when interacting with Japanese people. If my experience in Japan so far was that of an "outsider within" (Collins 1986, 1991, 1998, 1999; Harris 2008; Rogers 2010), the perception I felt in my interactions with people in Korea (though it took me a long time to understand) was another peripheral, or "othering," experience—as co-ethnic other. I remember my perplexed feelings when I was corrected, criticized, and sometimes laughed at because my voice carried non-native intonations, while my Japanese friend who had recently started to study Korean was praised for her passion for learning. Less than ten years later, however, changes seemed to be happening in Korea. Interest among Korean scholars, media industries, and civic organizers regarding their co-ethnic comrades in Japan has increased drastically (Jeong 2016).

Identity, when it comes to representations of communal identities, as Hall (1989) asserts, is always "in context, *positioned*" (68). As such, a mediated representation of the communal identities of others is always interpreted and situated within particular historical and sociopolitical contexts. Then, representations of diasporic Koreans in Japan, or *Jaeil* (재일, Japan residing) Koreans,[3] in the Korean mediasphere too have been influenced by the country's historical and sociopolitical climate. Influenced by Korea's postcolonial relationship with Japan and its neocolonial relationship with the US, along with the dominant presence of the pro-North organization named *Chongryeon*,[4] *Jaeil* Koreans were historically positioned to be other—either not "fully" Korean, with the name of *Banjjokbari* (반쪽발이, half-Japanese), or *Bbalgaengi* (빨갱이, "red" Communist) (Chung 2016; S. Kweon 2008; M. Lee 2004). Yet, as Korea experiences the country's paradigm shift into neoliberalism and with changing policies and culture alongside it, representations of *Jaeil* Koreans in South Korean media culture are experiencing major changes as well. This shifting moment, therefore, deserves close attention among scholars with respect to the representations of Korea's co-ethnic other.

This chapter examines the representation of diasporic Koreans in Japan, highlighting the rather recent attention on Korean schools in Japan. Through a close textual analysis of the independent documentary film *Uri-Hakkyo* (우리 학교, Our School), the chapter illustrates how the representation of difference placed upon Korean students in the contemporary Korean mediasphere is redefined, reframed, and reshaped within the film. In particular, the chapter explores the ways in which cultural identities of this particular diasporic community in Japan are represented in this

Korean documentary film that gained popular attention. Applying the notion of "identification" (Burke 1969) with the concept of "ideograph" (McGee 1980), the chapter discusses the film's attempt to reinterpret the identities of the co-ethnic other in Japan, who traditionally was stigmatized within Korea's sociopolitical contexts of postcolonial/anti-Japanese and Cold War/anti-Communist sentiments. The chapter first positions diasporic Koreans in Japan as Korea's co-ethnic other, tracing the representations in Korean mainstream culture and media sphere, and then discusses methods of identification employed in the film through the ideographs of *uri*, or our-ness.

Diasporic Koreans in Japan as Co-Ethnic Other

Where do diasporic Koreans in Japan, or *Jaeil* Koreans, fit in Korea's postcolonial, neocolonial, and local logic of difference? In the introduction to this book, Oh clarifies othering in Korea as not based solely on racism but rather reflected in unique historical, sociopolitical, and local logics. How, then, are representations of Koreans in Japan positioned within the "map" of the other in the Korean mediasphere? Answering this question is a complex matter, as representations of this co-ethnic group in the Korean media sphere have been heavily dependent upon the nation's shifting sociopolitical contexts—its colonial experience; its postcolonial and neocolonial nationhood and Cold War politics; and, later, the nation's neoliberal, multicultural (*damunhwa*) policies. In this section, I discuss the historical trajectories regarding representations of *Jaeil* Koreans by focusing on their historical as well as their sociopolitical uniqueness, in an attempt to situate the film in Korea's dynamic and changing social, political, cultural, and media climates.

Among the various diasporic Koreans across the world, *Jaeil* Koreans have been uniquely positioned and othered within the societies of both Japan and Korea due to the burdened historical relations between the two countries (Chung 2012; S. Kweon 2008; Lee 2004). In Korea, because the presence of this co-ethnic population originated from Japan's annexation of Korea (Hukuoka 1998; S. Kweon 2008; Yoon 2001), the representations of *Jaeil* Koreans have been heavily influenced by Korea's postcolonial sentiment. As Suk-in Kweon (2008) analyzes, "Because of the (post)colonial relationship, many Koreans keep negative attitudes toward Japan, the Japanese, and Japanese culture and these negative feelings are often projected on ethnic returnees from Japan" (59). Kweon's study reveals the relatively higher expectation that Koreans have toward diasporic Koreans in Japan (i.e., speaking fluent Korean and embodying authentic Korean cultural codes) compared to other diasporic Koreans. For example, Kweon states that Koreans view Korean Americans as the most popular diasporic group and, therefore, show the highest tolerance with respect to differences in Korean Americans' language use and intonations. On the other hand, Koreans' expectations toward *Jaeil* Koreans are higher, with less tolerance for their differences due to Koreans' postcolonial sentiments. In this sense, othering *Jaeil* Koreans in Korean society has been a product of the historical relationship between Korea and Japan, and the colonial history has rightfully had more influence than their economic, social, or cultural differences (S. Kweon 2008).

Regarding the historically ambivalent, often negative attitude toward *Jaeil* Koreans, Hyuk-tae Kweon's (2007) work is also noteworthy. Kweon has analyzed representations of *Jaeil* Koreans in the Korean mediasphere. Through his analysis on various media texts such as newspapers, comics, TV programs, and movies, Kweon has critically discussed the three "filters" Korean society has imposed upon *Jaeil* Koreans. The first filter is "ethnic nationalism" (민족주의, *minjok-ju-ui*), which is the most important connection between Korea and *Jaeil* Koreans. Quite ironically, though, this first filter is distorted with the strong power of the second filter, "anti-Communism" (반공주의, *bangong-ju-ui*). Then, finally, the third filter is "developmentalism" (개발주의, *gaebal-ju-ui*), which views *Jaeil* Koreans as people from a country richer than Korea and therefore "useful" for the country's development. Importantly, Kweon argues that these three filters were created, amplified, and solidified within Korean society through distorted media representations and that the Korean mediasphere showed no interest in *Jaeil* Koreans' lifeworlds. These representations in turn promoted negative attitudes toward the diasporic communities in Japan with notions such as "half-Japanese" (with the ethnic nationalism filter), "Communists" or "spies" (with the anti-Communism filter), and the rich "parvenu" or the "upstart" (with the developmentalism filter).

It is also important to mention the influence of Korea's national policy, or more importantly the absence of it, on representing Koreans in Japan. After the country's liberation and soon after the division between the North and the South, the recovery of authentic cultural identities of Korea "by removing the legacy of Japanese colonialism has been an essential part of [Korea's] cultural policy" (Ministry of Culture and Information 1979, 248), and with the help of this national policy, too, Korea has taken a relatively reluctant policy toward Koreans in Japan (Jeong 2016; Kang 2004; S.

Ryang 1997, 2000; Morris-Suzuki 2007). South Korean cultural policies have evolved over time, with the gradual inclusion of "international exchange" in the late 1980s and early 1990s and the negotiation with Western cultural influence; however, diversions from its colonial legacy (Japanese culture) and Communism (North Korean culture and pro–North Korean activities) were strictly kept during these times.

According to Jo (2014), Koreans in Japan have been represented through conflicting senses of both "belonging" and "abandonment." During the Cold War era, for example, although Korean communities in Japan showed a strong sense of belonging to the politics of their homeland, their relations, especially those of the *Joseon* nationalities, were disconnected. Frequently, diasporic Koreans in Japan had been the "forgotten" co-ethnic other during the Cold War regime in Korea or even "suspicious" as evidenced by high "criminal rates" of *Jaeil* Koreans as political suspects until 1990s (H. Kweon 2007) and as witnessed by the tragic incident of a *Jaeil* Korean student who ended up spending nineteen years in jail as a political prisoner.[5]

The period from the late 1990s to the early 2000s, however, witnessed a turning point in Korea's cultural policy. The Kim Dae-Jung administration and its Sunshine Policy toward North Korea, for example, made cultural exchange with North Korea more available than was the case in previous governments (Yim 2002). Furthermore, the South Korean government announced an "open door policy" and the globalization of national culture, which allowed the entry of Japanese media. According to Yim (2002), "Japanese film, video and publishing" was allowed in 1998, followed by subsequent permission for "the performing industry of Japan" in 1999 and "animation, pop music, music recordings, games and broadcast programs from Japan" in 2000 (42).

The collapse of Cold War rhetoric in the early 1990s and its influence on the cultural realm of Korea, along with the national shift to neoliberal discourses, in turn, has brought significant change in the nation's relationship to diasporic Koreans in Japan (Jo 2007). Especially, those who had been "abandoned" and "suspected" due to their pro–North Korean affiliation started to gain new attention from South Korean media culture and academia. Around the time Korean mainstream media started to redefine the North Korean other through movies such as *Shiri* (1999), *JSA* (2000), *Taegukki* (2004), and *Welcome to Dongmakgol* (2005), scholars, broadcasting companies, and civic organizers started to learn the history of Korean communities in Japan, their lifeworlds, and their identities (Jeong 2016; M. Lee 2004).

The documentary film *Uri-Hakkyo* was created within this context of Korea's shifting gaze toward their co-ethnic other in Japan. In the next section, I situate the film within the study of visual cultural texts and provide the context, background information, and rationale for choosing this text.

Documentary, Representation, and *Uri-Hakkyo*

It has been an increasingly common phenomenon in academic disciplines to study visuality—the "practice of performing and seeing" (Olson, Finnegan, and Hope 2008, 1). Naturally, then, representations of the other are done in the realm where visual performance and discursive practices merge. The documentary, a "non-fiction text" (Bonner 2013, 62) where political and personal representations are carefully recorded "to make an argument about the historical (and real) world" (Nichols 1991, 111), is a symbolic/rhetorical resource that invites critical analysis. After all, a documentary film is a visual rhetorical text (Olson, Finnegan, and Hope 2008) that results from the "creative work of selection, editing, and developing into narrative" (Bonner 2011, 63) a story that has sociopolitical implications.

Drew (2016) defines Zainichi cinema[6] in a similar vein, with visual communication, when he places the films "as practices of producing, curating, exhibiting, viewing, and critiquing film images of Koreans in Japan" (1). As such, the cinematic representation of Koreans in Japan has a unique history that dates back to the 1960s as the prehistory of Zainichi cinema (i.e., the storied representation of a Zainichi youth who would "return" to North Korea in *Kyuporano Aru Machi*, 1962); followed by representations in the 1970s and onward as formations of Zainichi identities (i.e., *All in the Moon*, 1993; *Go*, 2001); then the retrospective narratives in the 1990s and 2000s (i.e., *Rikidozan*, 2006); and finally the diversifications and reassessment of the Zainichi cinema experience that have continued into the twenty-first century (Drew 2016).

It is particularly noteworthy to mention the emergence of the films in the early 2000s that attempted to reassess the history and experience of Zainichi in relation to their homeland. Yong-Hi Ryang's (2005) documentary film *Dear Pyeongyang*, for example, could be a critical reassessment of the repatriation history of *Chongryeon* Koreans, as Ryang presents her own familial experience of living through the aftermath of the repatriation to North Korea. Coincidentally, the redefinition of Zainichi, or *Jaeil* Koreans, happened in the South Korean mediasphere upon the historically pro-North Korean subject and the schools. Therefore, situated within Zainichi cinema, and documentaries in particular, *Uri-Hakkyo* (2006), directed by the South Korean director Myungjun Kim, was a new and unique reassessment of Korea's co-ethnic other.

Uri-Hakkyo narrates the everyday lives of students at a small Korean school in Hokkaido, Japan. The school has a total of 162 students from elementary through high school. The film focuses especially on senior high school students, depicting their cultural identities as Koreans in Japan. The film provides the historical origin of Korean schools in Japan, their relationship with the two Koreas, and their struggle to survive in Japan, where discrimination and hate toward Koreans have been ever prominent. Contrary to the stigmatic social representations that Korean schools have in Japan and in South Korea (as *Chongryoen* schools), the film records a joyful and vibrant school atmosphere where students and teachers are close like families.

The film was released as an opening film at the Seoul Independent Documentary Festival in 2006 and also at the Busan International Film Festival, where it received an "Un-pa" award (운파상). The film, which was later shown in various places within Korea and in Japan, was watched more than 10,000 times in the first week and around 110,000 times by the end of 2006 (Park 2007). I chose this documentary film as an analytical text for two main reasons. First, the film has successfully gained visibility in both South Korea and the Korean communities in Japan, reaching a record audience for an independent documentary film. Second, I am interested in analyzing the film's narrative gaze in an attempt to understand how the representation of Koreans in Japan as co-ethnic other is reframed, by deconstructing the previous normative image of *Chongryeon* Korean schools in Japan. I draw upon Burke's (1969) notion of identification as a method to analyze the ways in which image deconstructions as well as reconstructions are made. I use a conceptual notion of ideograph (McGee 1980) to examine symbolic resources where identification occurs in this mediated text.

Identification and the Ideograph of *Uri*

In his book *A Rhetoric of Motives* (1969), Burke defines the concept of identification as follows:

> A is not identical with his colleague, B. But in so far as their interests are joined, A is identified with B. Or he may identify himself

> with B even when their interests are not joined, if he assumes that they are, or is persuaded to believe so. . . . In being identified with B, A is "substantially one" with a person other than himself. Yet at the same time he remains unique, an individual locus of motives. Thus he is both joined and separate, at once a distinct substance and consubstantial with another. . . . To identify A with B is to make A "consubstantial" with B. (20–21)

This notion of identification serves as a powerful tool for analyzing processes of persuasive communication, how messages recreate us in relation to communication, and what counts as "consubstantiality" between text and the audience.

In addition to this Burkean identification, I utilize McGee's (1980) notion of "ideograph" as a rhetorical tool to explore the power of language. Ideographs are explained as "one-term sums" that symbolize terms that people in a society are "conditioned to" believe as *their language*. Ideographs illustrate the social realities that people live without questioning the ideological force in them. Ideograph, then, can be explained as something that "alters" reality among people; it is an ideological tool that unites (and also separates) people together. Applied to the Korean context, the use of *uri*, or our-ness, represents unique cultural assumptions of collectivity. It connects people together by implying that the interlocuter and the audience, be they in personal interactions or in public discourses, have shared knowledge and common cultural codes.

An Analysis of *Uri-Hakkyo*

To analyze the documentary *Uri-Hakkyo*, I explore how the notion of ideograph is applied in the film. Specifically, I examine the film's use of *uri* as an ideograph in three ways: (1) the naming of the school *uri* or "our" school (as opposed to *Joseon*, or "North Korean" school); (2) the metaphoric meaning of sports (soccer in the case of this film) for the diasporic community; and (3) the function of songs to sustain ideological practices and shared cultural identities. I argue that ideographic uses in naming sports and songs can serve as tools for identification among the Korean audience, thus transcending the image of co-ethnic other into more familiar and humane perceptions and therefore identifying more easily with them. Further, I argue that anti-Japanese sentiment, which defines Korean education as a fight against discrimination and a struggle against racism in Japan, serves as a core symbolic resource for identification presented in this film.

First, naming serves as a tool of identification. A title slide that reads "*Uri-Hakkyo*" in Korean is based on handwriting, in multiple colors, of elementary students at Hokkaido Korean School. A common representation of Korean schools in Japan, especially those of *Chongryeon*, has been *Joseon Hakkyo*, which symbolically represents "North Korean" schools. Though *Joseon* for diasporic Koreans in Japan can have two meanings—the country before its liberation from Japan and their political affiliation to North Korea (Jeong 2012)—this naming symbolically has represented North Korea. This is especially true as *Hanguk Hakkyo* (한국학교), schools affiliated with South Korea, are political counterparts. As Chung (2016) observes, divisions between these categorically different schools have continued since 1948 (214). In the Korean mediasphere, it has been (and still is) common to represent *Chongryeon* schools as "*Joseon*" schools, and, therefore, titling the documentary *Uri-Hakkyo*, as opposed to *Joseon Hakkyo*, invites an opportunity to reframe the representation of this co-ethnic other differently from the traditional way. This identification is achieved through a consubstantiality of ethnic nationalism, as I discuss later in the chapter.

The documentary opens with a written narrative that explains the history of *Uri-Hakkyo*:

> After liberation, first-generation *Jaeil* Koreans built *Hakkyo* [schools] first so that their children who do not know our (*uri*) language [Korean] would not feel any inconvenience even after they return to their homeland. Before the country's division, around 5,400 Koreans schools were built in Japan. In the mid-50s, Korea University was built in Tokyo, and since then, the ethnic education system [among *Jaeil* Koreans] from elementary, middle, high school, through university has been completed.[7]

The first line indicates the common desire among postcolonial Koreans to regain their language after the liberation. According to Chung (2016), the history of Korean schools in Japan can be divided into three periods: (1) a common desire among Koreans to fight for their educational rights (colonial period to 1947); (2) a division among Korean schools (into *Joseon*/North Korean and *Hanguk*/South Korean schools) and the definitive surpassing of the *Joseon Hakkyo* (1948–80); and (3) practicalization, diversification, and mergers (after the 1990s) (214). Rather than focusing on ideologically driven divisions, this narrative rationalizes the processes of building Korean schools in Japan as the common desire among the postcolonial individuals. *Uri-*

Hakkyo is the name commonly used for Korean schools in Japan among the community, and because the term *uri* is such a familiar term among Korean audiences, using this title for the film invites the audience to feel the life-world of this co-ethnic other as closer to them.

Second, throughout the film, the notion of *uri* is used metaphorically to explain the ideological orientation among the schoolchildren to serve the community. Soccer, in particular, has a more significant meaning for them than just winning or losing. The documentary narrates that they are playing not for their individual achievement but rather for solidarity among Korean communities in Japan. "'*Uri-Dongpo*' [우리 동포, our community people] is often used to indicate the reasons why they need to play their best and how it gives them hope and pride as Koreans in Japan. While it is known about the power of sports in developing collective identities" (Jaksa 2011), it is particularly true for the Korean community in Japan, where sports serve as windows to represent their presences, cultural pride, and communal identities (Shin 2010, 2013). Furthermore, this is an important demonstration of vernacular power and identities against Japanese society, where Koreans are historically viewed inferiorly as second-class citizens (Chapman 2006; Itagaki 2015).

Finally, an ideographic use of *uri*, or our-ness, is prominent in songs in the documentary. As recognized in the field of ethnomusicology, music can serve as situated social practices of creating communal identities (Beaster-Jones 2019). The film *Uri-Hakkyo* shows the central role music plays among the Korean school students.[8] For example, the song "Bungaeseon Cosmos" (분계선 코스모스, The Cosmos Flower at DMZ) is used as a soundtrack in this film, along with the song "Urilul Boshila" (우리를 보시라, Please Look at Us). Both songs were created by *Jaeil* Koreans, who narrate their collective identities as diasporic Koreans. The first song is a rather old (or "traditional," among Korean school students) song that has been sung widely among Korean school students. The song's lyrics narrate the voice of *uri* talking to the flourishing flowers in the demilitarized zone (DMZ) area. The song starts with a question: "Nobody sees and praises the beauty of the flower there, but why are you flourishing here?"[9] The first verse ends with an observational answer that the flowers flourish there to feel the wind between the South and the North freely. The second verse ends with the phrase "You flourish here thinking of the day on which our wish ["*uri-ui-soweon*," 우리의 소원] would come true." The song metaphorically depicts the position of diasporic Koreans as an invisible minority, their envisioning of the homeland as one Korea, and the sorrow of the country's division.

The second song, "Urilul Boshila," plays a more central role in the film. The song narrates the students' stories about their school, especially the meaning of school as a place to protect their identities as Korean.[10] The song particularly focuses on experiences of the students who transferred from Japanese schools to the Korean school, a process of their transformation to a true self. While the song plays, the film shows the lifeworld of Korean school students: students in their uniforms commuting to school; a teacher hugging a small student in her dance uniform; students learning Korean language in the classroom; smiling students taking pictures; teams playing sports; female students dancing with smiles. The song appeals to the audience's humanistic feelings: their natural reaction to the smiles of children, the warmth of hugging, and the joy of learning, singing, and playing. The film shows the lifeworld of the students within the framework of *uri* and invites identification through this ideograph.

Finally, and most importantly, a core ideology that runs throughout the film is defining the Korean school as a protected space against historically persistent racism and hate among Japanese toward Koreans. The ideograph of *uri* is reflected through collective memory of the historic education fight among Koreans in Japan, known as the 4.24 (or Hanshin) Education Fight,[11] as well as through the reality of struggles with hate speeches and attacks toward Koreans, "our" children in particular, in Japan. The film *Uri-Hakkyo* is represented as a memory space, in which collective memories of the community's past serve as a discursive vehicle by which to circulate, pass on, and negotiate the community's identities.

Memory's ties to location, or a location of memory, have been widely discussed across disciplinary boundaries (Basso 1996; Blair 1999, 2006; J. Lee 2016). As JongHwa Lee (2016) claims, a "discussion on 'memory place' provides important starting points for the 'embodied-ness/situated-ness' of memory—the materiality and rhetoricity of memory on the one hand, and its discursivity and interactivity on the other" (371). In the documentary *Uri-Hakkyo* (and from then on in other documentaries on Korean schools in Japan), a communal memory of fighting for Korean students' educational right serves as a strong rationale to keep the community's solidarity. In the film, a first-generation woman who lived through the time of constructing and protecting the schools narrates the story, highlighting Koreans' postcolonial consciousness after liberation, persistent threats from the Japanese political authorities, and constant struggle to protect schools.

Narrating her experience of the education fight in 1948, she states, "Police came into our schools with black sticks. . . . Students gathered to protect our schools. Especially for male students, fighting became their job, a more important duty than studying. . . . They did not go back home and slept at schools for nights. . . . So many Koreans protested, and even one student passed away. . . . This incident remains as one of the most important histories in our community."[12]

Importantly, the memory of oppression, with the spirit of "fight" and solidarity, is placed in continuity with the current reality of the school. Perhaps the most serious tone that appears in this film is the threat the school receives from Japanese extremists. One day, the school receives a call. A teacher picks up and says, "Hello, this is [Korean] *Hakkyo*." A man's voice with a threatening tone says, "Your school's kids! I will kill any one of them, you so dirty *Chosenjin*! Remember, you guys are animals! I will kill you!" Korean schools in Japan, with their representation of the ethnic/cultural/political other, have always been a target of attack among Japan's political extremists. Yet, anti-Korean sentiments and racist hate speech escalated in Japan after the 2000s due to various economic, political, and cultural reasons (Itagaki 2015; Iwabuchi 2017; Han 2020). This hostile sociopolitical climate in Japan has a direct impact on Korean schools in Japan.[13] Korean school students across Japan have been targeted for verbal and physical attack, and the film depicts direct threats this particular school experiences. Historically persistent racism in Japan, with more intensified hate speech toward Koreans in Japan, appeals to a strong notion of *uri*, or our-ness, and the protection of "our" children, providing a strong rationale for protecting the school. The Korean school, then, is no longer a representation of North Korea but rather a symbolic representation of Korean pride against Japan. This anti-Japanese sentiment, as a response to Japan's anti-Korean sentiment, serves as a strong means of identification, a sense of *uri* that invites sympathy among the Korean audience toward the nation's postcolonial exile.

Applying the Burkean theory of identification, there are three "consubstantialities" the film has successfully used to appeal to Korean audiences. First is ethnic nationalism, or the sense of "we proud Koreans." That is, an inclusion of *Joseon* school into the notion of *uri* is achieved through a common sentiment of ethnic nationalism, "we proud Koreans." In the film, Korean students' identities are often reflected through narratives of "pride as Koreans." For example, the story of a female high school student who transferred from a Japanese school mentions that "Korean school has given me courage to be me," contrary to the inferiority she had to carry in a Japanese school. Winning in a soccer game is another important event that demonstrates their ethnic pride. The lyrics in the songs that Korean school students sing narrate the ethnic spirit that desires one Korea, despite Koreans' invisibility in history. All of this evidence of ethnic pride serves as an essence of identification with Korean audiences. Importantly, the reevaluation of *Joseon* schools in South Korean society is achieved with the weakened anti-Communism sentiment. With the weakening of the anti-Communist filter, the power of identification with the notion of ethnic pride, or "we proud Koreans," is intensified.

Second, and related to the first point, the sociocultural memory of colonial experience serves as an important consubstantiality between the *Joseon* schools and the South Korean audience. Again, this identification is enabled only with the weakened anti-Communist framework in Korea. The direct experience of colonialism the *Jaeil* Korean communities have is in fact the most important "common historical experience" with Koreans (H. Kweon 2007, 259). Yet, this postcolonial sentiment had been dominated by the anti-Communist climate, or as Kwon (2007) names it, "the anti-Communization of the anti-Japanese logic" (255). With a loosened anti-Communist filter, students' attendance at Korean schools in Japan despite the escalating discriminatory environment appears to be even "brave" for South Korean audiences (K. Cho 2007).

Finally, an appeal to a humanistic perspective could serve as a powerful consubstantiality for a Korean audience. Perhaps this is the most common, and therefore the most powerful, identification tool. The ethnographic approach to the students' lifeworlds enabled the audience to view *Joseon* (or *Chongryeon*) Koreans as human beings just like "us." As "the presence of *Chongryeon* had long been a mere national [North Korean] institution in South Korean society," (K. Cho 2007, 129), this "humanization" of the co-ethnic other could serve as a significant identification tool. For example, in an interview in 2017, the director Kim reflects on his initial ignorance toward the *Joseon* Korean schools. He first visited a teacher affiliated with Mindan (a pro-South organization) who taught Korean classes at a Japanese school. Surprisingly, he was told that he should visit *Joseon* Korean schools first if he wanted to learn about the history of ethnic education. Though he was initially fearful of visiting a pro–North Korean school (as he says, he is from a generation with "anti-Communist education"), within one hour of talking with the students, he realized that a big change was happening in his mind. Kim states, "I knew that I was facing some very important issue here. . . . Beyond ideologies, I believe that anybody, at least if that person is a Korean, would experience a big change after meeting and talking with these students." This attempt to understand pro–North Korean schools with a focus on their humanity has continued since this film (Baek 2017).

Conclusion

Situated within both postcolonial and Cold War politics in and between Japan and Korea, the issue of media representations of *Jaeil* Koreans serves as an interesting arena of inquiry. In Japan, Zainichi Koreans have been portrayed as stigmatized minorities within the nation's postcolonial structure. Although Zainichi Koreans have been integrated into Japan under the same racial category, they have suffered discrimination based on Japanese ethnic hierarchies. In Korea, *Jaeil* Koreans, and *Chongryeon* Koreans in particular, have been othered due to the stigmatized representations attached to Communism as well as to Japanese colonial legacies. In a way, Koreans in and from Japan bear ambivalent social identities as a stigmatized other either through their ethnicity (as they are the ethnic other in Japan) or through their former nation of residence (co-ethnic other in Korea).

Paying particular attention to the active redefinition of Zainichi/*Jaeil* as Korea's co-ethnic other by resituating them within the cultural framework of Koreanness, or an ideograph of *uri*, was a meaningful attempt in several ways. First, this attempt reveals how *Jaeil* Koreans are positioned in Korea's anthrocategorism with their unique historicity. That is, in Korea at least, the othering mechanism for *Jaeil* Koreans was based not on the ethnicity but rather on the ideologies of anti-Communism and postcolonial conditions. Thus, second, studying the effort to redefine the nation's co-ethnic other reacts to the historical absence of interests from homeland to the lifeworld of *Chongryeon* Koreans. The images of the pro-North *Jaeil* Koreans are reassessed, or altered, from the ideologically contaminated (by Communism), troubled (by colonial legacies) other to the sympathetic victim of brutal Japanese colonial rule and oppression. Finally, this shift hints at renewed imaginations toward the co-ethnic other and transnational solidarity. Theoretically, the notion of *uri* as an ideograph helps us understand the shift in the notions of self and other from modern to postmodern representations, from fixed and essentialized presentations to more deconstructed ones, resituated in the different discursive system, context, and historicity. Relocating the mediated representation of diasporic Koreans in Japan, and the effort of Korean media to highlight their lifeworlds, stood as a significant inclusion of them as the "forgotten history" in South Korea.

NOTES

1. The *Joseon* nationality, or *Chosen-seki* in Japanese, does not mean North Korean nationality. It is a category that was given to Koreans in Japan after the liberation, and for those Koreans who did not choose to obtain South Korean or Japanese citizenship, this "nationality" has been kept. For detailed discussions on issues of nationality among Koreans in Japan, see Y. Ryang (2005).

2. Entry to South Korea with the *Joseon* nationality has not been allowed without certain exceptional cases.

3. There are several different names to represent Koreans in Japan, each of which, according to Jeong (2012), has unique historical roots. For example, "Koreans in Japan" can include several different names, such as *Jaeil Hannin* (재일한인) or Japan-residing (South) Koreans; *Jaeil Josunin* (재일조선인) or Japan-residing (North) Koreans; *Jaeil* (or *Zainichi* in Japanese); *Jaeil* Koreans; and *Jaeil Kyopo* (재일교포). While it is common for other diasporic communities to be represented with the place they migrated to (e.g., Korean American), naming for Koreans in Japan is in general categorized in relation to three typologies: (1) nationality, (2) sense of belonging, and (3) time of migration. Given this complex context, in this chapter, I use the name "diasporic Koreans in Japan" and "*Jaeil* Koreans" interchangeably. I chose to use "*Jaeil*" as this is the name consistently used in contemporary South Korean society (Jeong 2012) to accurately represent the local logic of naming the co-ethnic other in South Korea. I also use "diasporic Koreans in Japan" as opposed to "Koreans in Japan" to emphasize this particular community's characteristic as an "old-comer" in the Japanese multicultural context (Chapman 2006).

4. *Chongryeon* is an abbreviation of the General Association of Korean Residents in Japan, or *Jaeilbon Joseonin Chong-Ryeonhaphoe* (재일본조선인총련합회). The organization has also been known as *Jo-Chong-Ryeon* (조총련) in South Korea.

In response to Korea's sociopolitical climate in the Cold War era, in the 1970s and 1980s, diasporic Koreans in Japan were politically divided too. When it comes to national/ethnic education in Japan, note that the schools under *Chongryeon* had exerted overwhelming dominance in Japan during this time. For more discussion, see Chung (2016).

5. Suh Sung was a Korean in Japan (born in Kyoto, Japan, in 1941) who visited South Korea for study but was unjustly imprisoned. He wrote a book that reflects on his time in prison, published in Korean, Japanese, and English. For the English version, see *Unbroken Spirits: Nineteen Years in South Korea's Gulag* (2001).

6. *Zainichi* represents a Japanese translation of *Jaeil* Koreans—Koreans in Japan. Used as a unique name as it is (without followed by Korean), *Zainichi* refers to Koreans in Japan as old-comer "resident or denizen of Japan" (Chapman 2006, 90).

7. Translated by author.

8. For example, as Ha's (2018) ethnographically based work on Korean schools in Japan witnessed, music serves as a cultural means for the students to transgress the South-North boundaries.

9. The full lyrics of the song's first verse is as follows:

곱다고 보아주는 사람도 없느데 어이하여 너는 여기에 피었느냐
(Nobody sees you and praise your beauty, but for what are you flourishing here)
림진강기슭에 새하얀 코스모스 살랑살랑
(The cosmos flower on the shore of Rim-Jin River)
남북을 오고가는 그 바람에 설레고 싶어서 피어났느냐
(To feel the wind that goes the South and the North, did you flourish here)

10. The full lyrics of the song's first verse is as follows:

그 언제나 나를 보는 눈길들, 내가 서는 자리마저 하나 없듯이
(The gazes that see me always; As if there is no place that I can stand)
마음을 숨기며 발자취도 감추며 세상에는 저혼자라 알았왔네
(Hiding my mind and footsteps, though I thought that there is only me in the world)
단하나의 이름을 불러주는 동무들이 나를나를 이루어 주고
(Friends who call me in my sole name would make me and my self)
두팔을 크게 벌려 여기 오라고 안아주는 나의 학교
(My school that calls me with their two arms wide open)
우리를 보시라 그 어디 부럼 있으랴, 마음껏 배워가는 이 행복넘치네
(Please watch us, we do not envy, full of happiness to learn and grow)
아침의 햇빛이 아름답고 고운 그 모습을 그려 살리라
(We will live with the picture of beautiful morning sunshine)

11. In January 1948, the Japanese Ministry of Education ordered that Korean schools (there were around six hundred Korean schools then) comply with Japan's School Education Law in order to be accredited in Japan. Japan's School Education Law required that all classes would be conducted in Japanese, following the Japanese education curricula, but in the newly built Korean schools across Japan, teaching all subjects in Korean was an important mission with their postcolonial mentality. Many Koreans protested against this order, viewing it as a revival of the past colonial experience. "The uncompromising attitudes of both Koreans and the Japanese authorities eventuated in violence" (C. Lee 1981, 165). On April 24, 1948, a large-scale demonstration occurred in the Osaka-Kobe area (called the Hanshin area in Japan), which resulted in thousands of Koreans arrested, and "two Koreans were shot dead by the U.S. military police and many were injured" (S. Ryang 1997, 86). The incident is called the "4.24 Education Fight," named after the date on which the demonstration happened, or the "Hanshin Education Fight," named after the area in which the demonstration occurred.

12. The narration was translated by author.

13. For fuller descriptions of the impact of hate speeches and racism on Korean schools, see Ha (2018).

REFERENCES

Basso, Keith. 1996. *Wisdom Sits in Places: Landscape and Language among the Western Apache*. Albuquerque: University of New Mexico Press.

Beaster-Jones, Jayson. 2019. "Linguistic and Semiotic Approaches to Ethnomusicology:

From Abstract Structure to Situated Practice." In *Theory for Ethnomusicology: Histories, Conversations, Insights*, edited by Harris M. Berger and Ruth M. Stone, 26–50. New York: Routledge.

Bek, Seong-Soo. 2017. "Documentari Eiga 'Uri-Hakkyo'wo Meguru 3tsuno Communitino Kousatsu: Kankoku, Nihon, Zainichi Korean Shakaino Dainamizumu" ドキュメンタリー映画「ウリハッキョ」をめぐる3つのコミュニティの考察：韓国、日本、在日社会のダイナミズム [An analysis of three communities on the documentary film "Uri-Hakkyo": Dynamisms of Korea, Japan, and Zainichi communities]. *Kanda Gaigodai Kiyou* 神田外語大紀要 [Journal of Kanda University of International Studies] 29:431–55.

Blair, Carole. 1999. "Contemporary U.S. Memorial Sites as Exemplars of Rhetoric's Materiality." In *Rhetorical Bodies*, edited by Jack Selzer and Sharon Crowley, 16–57. Madison: University of Wisconsin Press.

Blair, Carole. 2006. "Collective Memory." In *Communication as . . . : Perspectives on Theory*, edited by Gregory J. Sheperd, Jeffrey St. John, and Ted Striphas, 51–59. Thousand Oaks, CA: Sage.

Bonner, Frances. 2013. "Recording Reality: Documentary Film and Television." In *Representation*, 2nd ed., edited by Stuart Hall, Jessica Evans, and Sean Nixon, 60–99. Los Angeles: Sage.

Burke, Kenneth. 1969. *A Rhetoric of Motives*. Berkeley: University of California Press.

Chapman, David. 2006. "Discourses of Multicultural Coexistence (Kyosei) and the Old-Comer Korean Residents in Japan." *Asian Ethnicity* 7 (1): 89–102.

Cho, Hae-Joang. 1998. "Constructing and Deconstructing Koreanness." In *Making Majorities: Constituting the Nation in Japan, Korea, China, Malaysia, Fiji, Turkey, and the United States*, edited by Dru C. Gladney, 73–94. Stanford: Stanford University Press.

Cho, Kyeong-Hee. 2007. "Kankokushakaini Okeru Zainichi Chosenjinninsikino Hensen" 韓国社会における在日朝鮮人認識の変遷 [Historical development of the perceptions toward Zainichi Choseon Koreans in Korean society]. *Hwanghae Munhwa* 황해문화 [Hwanghae Review] 57:46–75.

Chung, Chin Sung. 2016. "Jaeildonpo Minjokhakkyo" 재일동포 민족학교: 분단과 탈식민의 역사 [Korean schools in Japan: Their history of division and (post-)colonialism]. *Ilbon Bipyeong* 일본비평 [Japanese Critique] 16:208–42.

Collins, Patricia Hill. 1986. "Learning from the Outsider Within: The Sociological Significance of Black Feminist Thought." *Social Problems* 33 (6): S14–S32.

Collins, Patricia Hill. 1991. *Black Feminist Thought: Knowledge, Consciousness, and the Politics of Empowerment*. New York: Routledge.

Collins, Patricia Hill. 1998. "Intersections of Race, Gender, and Nation: Some Indications for Black Family Studies." *Journal of Comparative Family Studies* 29 (1): 27–37.

Collins, Patricia Hill. 1999. "Reflections on the Outsider Within." *Journal of Career Development* 26 (1): 85–89.

Drew, Oliver. 2016. *Zainichi Cinema: Koreans in Japan Film Culture*. London: Palgrave Macmillan.

Ha, Kyung Hee. 2018. "Cultural Politics of Transgressive Living: Socialism Meets Neoliberalism in Pro-North Korean Schools in Japan." *Social Identities* 24 (2): 189–205.

Hall, Stuart. 1989. "Cultural Identity and Cinematic Representation." *Framework: Journal of Cinema and Media* 36:68–81.

Han, Min Wha, and JongHwa Lee. 2011. "Transforming the Image of the *Other*: Representations of North Korea/ns in *Hallyu* Cinema." In *Hallyu: Korean Pop Culture Waves in Asia and Beyond*, edited by Do Kyun Kim and Min Sun Kim, 155–80. Seoul: Seoul National University Press.

Han, Soo-Hye. 2020. "'Trash to the Trash Cans, Koreans to the Korean Peninsula!': Diehard Racism and the Rise of Hate Speech against Korean Residents in Japan." In *Korean Diaspora across the World: Homeland in History, Memory, Imagination, Media, and Reality*, edited by Eun-Jeong Han, Min Wha Han, and JongHwa Lee, 147–72. Lanham, MD: Lexington Books.

Hoover, Kathy McKibben. 2010. "Outsiders/Within and In/Outsiders: Varieties of Multiculturalism." *Journal of Educational Controversy* 5 (2): 1–9.

Hukuoka, Yasunori. 1998. *Zainichi Chosen Kankokujin: Wakai Sedaino Aidentiti* 在日韓国朝鮮人：若い世代のアイデンティティ [*Zainichi Koreans: Identities among young generations*]. Tokyo: Chuko Shinsho.

Itagaki, Ryuta. 2015. "The Anatomy of Korea-phobia in Japan." *Japanese Studies* 35 (1): 49–66.

Iwabuchi, Koichi. 2017. "In Search of Proximate Enemies." *Japan Forum* 29 (4): 437–49.

Jeong, Jin Seong. 2016. "Jaeildongpo Hochingui Eoksaseonggwa Hyeonjaeseong" '재일동포' 호칭의 역사성과 현재성 [The historical consequence and contemporary state of phraseology concerning Koreans in Japan]. *Ilbon Bipyeong* 일본비평 [*Japanese Critique*] 7:258–334.

Jo, Gwan-ja. 2015. "Jaeil Choseonin Damnonae Natanan Kiminuishikul Neomeoseo" 재일조선인 담론에 나타난 "기민(棄民)의식을" 넘어서[Beyond the consciousness of 'abandoned people' in the discourses of *Jaeil Choseonin*]. *Tongilgwa Pyeonghwa* 통일과 평화 [*Journal of Peace and Unification Studies*] 7 (1): 176–216.

Kim, Meong Jun. 2006. *Uri-Hakkyo* 우리 학교 [*Our school*]. A Documentary film.

Kweon, Heok-Tae. 2007. "Jaeil Choseoningwa Hankuksahoe: Hankuksahoeneun Jaeil Choseonineul Eotteokae Pyosang haeowanneunga" 재일조선인과 한국사회: 한국사회는 재일조선인을 어떻게 '표상'해왔는가 [Zainichi Koreans and Korean Society: How Have Zainichi Koreans been Represented?]. *Yeoksa Bipyeong* 역사비평 [*Critical Review of History*], 2:234–67.

Kweon, Sug-In. 2008. "Diaspora Jaeil Choseoninui 'Kuihwan': Hankuksahoeaeseoui Keongheomseonggwa Jungchaeseong" 디아스포라 재일한인의 '귀환': 한국사회에서의 경험성과 정체성 [Returning ethnic Koreans from Japan in Korea]. *Kukjae Jiyeok Yeongu* 국제.지역연구 [*International Area Studies Review*] 17 (4): 33–60.

Lee, Chang Soo. 1981. "The Legal Status of Koreans in Japan." In *Koreans in Japan: Ethnic Conflict and Accommodation*, edited by Chang Soo Lee and George De Vos, 133–58. Berkeley: University of California Press.

Lee, JongHwa. 2016. "The 'Sacred Standing' for the 'Fallen' Spirits: Yasukuni Shrine and Memory of War." *Journal of International and Intercultural Communication* 9 (4): 368–88.

Lee, Mun-Woong. 2004. "Chongryeongye Jaeil Choseoninui Saenghwalsegye: Illyuhakjeok Jeopgeun" 총련계 재일 조선인의 생활세계: 인류학적 접근 [The lifeworld of the North Koreans in Japan: An anthropological approach]. *Sahoe Kwahak* 사회과학 [*Korean Social Science*] 26 (1–2): 163–224.

McGee, Michael C. 1980. "The 'Ideograph': A Link between Rhetoric and Ideology." *Quarterly Journal of Speech* 66:1–16.

Ministry of Culture and Information. 1979. *Culture and Communication for 30 years (1948–1978)*. Seoul: Ministry of Culture.
Morris-Suzuki, Tessa. 2007. *Exodus to North Korea: Shadows from Japan's Cold War*. Lanham: Rowman & Littlefield.
Nichols, Bill. 1991. *Representing Reality: Issues and Concepts in Documentary*. Bloomington: Indiana University Press.
Oh, Ingyu. 2012. "From Nationalistic Diaspora to Transnational Diaspora: The Evolution of Identity Crisis among the Korean-Japanese." *Journal of Ethnic and Migration Studies* 38 (4): 651–69. https://doi.org/10.1080/1369183X.2012.659127
Olson, Lester C., Cara A. Finnegan, and Diane Hope. 2008. "Visual Rhetoric in Communication: Continuing Questions and Contemporary Issues." In *Visual Rhetoric: A Reader in Communication and American Culture*, edited by Lester C. Olson, Cara A. Finnegan, and Diane S. Hope, 1–13. Thousand Oaks, CA: Sage.
Park, Yun Soo. 2007. "The Director Kim, Myeong-Jun in *Uri-Hakkyo*." *Women's News*, April 6. https://www.womennews.co.kr/news/articleView.html?idxno=33103
Rogers, Mary F. 2010. "Outsiders/within and In/outsiders: Varieties of Multiculturalism." *Journal of Educational Controversy* 5 (2): 1–9.
Ryang, Sonia. 1997. *North Koreans in Japan: Language, Ideology, and Identity*. Boulder: Westview Press.
Ryang, Sonia, ed. 2000. *Koreans in Japan: Critical Voices from Margin*. London: Routledge.
Ryang, Yong-Hi. 2005. *Dear Pyeongyang*. A documentary film.
Suh, Kuk-Sung, ed. 1983. *The Identity of the Korean People*. Seoul: National Unification Board.
Yim, Haksoon. 2002. "Cultural Identity and Cultural Policy in South Korea." *International Journal of Cultural Policy* 8 (1): 37–48.
Yoon, Kwoncha. 2001. *Zainichiwo Kangaeru* 在日を考える [*Thinking Zainichi*]. Tokyo: Heihansha.

10

The Other at Home

A Comparative Analysis of Coverage of an Exiled Korean American K-Pop Star

Alice Nahyeon Kim and Sherry S. Yu

Steve Seung Jun Yoo (유승준) was a legendary South Korean popular music (hereafter K-pop) star in the 1990s who had exceptional cross-generational popularity. Yet his sudden decision in 2002 to relinquish his Korean citizenship to become a US citizen, and the murkiness of his stance during the process, was considered a betrayal to his dedicated fans and the Korean public. The government also considered his case to be intentional avoidance of military service and therefore banned his entry into Korea. Since then, for nearly twenty years, Yoo has been forbidden from entering what he calls his "home country" (Jin-hyung Cho 2017).

This case is worthy of research attention, not because it is a story about a once famous K-pop star but because it is the case of a Korean American (or America-raised Korean) becoming the other in his country of origin, similar yet different to the case of Korean Americans being the other in their country of settlement. While the latter has been well documented, especially how minorities are considered as the other in the "white world" (Bhabha 1996, 56; Hall 2001), how Korean Americans as minorities can be double-marginalized in their homeland is less explored (John Cho 2012; C. Oh 2014; D. Oh 2017). Yoo's case also opened up heated public debates on citizenship, military service, and hybrid identity, not only in Korea but also within the Korean American community, and influenced the making and remaking of relevant citizenship and military service laws that govern the ways Korean Americans navigate their hybrid identities in both worlds. The story of Yoo and the questions of his belonging ultimately disclose the complicated case of othering manifest in Korea that the Western-centered lens of racism cannot fully explain.

This study traces the coverage of Steve Yoo as documented by both Korean and Korean American newspapers within the past eighteen years (2002–20), equivalent to a total of 638 news items from *The Korea Times* and *The Korea Daily* of South Korea and their respective Korean American branches, *The Korea Times U.S.A* and *The Korea Daily U.S.A*. Newspapers are one way to explore how the discourse around a particular event is initiated and developed. The popularity of Yoo as a K-pop star and the subsequently significant media coverage of his case provide researchers with rich data through which the discussion of Yoo's case in Korea as well as in the Korean American community can be explored. By using Homi Bhabha's notion of the other, a textual analysis of coverage attempts to reveal the discourse around Yoo and what that means for Korean Americans.[1]

Background

Korean Citizenship and Military Service

To understand the context in which the case of Yoo's citizenship issue is situated, a brief introduction to Korean citizenship and the mandatory military service as citizenry duty is necessary. The Korean constitution stipulates that all male citizens aged eighteen years or older have the duty to perform military service for eighteen to twenty-two months, and dodging this service is considered a punishable crime, primarily because the country is still in a state of armistice with North Korea. The long service period, which requires young men to pause their academic or professional careers, and the constant danger of injuries during their service, however, impose a substantial burden on young men (C. Lee 2019).

Military dodging further complicates the lives of overseas Koreans, as the citizenship law is often amended to regulate this dodging and creates legal hurdles for them (Y. Lee 2013). Korea confers citizenship based on the nationality of one or both parents, and children born outside of Korea to Korean parent(s), including those with permanent residency in another country, are immediately subject to Korean citizenship and are thereby dual citizens by birth. If dual citizens wish to retain their Korean citizenship, they must fulfill military service in the case of male children, and if they choose not to, they must formally renounce their Korean citizenship before they reach the age of eighteen (Umeda 2010). If they do not conform, legal consequences may follow, including an entry ban ("Brief Introduction of Korean Nationality Laws" 2018). Korean citizens with permanent residency in other countries (which was the case of Steve Yoo), on the other hand, can delay their military service until the age of thirty-eight under the current law, if they stay outside of Korea and do not seek to enter or generate income in Korea (Military Manpower Administration 2017).

Military Service and K-Pop Stars

Aside from these legal aspects of military service, there are also social implications. Korean native men who did not fulfill their military duty often become alienated among those who did, even if they were exempt with a legally legitimate reason (I. Kwon 2005). As sensitive as the issue is, the entertainment industry holds high expectations for male celebrities to comply with military duty (S. Lee 2004). However, for male celebrities, military service puts a great pause on their careers, since not only well-managed but also frequent public appearances are critical to their survival in the competitive entertainment industry (Yu and Kim 2015). Also, fans do not want to let their stars go. In some cases, K-pop idol fans filed appeals to the Blue House for exemption of military service for their adored stars (J. Kwon 2019; McCurry 2019). Thus, it is not unexpected to see varying cases in which celebrities either are embroiled in military-dodging scandals and the subsequent public outrage, such as a Korean native singer MC Mong (C. Lee 2010), or have improved their public image by voluntarily giving up their US permanent residency and choosing to fulfill military service, such as singer Taecyeon of the K-pop group 2PM (D. Jang 2017). Most often, however, these cases tend to be evaluated based on whether or not celebrities fulfilled their duty, with little consideration of the nature of their transnational lives and the subsequent socioeconomic and legal situations they have to deal with.

Steve Seung Jun Yoo's case reflects the former, as his public image prior to the military scandal was positive. Born in 1976 in Seoul, his family immigrated to the US when he was thirteen years old and settled in Buena Park, California (C. Lee 2019; "Yoo Seung Jun" 2020). In 1997, Yoo debuted as a singer in Korea and quickly climbed to stardom (H. Kim 2019). Yoo's celebrity was multifaceted: he was a rapper, an athletic man, and also a Christian (H. Park 2002). His positive public image, as conveyed in his nickname, "beautiful young man" (아름다운 청년), turned sour when he renounced his Korean citizenship to obtain US citizenship just months before he was scheduled to be drafted into military service in 2002 (G. Kim 2019; McCurry 2019; Shim 2015). Yoo's unexpected decision sparked public outrage because not only had media reported multiple times that he expressed his intention to fulfill his military duty—although Yoo currently denies that he made any public affirmation about his decision regarding military service—but also he had completed his medical test and was assigned to serve the term as a public service worker (J. Kim 2002; Kwak 2019; Son 2016).

The Military Manpower Administration (병무청) and the Korean government considered his action to be intentional dodging, as Yoo's renouncement of his Korean citizenship happened while he was out of the country for a concert in Japan, for which he had been granted a travel exception, uncommon for those who are expecting to be drafted (Son 2016). Consequently, the government placed an entry ban on Yoo based on article 11 of the Immigration Act, which prohibits the entry of people who are against the "interests and safety of the Republic of Korea" (Choi 2019; C. Lee 2019; Son 2016).

Since then, working as an actor in China, Yoo has tried several times to make his way "home" (Jin-hyung Cho 2017). He filed a lawsuit against the Korean embassy in Los Angeles for its refusal to grant him an F-4 visa, which was applied for when he reached the age of thirty-eight and the military draft was no longer applicable (Ock 2019). The F-4 visa, which is for overseas Koreans, allows for almost all employment activities in Korea (J. Lee 2020; "Visa Categories" 2016). In March 2020, the Supreme Court of Korea ruled in favor of Yoo in a lawsuit arguing that the visa refusal was improper, referring to a fault in administrative procedure (J. Lee 2020). However, this ruling does not mean that Yoo can automatically enter Korea. The controversies around him surfaced once again in December 2020, when Yoo publicly criticized the Korean government via his personal YouTube channel (Jun 2020).

Literature Review

The Other in the "White World" versus the Homeland

Immigration laws determine the legal status of immigrants in the host country and, by doing so, dictate who belongs and who does not. Exclusionary immigration laws in the US such as the 1882 Chinese Exclusion Act and the 1907 Immigration Act continued until the 1965 Hart-Celler Immigration Act, which eliminated the immigration quota by country of origin, and clearly expressed the government's intention not to accept immigrants as full members of society (James 2000; Waldinger and Mehdi Bozorgmehr 1996). Korean immigration to the US rose dramatically because of economic opportunities amid political instability in Korea and the formidable Korea-US military relations in the post–Cold War era (Min 2006). In 2010, approximately 1.8 million Korean descendants were living in the US. However, by 2017, the number had dwindled to approximately 1 million (O'Connor and Batalova 2019). Reverse immigration to Korea has also risen, as Korea experiences exponential social and economic growth, which makes the benefits of emigration less appealing (Han 2012).

The reality of living as the other may also have contributed to Koreans' decision not to immigrate to the US or to move back to Korea. The elimination of racial quotas and the growth of the Korean population in the US did not necessarily mean the elimination of exclusion or othering. The exclusionary laws are still alive, mediated through racialized images of Asians as the other or as the model minority, and continue the legacy of discrimination (Hamamoto 1994; L. Kim 2004; Wing 2007). The differences are considered as the markers of inferiority rather than as the benefits of diversity. Homi Bhabha (1996, 56) argues, in the words of Frantz Fanon, that such differentiation is "historically untimely," that is, "You come too late, much too late. There will always be a world—a white world—between you and us." The hegemonic inequality embedded in the structure for the benefit of the White world prevents minorities from fully demonstrating their hybrid potential in real life (Bhabha 1996; Hamamoto 1994; Kraidy 2006).

Korean Americans in Korea face another form of othering. The cultural, social, and political dissociations that Korean Americans experience in Korea make them feel like they are an "insider-outsider" (D. Oh 2018). Christian Park (2019, 125) argues that the perception of Korean Americans in Korea is not "static or homogeneous but constantly changing," showing contradicting images of Korean Americans. That is, Korean Americans are seen as either the traitors who deserted the motherland or the subject of envy. Simultaneously, they are compatriots who suffer through hard labor and discrimination in the foreign country (C. Park 2019). In between these images, a variety of terms are used to refer to Korean Americans, including *gyopo* (overseas Koreans), *dongpo* (compatriots), and, more recently, *hanin* (people of Korean ethnicity) (C. Park 2019). These mixed perceptions of Korean Americans complicate their identities and experiences in Korea. For example, Cho (2012, 220) argues that Korean American English teachers in Korea enjoy advantages, such as employment and social privilege, by utilizing the highly valued linguistic capital of English but that, simultaneously, they are also deemed "failed immigrants and inauthentic English-speakers."

Young Yun Kim (2001, 17) explains that immigrants experience "reentry shock" when they return to the homeland after being a sojourner in another culture. "Uprooted" from the home culture and striving to fit in to their host society, Korean Americans experience personal reinvention and existential transformation, eventually "becoming" intercultural (9). Within this transformed existence, when they reenter the homeland, Korean Americans realize that they are, in the words of Bhabha (1996, 53), "in-between" two countries in a hybrid form, or are "'both-and' people," which could conversely mean "'neither-nor' people" (Harinen 2001, 39) and possibly subject to double marginalization. In this context, the "Third Space" in which Korean Americans can represent themselves becomes meaningful as they are often represented neither in the mainstream media in the US nor in Korea (Bhabha 1994).

Korean Diasporic Media in Response to Othering

Diasporic media, that is, media by and primarily for immigrants and ethnic minorities (Matsaganis, Katz, and Ball-Rokeach 2011), play a significant role in negotiating the complex experiences that hyphenated individuals endure. Their "reactive and proactive" and "outward and inward" roles in solidifying the community and voicing out to broader society (Fleras 2009, 726) are useful particularly in countering the images of Korean Americans as the other in the White world. Bhabha's (1994) Third Space is relevant here, as a space of resistance to the perpetuating imagery of immigrants as the other and the representation of the perspectives of immigrants that are often not covered in mainstream media.

A much less explored role of diasporic media is countering the image of Korean Americans as the other in the homeland. Diasporic media, let alone diasporic Koreans, are often considered second-class (Yu 2017). Particularly, locally grown immigrant media, as opposed to the branches of transnational media, are looked down on even more due to the quality of journalism, which is perceived to be produced by those who are not professionally trained (Yu 2017). Nonetheless, diasporic media are valued for "geo-ethnic storytelling," that is "a practice that aims to produce culturally relevant and locally vital information to immigrants in the host society" (Lin and Song 2006, 364). Korean diasporic storytelling, unique to the local Korean community, is distinctively Korean American and is different from that of Korean media, although the presence of Korean perspectives through imported news from Korea should be acknowledged (Yu 2018). As media for the community in between Korea and America, Korean American media offer a space where hybrid identities can be represented and transnational experiences can be shared. This aspect of Korean media is particularly important for examining how this space of resistance and representation documents the case of Steve Yoo.

Methodology

This study conducts a textual analysis of the coverage of Steve Yoo. Textual analysis is a methodology that examines language, symbols, or pictures present in texts to understand the broader meaning of the messages and the historical, cultural, and political contexts of communication (Allen 2017). We examined the coverage of Yoo in Korean-language daily newspapers published in Korea and in the Korean American community in Los Angeles: *The Korea Times* (한국일보; hereafter KTKR), *The Korea Daily* (중앙일보; hereafter KDKR), *The Korea Times U.S.A.* (hereafter KTLA), and *The Korea Daily U.S.A.* (hereafter KDLA). KTKR has operated KTLA, its US branch, since 1969, and KDKR has operated KDLA since 1974 ("The Korea Times" n.d.; "JMnet USA" n.d.). The two Korean American newspapers are the leading daily newspapers in the Korean American community.

The search term "유승준," which is the Korean name of Steve Yoo, was used to retrieve the articles from individual newspapers' search engines on their Korean websites. The website search engine is an appropriate choice as it provides more reliable search results compared to other databases such as Factiva or Google Advanced Search due to the language. Archiving is also part of business for KDLA and KTLA: they have operated subscription-based archive services since 2000 and 2006, respectively; thus, reliability is ensured to a certain extent (Kang and Kim 2011; "History" n.d.). This study drew from news articles published between January 2002, when Yoo's military-dodging scandal was first reported, and March 2020, including the most recent court trial for Yoo's visa application to Korea.

Preliminary coding was based on relevance, news category, and news topic. For relevance, the articles were categorized into Yoo as "a primary focus in relation to the citizenship/military issue," as "a secondary focus in relation to the citizenship/military issue," and as "an artist or individual." For news category, the articles were categorized into "news report," "editorial," and "op-ed." Only "news reports" were included in the final sample in order to focus on news, not individual opinions. News topics were mainly "citizenship issues" (e.g., identity, entry ban, lawsuit, visa application), but they also included Yoo's "professional work" as an artist (e.g., media interviews, concerts, new albums) and his "personal life" as an individual (e.g., social media, family, volunteer work, religious activities). All of these were included in the sample to understand variations in coverage across newspapers. Finally, the ways in which Steve Yoo's name is addressed were coded—whether his Korean name (Yoo Seung Joon or 유승준) or his English name (Steve Seung Joon Yoo or 스티브 승준 유], or both)—since naming is an important indicator of othering.

With this, the final sample is a total of 638 articles: 109 articles in KTKR, 177 articles in KDKR, 228 articles in KTLA, and 124 articles in KDLA. It is important to note that the articles from KTLA and KDLA may not be entirely locally produced in Los Angeles. Previous studies have found that only about 30–40 percent of news articles presented in Korean American media in Los Angeles are locally produced by in-house staff writers, with the rest imported from other sources (including articles with no bylines) (Ling and Song 2016; Yu 2018). The analysis below refers to local production only when there are clear indicators in the byline, such as the reporter's email address and the city.

Findings

From Us to the Other: Steve Yoo in Korean Newspapers

Both KTKR and KDKR started reporting on Yoo's case in January 2002. A majority of articles were directly dedicated to Yoo's citizenship, entry ban, or lawsuits with the government, specifically, naturalization and public reaction. In these articles, Yoo was often described as "popular star Yoo Seung Joon" (KTKR 2002-01-21) or "singer Yoo Seung Joon" (KTKR 2003-06-02). As time passes, Yoo is referred to in relation to his earlier fame, such as "*the* star of the 1990's" (주름잡던 스타) and "once-beloved beautiful young man" (한 때 아름다운 청년) (KDKR 2015-05-21; KTKR 2019-

07-11). The words "shock" (쇼크) (KDKR 2002-01-22) and "criticism" (비난) often appeared to describe the public reaction toward him (KTKR-2003-06-02; KTKR 2005-05-26). The main discourse was that Yoo had promised to fulfill his military duty, and, therefore, his decision to break this promise in order to obtain US citizenship was "betrayal" (배신) of the love of his fans and a "disappointment" (실망) to the Korean public (KTKR 2019-07-11; KDKR 2002-01-22; KDKR 2002-01-31). In these reports, Yoo was mostly referred to as "Yoo Seung Joon" (유승준) instead of his English name. Occasionally, some articles referred to Yoo as a "Korean American gyopo singer" (재미교포 가수) (KDLA 2003-05-30; KDLA 2003-07-28).

After the entry ban in 2002, Korean newspapers occasionally reported on his personal and professional activities. Personal events included Yoo's short visit to Korea for the funeral of his fiancée's father in 2003 (when he was permitted an exception by the government to express his condolences) and his marriage in 2004. Professional activities included his work as an actor and singer in the US and China and his plan to debut in Hollywood. His potential comeback to Korea's entertainment scene was reported negatively. For example, articles published in 2005 reported that Yoo's planned documentary TV show "유승준 99.8: Westside Story" on M.net was cancelled due to the public outcry against him (e.g., KTKR 2005-05-26). In 2006, one article also reported that 60 percent of the respondents in a public opinion poll opposed Yoo's entry to Korea (KDKR 2006-08-25). The rest of the articles published up until 2014 mostly reported Yoo's case in relation to the military issue and the public debates about whether the government's decision on the entry ban was rightful or not. In these reports, Yoo was still referred to by his Korean name (e.g., KDKR 2006-08-25).

Yoo emerged again at the center of public debate in 2014, when a rumor started to spread that he was attempting to reenter Korea. Soon after, he publicly expressed his wish to return to Korea, and thereafter he received more frequent coverage in Korean newspapers. The articles reported on the still negative public opinion toward Yoo (e.g., KDKR 2015-05-20). One particular article depicted Yoo as a "fake man" who only wants to work in Korea as a celebrity but does not wish to fulfill his duty as a Korean (KTKR 2014-01-01). This article seemed to directly question Yoo's authenticity as a Korean and, by doing so, further highlighted his otherness. In May 2015, news articles reported on Yoo's tearful apologies in a self-arranged interview on Afreeca TV, a Korean live video-streaming platform. The articles reported on the confused reaction from the public, pointing out that Yoo's apology and his attempt to regain the public's favor seemed conveniently timed, since he had reached the age of thirty-eight and could therefore be exempted from military duty (e.g., KTKR 2015-05-19). In November 2015, newspapers reported that Yoo had filed a lawsuit against the government on the entry ban, covering every step in the course of his lawsuit. Yet, many articles conveyed suspicion that his intentions were driven not by his longing for Korea but by an attempt at financial gain. These news articles provided detailed information on how the F-4 visa works, allowing overseas Koreans to make income through economic activities in Korea (e.g., KDKR 2018-02-16). Some articles also reported on Yoo's interviews addressing such accusations (KDKR 2019-09-17).

Articles reported that while there were mixed responses from Koreans toward Yoo, negative opinions were more prevalent (e.g., KDKR 2003-06-01). Only a few articles, 5 out of 206, focused on the perspective of Korean Americans, specifically highlighting the complexity of the identity of overseas Koreans. One article, published in 2005, reported that the biggest concerns of the overseas Koreans are military service and identity (KDKR 2005-04-14). Another article published in 2005 questions the distinction between "overseas Koreans" (재외동포) and foreigners (KDKR 2005-05-25). The article also emphasized how little consideration has been given to the complicated identities of overseas Koreans and their transnational experiences.

In most of the articles published between 2014 and 2018, about half referred to Yoo with both his Korean and English names. The aforementioned article that referred to Yoo as a "fake man" mainly used his English name, Steve (스티브) (KTKR 2014-01-01). The emphasis on his English name works to highlight that Yoo is not an *authentic* Korean because he did not perform his duty as a Korean, and is thus the other. Another article also stated that the name "Steve Yoo" had now become more familiar (KTKR 2019-07-11). In more recent articles, Yoo is referred to by both his Korean name and his English name. This change from his Korean name to the dual names (or even his English name only) over the course of time demonstrates the gradual disassociation of Yoo from any connection with Korea in the public discourse.

In general, news articles in both KTKR and KDKR reported on the case of Steve Yoo in relation to his military service. Yoo's citizenship and his transnational, hybrid experiences as a person who was born in Korea but raised in the US were not the focus of most of the news reports. This coverage shows that Korean newspapers largely reported on Yoo's case from the legal perspective of whether a person performed citizenship duty for the nation or not and whether that legal decision is just or not. As a result, Yoo's case was simplified as a choice of a "Korean" man, not a choice of an America-raised Korean man who had to consider multilayered factors and potential consequences that would affect his life in between Korea and America, although it is not to say that this complexity should exempt him from any legal actions against him.

In-Between Hybridity: Steve Yoo in Korean American Newspapers

KTLA and KDLA also closely reported the case of Yoo. In general, their focus was on the legal equity (형평성) of the entry ban, not only from the perspective of Yoo specifically but also from the perspective of Korean Americans broadly; on the importance of understanding the complicated circumstances in which Korean Americans are situated; and on the legal and social consequences they have to consider (KDLA 2002-01-25).

Most articles published after Yoo's entry ban in 2002 focused on the government's decision on Yoo's case. A majority of the articles reported that the decision was based on public opinion rather than consideration of equity in applying the law. Words and phrases such as "emotional" (감정적인), "concerning" (우려), "unjust" (부당), "excessive" (너무해), and "based on the public opinion" (여론 편승) often appeared (e.g., KTLA 2002-02-05; KDLA 2002-02-01). The articles were written based on an understanding of Yoo and his family, sometimes directly quoting the words of Yoo's parents, such as "the government's decision is too harsh" or "Korean media are biased" (KTLA 2002-02-02; KDLA 2002-02-02). The articles also reported on protests organized by the Korean American community in support of Yoo (e.g., KDLA 2002-02-06).

The Korean American newspapers also focused on the impacts that Yoo's case could have on the Korean American community in general. Most articles reported on how the case could lead to animosity from the Korean public at home toward overseas Koreans. One specific article, "Bashing Steve Yoo Spreading Like Wildfire toward Korean Americans" (유승준 때리기 미주한인 "불똥"), reported that the Korean public outcry against Yoo had led to outright hatred against Korean Americans (KDLA 2002-01-23). The article further reported that the Korean public was criticizing Yoo and treating all Korean Americans as betrayers who visit Korea only when they run out of money. Some articles also focused on the laws relevant to Korean American citizens. One article reported on the strengthened military service law, which Korean Americans should be aware of in order to avoid unexpected disadvantages (KTLA 2016-05-20). In these reports, Yoo was referred to as "Yoo Seung Jun" (유승준), his

Korean name. Multiple articles emphasized Yoo's relationship to the Korean American community by referring to him as a "popular singer from LA" (LA출신 유명가수) (KDLA 2002-02-01; KDLA 2002-04-16). One specific article introduced him as an "outstanding star that Korean American society has generated" (미주 한인사회가 배출한 걸출한 스타) (KDLA 2002-02-23).

The rest of the articles published up until 2014 are about Yoo's personal and professional activities. Not only Yoo's personal milestones, such as his marriage, but also his concerts and participation in Korean American community events were closely reported. Surprisingly, a significant number of articles, written by local reporters, were dedicated to promoting Yoo's religious and philanthropic activities in the US and Africa. In these articles, Yoo was also referred to by his Korean name.

In 2015, Korean American newspapers started actively reporting again on Yoo's attempt to reenter Korea. A majority of articles reported on Yoo's lawsuit in relation to the F-4 visa. The articles focused on how negative the Korean public's opinion was toward the visa situation, for example, "As the case of Yoo become rekindled, the Korean society is turning hostile toward the F-4 visa" (KDLA 2019-07-17) and "Korean American society is concerned as the Korean society is forming negative opinions about the visa for overseas Koreans" (KDLA 2019-11-11). The articles also focused on the Korean government's attempt to strengthen the qualification criteria for the F-4 visa and the potential impacts on Korean Americans, as revealed through language such as "Raising the bar for F-4 visa application may violate the right of 1.5 or 2nd generation overseas Koreans" (KDLA 2019-07-24). Since 2015, most Korean American newspaper articles have included Yoo's English name as well as his Korean name. Both Korean and Korean American newspapers switched from addressing Yoo by his Korean name to his dual name, but there is a difference of emphasis. Korean American newspapers emphasized Yoo's in-between hybridity while Korean newspapers emphasized Yoo as the other and his subsequent disassociation from Korea.

In general, Korean American newspapers were relatively more understanding of Yoo's case and reported with consideration for the complexity of the lives of overseas Koreans. Some articles that discussed Yoo as a secondary focus in relation to the citizenship issue reported on the sorrow Korean Americans have toward the Korean government (KDLA 2019-07-14). For example, according to the article "Are We Sinners for Living in America?" (미국산다고 우리가 죄인인가요?): "If Korean Americans are successful, they are considered as *Koreans*, and when they fail, they become *American*" (성공하면 한국인 [Korean], 실패하면 현지인 [American]) (KDLA 2020-01-14). Another article criticized the ironic situation that Korean Americans cannot freely enter Korea for fear of military enlistment (KDLA 2019-04-08). In other articles, the distinction between 1.5-generation Korean Americans, who were born in Korea but raised in the US, and second-generation Korean Americans, who were born and raised in the US, was emphasized to disassociate Yoo's case from the latter. One article reported on the opinion of Korean Americans that differentiated Yoo's case from the case of Major League Baseball player Shin-Soo Choo (of the Texas Rangers), whose two US-born sons renounced their Korean citizenship (KDLA 2019-08-06). The article delivered the sense of outrage that the Korean American community felt about Choo's sons being blamed for exercising their rights and being treated as criminals, when Yoo's and Choo's cases were clearly different, that is, cases of 1.5 generation versus second generation, respectively.

Discussion and Conclusion

Citizenship represents various aspects of an individual. Volpp (2007) explains citizenship of Asian Americans in terms of legal status, rights, political activity, and identity, as well as how the racialized debates around their incapability to engage in citizenry activities delayed the installment of citizenship for them in the US. The case of Yoo is not about racialization, but many of these aspects of citizenship do apply. His decision to choose US citizenship over Korean citizenship brought about repercussions he did not anticipate, not only as an individual but also as an artist at the peak of his career. Interestingly, Yoo's case is more about duty than rights and focuses on economic rather than political activity.

The fulfillment of military duty is seen as making male Korean citizens truly *Korean*, whereas not doing so can make them the *other* regardless of legal legitimacy or citizenship status. The discourse of betrayal prevailed in the Korean newspapers: Korean Americans are one of *us* when they are *Korean*, but they immediately become *them* when their *other* affiliation gives them options (e.g., citizenship, military service) that Korean natives do not have. What is missing in the discussion is that the citizenship and military service laws have changed since the start of Yoo's case. For example, in 2004, the government introduced a special military program for people with permanent residency outside of Korea so that they can protect their permanent resident status and also be supported with benefits such as free flights to their country of residence (Han 2010). The introduction of this program has significantly increased the number of military service applications from overseas permanent residents, a growth of more than 30 percent annually (C. Kim 2019). The age for military service exemption was also increased in 2005, from thirty-six to thirty-eight years old, although how this works for Korean Americans can be subjective (H. Jang 2019). These changes may not be unrelated to Yoo, but these options were not available in 2002 when Yoo had to forgo his Korean citizenship and obtain US citizenship.

In contrast, the Korean American discourse reveals an emphasis on the complexity associated with hybrid identity as a Korean American—which was rarely discussed in the Korean newspapers, although not absent. The stories were narrated from the perspectives of Yoo or Korean Americans in general rather than from the viewpoint of the Korean public. The stories also focused on the broader implications of Yoo's case for Korean Americans, specifically, how the changes in the citizenship and military service laws and the subsequent inconveniences may affect the lives of Korean Americans. A mix of love and hatred (or understanding and blame) toward Yoo seems to coexist here. While there was empathy toward Yoo as a Korean American in general, the heterogeneity or varying levels of hybridity within the Korean community were overtly emphasized, that is, the difference between 1.5 and second generations. Essentially, Yoo was a 1.5-generation Korean American, not a second-generation one, and a US permanent resident, not a US citizen. Therefore, his case is not at all representative of all younger-generation Korean Americans. The discussion in Korean American newspapers focused on how the changed laws should be applied differently—which is again another layer of discussion unseen in the Korean newspapers.

The comparison of the Korean and the Korean American discourses around the case of Yoo both challenges and confirms the notion of the other. The findings challenge the conventional understanding of the other. Immigrants or ethnic minorities in the "white world" (in the words of Frantz Fanon) have been othered through the exclusionary immigration laws and the reinforcement of constructed inferiority in media representations. They came to the White world "too late" and therefore can never win. This argument of injustice implies to a certain extent that minorities are not subject to othering in their own homeland. The case of Yoo, however, demonstrates that the opposite is possible—although not at the fault of the majority but still with less consideration of the complexity of in-between lives. It is important to note, however, that if Korean Americans are *perpetually* or *non-negotiably* other in the White world regardless of their birthplace, they are othered in the homeland when duties that are mandatory for Koreans become optional for Korean Americans. In other words, othering is contextual rather than perpetual.

Simultaneously, the case of Yoo also confirms the notion of the other in that hybridity is a source of othering wherever Korean Americans exist. Hybridity is considered as difference, thus a problem despite its potential benefits. This perspective corresponds to the mixed public perceptions toward Korean Americans in Korea, in that Yoo is *one of us* because he is ethnically Korean but he is immediately *them* if he does not fulfill *our* duty. The only place where hybridity is accepted and understood is Korean American media, or what Homi Bhabha termed the Third Space, where the resistance of othering and the representation of the Korean American community emerge, even if a mix of love and hatred may also exist. The narratives from the perspectives of Korean Americans in general and Yoo in particular emerge mostly here. The narratives of hybridity (and the degree of hybridity) also emerge here. In this sense, the significance of diasporic media as a space for countering or negotiating othering is confirmed yet again, but this time not only in the White world but also in the homeland, a new finding realized through this study.

NOTE

1 Note that this paper does not take a stance on the decision of the Korean government or the legal matters surrounding the case of Yoo.

REFERENCES

Allen, Mike. 2017. *The Sage Encyclopedia of Communication Research Methods*. Thousand Oaks, CA: Sage.
Bhabha, Homi K. 1994. *The Location of Culture*. London: Routledge.
Bhabha, Homi K. 1996. "Culture's In-Between." In *Questions of Cultural Identity*, edited by Stuart Hall and Paul Du Gay. London: Sage.
"Brief Introduction of Korean Nationality Laws." 2018. Consulate General of the Republic of Korea in Houston, June 30. http://overseas.mofa.go.kr/us-houston-en/brd/m_5578/view.do?seq=746000
Cho, Jin-hyung. 2017. "Fighting to Be Able to Return Home: After Enlistment Scandal, Steve Yoo Is Battling to Come Back to Korea." *Korea JoongAng Daily*, February 12. https://koreajoongangdaily.joins.com/2017/02/12/etc/Fighting-to-be-able-to-return-home-After-enlistment-scandal-Steve-Yoo-is-battling-to-come-back-to-Korea/3029767.html
Cho, John. 2012. "Global Fatigue: Transnational Markets, Linguistic Capital, and

Korean-American Male English Teachers in South Korea." *Journal of Sociolinguistics* 16 (2): 218–37.
Choi, Si-young. 2019. "[News Focus] Will K-Pop Singer Steve Yoo Be Allowed into South Korea?" *Korea Herald*, November 13. http://www.koreaherald.com/view.php?ud=20191113000780
Fleras, Augie. 2009. "Theorizing Multicultural Media as Social Capital: Crossing Borders, Constructing Buffers, Creating Bonds, Building Bridges." *Canadian Journal of Communication* 34 (4): 725–29. https://doi.org/10.22230/cjc.2009v34n4a2296
Hall, Stuart. 2001. "The Spectacle of the 'Other'." In *Discourse Theory and Practice: A Reader*, edited by Margaret Wetherell, Stephanie Taylor, and Simeon J. Yates, 324–44. London: Sage.
Hamamoto, Darrell Y. 1994. *Monitored Peril: Asian Americans and the Politics of TV Representation*. Minneapolis: University of Minnesota Press.
Han, Jane. 2010. "Korean Army Tries to Entice US Green Card Holders." *Korea Times*, May 23. http://www.koreatimes.co.kr/www/news/nation/2013/08/117_66355.html
Han, Jane. 2012. "Reverse Immigration from US Rising." *Korea Times*, May 20. http://www.koreatimes.co.kr/www/nation/2020/02/182_111361.html
Harinen, Päivi. 2001. "Young Dual Citizens—People of 'the Third Space'?" *Young* 9 (3): 29–42.
"History." n.d. *Korea Times*. Accessed June 17, 2020. http://service.koreatimes.com/info/history.html
James, Alvin. 2000. "Demographic Shifts and the Challenge for Planners: Insights from a Practitioner." In *Urban Planning in a Multicultural Society*, edited by Michael A. Burayidi, 15–35. Westport, CT: Praeger.
Jang, Dongwoo. 2017. "2PM's Ok Taecyeon Begins Mandatory Military Duty." *Yonhap News Agency*, September 4. https://en.yna.co.kr/view/AEN20170904006700315
Jang, Hyukjin. 2019. "Yu-seung-jun, han-gug ol su iss-eul-kka?tss-4-5-se-kka-ji che-lyu mag-neun t-yu-seung-jun-beob-t chu-jin" [Yoo Seung Joon, can we come back to Korea? . . . Introduction of the "Steve Yoo" law that prohibits entry until the age of 45]. *KBS News*, July 22. http://news.kbs.co.kr/news/view.do?ncd=4247145
Jun, Jihhye. 2020. "'Young People Enraged by Choo Mi-ae, Cho Kuk, Not Me.'" *Korea Times*, December 20. https://www.koreatimes.co.kr/www/nation/2020/12/113_301154.html
"JMnet USA, the Largest Korean Media Group in the US." n.d. JMnet USA. Accessed June 17, 2020. http://corp.koreadaily.com/eng/about/index.html
Kim, Chulsoo. 2019. "Yeongjugwonja hangukgun ipdae 800 myeong dalhaldeun" [Almost 800 foreign permanent residents joining Korean military]. *Korea Times L.A.*, July 6. http://www.koreatimes.com/article/1256675
Kim, Gayeon. 2019. "[Jeon-mun] yeong-won-han t-a-leum-da-un cheong-nyeon-t yu-seung-jun bog-gwi hui-mang-han-da" [Forever "beautiful young man" wishes to come back]. *Asia Business Daily*, July 11. https://www.asiae.co.kr/article/2019071115425241224
Kim, Hyun-bin. 2019. "Ruling Opens Chance for Ostracized K-Pop Singer to Enter Korea after 17 Years." *Korea Times*, November 15. http://www.koreatimes.co.kr/www/nation/2020/06/251_278803.html
Kim, Ji young. 2002. "Gun-dae ga-gess-da-deon yu-seung-jun dd-si-min-gwon chwi-deug balg-hyeo-jyeo" [Yoo Seung Joon, who said he would go to the military,

revealed to achieve American citizenship]. *Korea Times*, January 21. https://www.hankookilbo.com/News/Read/200201210066168577

Kim, L. S. 2004. "Be the One That You Want: Asian Americans in Television Culture, Onscreen and Beyond." *Amerasia Journal* 30 (1): 125–46. https://doi.org/10.17953/amer.30.1.356381678qj14622

Kim, Young Yun. 2000. *Becoming Intercultural: An Integrative Theory of Communication and Cross-Cultural Adaptation.* Thousand Oaks, CA: Sage.

"The Korea Times." n.d. *Korea Times.* Accessed June 17, 2020. http://service.koreatimes.com/info/about.html

Kraidy, Marwan. 2006. *Hybridity, or the Cultural Logic of Globalization.* Philadelphia: Temple University Press. https://library.oapen.org/handle/20.500.12657/31581

Kwak, Yeon-soo. 2019. "Former K-Pop Star's Return Sparks Controversy." *Korea Times*, January 20. http://www.koreatimes.co.kr/www/art/2020/06/732_262342.html

Kwon, Insook. 2005. "Hegemonic Masculinity and Conscription: Focusing on the Masculinity of KATUSA." *Journal of Korean Women's Studies* 21 (2): 223–53.

Kwon, Jen. 2019. "South Korean Boy Band BTS Won't Get a Pass on Mandatory Military Service." *CBS News*, November 22. https://www.cbsnews.com/news/bts-must-serve-south-korean-military-starting-next-year-defense-ministry-rules-today-2019-11-22/

Lee, Claire. 2010. "MC Mong Charged with Dodging Military Duty." *Korea Herald*, September 13. http://www.koreaherald.com/view.php?ud=20100912000296

Lee, Claire. 2019. "Exiled K-Pop Star May Finally Return to Korea after 17 Years." *Breaking Asia*, November 15. https://www.breakingasia.com/news/exiled-k-pop-star-may-finally-return-to-korea-after-17-years

Lee, Jae-lim. 2020. "Court Rules in Favor of Steve Yoo: Singer Wins Lawsuit against the Consulate That Denied Him a Visa." *Korea JoongAng Daily*, March 15. https://koreajoongangdaily.joins.com/2020/03/15/etc/Court-rules-in-favor-of-Steve-Yoo-Singer-wins-lawsuit-against-the-consulate-that-denied-him-a-visa/3074934.html

Lee, Seung-Sun. 2004. "A Study on the Characteristics of Celebrity Entertainers as 'Public Figures' in the Defamation Lawsuits." *Korean Journal of Broadcasting and Telecommunication Studies* 18 (3): 293–334.

Lee, Yeon Woo. 2013. "Jurisprudential Review of Management System of Persons Residing abroad with Military Service Obligation." *Chungnam Law Review* 24 (1): 79–115.

Lin, Wan-Ying, and Hayeon Song. 2006. "Geo-Ethnic Storytelling: An Examination of Ethnic Media Content in Contemporary Immigrant Communities." *Journalism* 7 (3): 362–88. https://doi.org/10.1177/1464884906065518

Matsaganis, Matthew D., Vikki S. Katz, and Sandra J. Ball-Rokeach. 2011. *Understanding Ethnic Media: Producers, Consumers, and Societies.* Thousand Oaks, CA: Sage.

McCurry, Justin. 2019. "BTS K-Pop Band Members Must Do Military Service, South Korea Says." *The Guardian*, November 22. https://www.theguardian.com/world/2019/nov/22/bts-k-pop-band-members-must-do-military-service-south-korea-says

Military Manpower Administration. 2017. "Yeong-ju-gwon-ja si-min-gwon-ja heo-ga—gug-oe-i-ju heo-ga—gug-oe-yeo-haeng, gug-oe-che-jae—byeong-yeog-i-haeng-an-nae" [Guide for military service for foreign citizens and permanent residents]. Military Manpower Administration. https://www.mma.go.kr/contents.do?mc=mma0000801

Min, Pyong Gap. 2006. *Asian Americans: Contemporary Trends and Issues.* Thousand Oaks, CA: Pine Forge Press.

Ock, Hyun-ju. 2019. "[Newsmaker] Entry Ban on Koran American Singer Illegal: Top Court." *Korea Herald*, July 11. http://www.koreaherald.com/view.php?ud=20190711 000617

O'Connor, Allison, and Jeanne Batalova. 2019. "Korean Immigrants in the United States in 2017." *Migration Policy*, April 8. https://www.migrationpolicy.org/article/korean-immigrants-united-states-2017

Oh, Chuyun. 2014. "Performing Post-Racial Asianness: K-Pop's Appropriation of Hip-Hop Culture." *Congress on Research in Dance Conference Proceedings* 2014:121–25. https://doi.org/10.1017/cor.2014.17

Oh, David C. 2017. "K-Pop Fans React: Hybridity and the White Celebrity-Fan on YouTube." *International Journal of Communication* 11:2270–87.

Oh, David C. 2018. "Seeing Myself through Film: Diasporic Belongings and Racial Identifications." *Cultural Studies↔Critical Methodologies* 18 (2): 107–15.

Park, Christian J. 2019. "Ethnic Return Migration of Miguk Hanin (Korean Americans): Entanglement of Diaspora and Transnationalism." In *Diasporic Returns to the Ethnic Homeland: The Korean Diaspora in Comparative Perspective*, edited by Takeyuki Tsuda and Changzoo Song, 121–42. Cham: Springer.

Park, Hyun young. 2002. "'Gun-dae gan-da-deo-ni-tss bae-sin-tss-t' yu-seung-jun syokeu" [After he said to go to the military . . . betrayal . . . "Yoo Seung Joon Shock"]. *JoongAng Ilbo*, January 22. https://news.joins.com/article/4213317

Shim, Jaegul. 2015. "Yu-seung-jun, 3gyae mi-seu-teo-li nun-mul-lo hae-myeong" [Yoo Seung Joon explains his three controversies in his tearful interview]. *Korea Times*, May 20. https://www.hankookilbo.com/News/Read/201505200022601750

Son, Hyun Sung. 2016. "Beobwon tyuseungjun, ipgung geumji jeongdang" [Court, "Yoo Seung Joon's entry ban was just"]. *Korea Times*, September 30. https://www.hankookilbo.com/News/Read/201609301530509304

Umeda, Sayuri. 2010. "South Korea: Permanent Dual Nationality Allowed after 60 Years | Global Legal Monitor." Library of Congress, August 24. https://www.loc.gov/law/foreign-news/article/south-korea-permanent-dual-nationality-allowed-after-60-years/

"Visa Categories." 2016. Embassy of the Republic of Korea to Canada. December 29. http://overseas.mofa.go.kr/ca-en/brd/m_5238/view.do?seq=727441&srchFr=&srchTo=&srchWord=&srchTp=&multi_itm_seq=0&itm_seq_1=0&itm_seq_2=0&company_cd=&company_nm=

Volpp, Leti. 2007. "'Obnoxious to Their Very Nature': Asian Americans and Constitutional citizenship." In *Contemporary Asian America: A Multidisciplinary Reader*, 2nd ed., edited by Min Zhou and J.V. Gatewood, 526–41. New York: New York University Press.

Waldinger, Roger, and Mehdi Bozorgmehr. 1996. "The Making of a Multicultural Metropolis." In *Ethnic Los Angeles*, edited by Roger Waldinger and Mehdi Bozorgmehr, 3–37. New York: Russell Sage Foundation.

Wing, Jean Yonemura. 2007. "Beyond Black and White: The Model Minority Myth and the Invisibility of Asian American Students." *Urban Review* 39 (4): 455–87. https://doi.org/10.1007/s11256-007-0058-6

"Yoo Seung Jun—Steve." n.d. JpopAsia. Accessed June 17, 2020. https://www.jpopasia.com/yooseungjun/

Yu, Seong-un, and Min-gwan Kim. 2015. "Army Duty Can Make or Break a Star's Reputation." *Korea JoongAng Daily*, June 7. https://koreajoongangdaily.joins.com/2015/06/07/features/Army-duty-can-make-or-break-a-stars-reputation/3005086.html

Yu, Sherry S. 2017. "Ethnic Media as Communities of Practice: The Cultural and Institutional Identities." *Journalism* 18 (10): 1309–26.

Yu, Sherry S. 2018. *Diasporic Media beyond the Diaspora: Korean Media in Vancouver and Los Angeles*. Vancouver: UBC Press.

Conclusion

David C. Oh

The purpose of the book has been to understand the ways South Korean media represent otherness and to elaborate upon the concept of anthrocategorism. To summarize briefly, I argued in the introduction that Koreans use the term *injongchabyeol* to discursively name ethnic, racial, national, and regional discrimination. Though this is often translated to racism because of the affective power of the term to describe unjustifiable and immoral treatment of others, the word is imprecise. As I mentioned earlier, using *injongchabyeol* as an indigenous term, which I translate with a neologism, anthrocategorism, not only is more precise but also decenters Western frameworks when describing spaces outside the West. Continuing to use terms such as "racism" to refer to othering in Korea unintentionally implies that Western frameworks of race are universal, natural, or most obvious. Relying exclusively on Western concepts and theories does not capture accurately what is happening. It is in some ways like the translation loss that happens when language is converted from one context to another (Sorby 2008), except that this is not a linguistic but a social mistranslation and application. Such as it is, new language is necessary to more accurately capture Korea's discursive terrain around difference. Following a decolonial impulse to privilege indigenous meaning-making practices, anthrocategorism is simply a translation to describe an existing local concept.

There are at least two critical concerns that should be addressed by introducing this term as an alternative to racism in understanding the mediated construction of otherness in Korea. First, one value of using "racism" is that there are few words with the counter-hegemonic, affective power of racism to challenge systems of domination. This concern is valid and important. My hope, then, is not to obscure the counter-hegemonic strength of naming racism as a cause for oppression but to argue that this same affective charge should and can be applied to different constructs. To do this is not an easy project, but it is a necessary one to argue that there are local harms that are comparable to the severity of Western-based racism but that the targets of oppression and the beneficiaries of the system differ.

Second, it might be easy to read an assertion of anthrocategorism as dismissive of racism. It is important to be very clear on this point. Arguing that the driving logic of othering in Korea is anthrocategorism does not invalidate concerns about racism because both coexist. In other words, racism constitutes part of the ways in which Korea/ns understand difference, particularly beyond the region. Anti-Black racism and the ambivalent endorsement of White supremacy exist in South Korea. Racism is not, however, a totalizing system as it is in the West, and anthrocategorism's articulations differ as well. What I mean, and which is articulated in these chapters, is that anthrocategorism consists of co-ethnic othering, racial othering, ethnic othering, othering based on different global regions, and othering based on national development. Anthrocategorism in Korea is an amalgam of all of these otherings simultaneously. As an example, Black Africans are treated differently than Black Americans, who are treated differently than mixed-race Black Koreans (Nadia Kim 2014). Though they might be read similarly in terms of race, they are read differently in terms of the national power of their countries of origin, imagined constructions of different regions, and, for mixed-race Black Koreans, co-ethnic stigma. White Eastern Europeans benefit from Whiteness but also are sometimes thought of as criminals and prostitutes because of their association with non-industrialized countries. The question "Are you Russian?" when asked to a White woman is not an innocent question, but, instead, it acts as code for whether the woman is a sex worker. Given Korea's own history of US military camptowns (Gage 2014; K. Moon 1997; S. Moon 2010), sex work, particularly cross-racial or cross-ethnic sex work, suggests hierarchies of power in which Korean men reassert masculinization by becoming the consumer of global power/sexual inequalities. *Joseonjok* are the othered group perhaps most associated with criminality, despite sharing racial and ethnic similarity with Koreans (Yang 2010; Yi and Jung 2015). As such, they are viewed as being corrupted by their diasporic lived experience abroad, while Korean Americans are more able to convert their diasporic identities into cultural capital (though this is contingent and liminal).

It is likely that anthrocategorism works in other societies as well. For instance, though the US tends to dissolve White ethnic difference into racial similarity, this is less true in Europe, where national and regional distinctions, for example, Southern Europe, Western Europe, and Eastern Europe, are more visible. This is despite the fact that Eurocentrism and White supremacy operate as a guiding logic and legacy of colonialism (Pieterse 1992; Shohat and Stam 1994). That said, national and regional differences are subsumed under racial difference when people of color rise in sufficient numbers that they become seen as a threat, as witnessed in the increased support for far-right, anti-immigrant discourse in Europe (Siapera 2019). Systemic racism, then, is the prevailing logic of difference. Anthrocategorism works differently in South Korea. As a non-White nation, it is not a direct beneficiary of White supremacy and racism as a system, so its investments in it are tenuous. To make this case, I draw a contrast with White supremacy to argue further that race is not the guiding logic of difference and to point to its different, more complex constructions of difference and desirability.

Colonial-era iterations of White supremacy functioned by assuming the biological and cultural superiority of White people (Shohat and Stam 1994; Pieterse 1992). White people were encouraged to identify with Europe as a racial project and to think of themselves as belonging to the apex of civilization, while the rest of the world was constructed as primitive, drawing particular contrast with Africa (Shohat and Stam 1994). While there were some contradictions and romanticized colonial fantasies about the mythical and "natural" essence of colonized people and the "simplicity" of non-industrialized life, this idea relies on the troubling notion that people of color have inferior intellects and morality. In contemporary discourse, notions of biological inferiority are largely abandoned except by those who assert overt racist bigotry (Prashad 2001). Instead, White supremacy asserts cultural racism (Jhally and Lewis 1992), mutating the biological claims of overt racism to assert that global inequalities between regions and societies as well as domestic and racial inequalities are because of *cultural* deficiencies (Bloch 2014). This allows (White) people to understand themselves as non-racist because they disavow biological racism while ostensibly believing any person or people group is capable of better outcomes while still holding onto beliefs about White supremacy. Thus, the causes of racial domination shift from biology to the cultures of the oppressed (Bonilla-Silva 2010). The non-recognition of systemic racism is strengthened by liberal claims of colorblindness, which hides racism's impacts, as racism and even race as a social construct are ignored as insignificant (Bonilla-Silva 2010; Watts 2017; Parameswaran 2009; Herakova et al. 2011; Cisneros and Nakayama 2015).[1]

Regardless of the form White supremacy takes, the contradictions and complexities of its hegemonic practice and the ideological cover that is used to conceal its function, it operates on a fairly simple logic: White is superior and normal. In this system, race is the prevailing way in which human difference is understood, even as people paradoxically argue for its insignificance. Ethnic differences are ignored and reduced to race. It is why Palumbo-Liu (1999) advanced the discursive construction of "Asian/American" to point to the ways in which ethnic difference and national similarity are ignored as Asian Americans—regardless of citizenship, family immigration history, cultural knowledge, and ethnic difference—are undifferentiated not only between one another in the US but also from Asians across the Pacific. Race is overdetermined, then, as a way of seeing difference.

Korean articulations of anthrocategorism are more complicated in two ways. First, Koreanness is not seen as the superior pole by which all other groups are judged as wanting, yet it is understood as what constitutes normality in the discursive terrain. White supremacy, in contrast, views itself in a bipolar hierarchy as superior and normal; a lack of one results in a lack in the other. Second, categorizing difference is based on multiple categories that have come together through Korea's distinctive experience with powerful neighbors, its postcolonial relationship to Japan, its neocolonial relationship to the US, and, less directly but still significantly, its neocolonial relationship to the West. Unlike in the US, where popular discourse obscures hierarchies to argue for meritocracy, there is a propensity in Korea to make hierarchies explicit. This is, for example, embedded in language with the use of different speech levels and complicated honorifics, and it is embedded in everyday life through class and university rankings and informally through the use of language such as the suffix *~jjang* (짱) in *eoljjang* (most beautiful face) and *momjjang* (best body). Of course, this hierarchization is not unique to Korea, but there is a fervor for it that is recognizable. It should, then, not be remarkable that this ranking has also extended to the categorization of people groups. Based on the chapters in this book and on available literature about the popular, discursive terrain, a pattern emerges that pulls together Korea's complicated relations with other major powers.

Before describing this hierarchization of people and its interactions with notions of normality, it is important to first mark another contrast with White supremacy. Unlike Whiteness, which is often rendered invisible through its construction as an identity formed in opposition to others (Nakayama and Krizek 1995; Oh 2012; Supriya 1999; Dyer 1997), Koreanness is made explicit. It is seen in the discursive habits of everyday Koreans as they/we refer to "our country" and "our language" in lieu of the names of the country or language and in frequent references to what Koreans believe. For the outsider and perhaps for the non-normative insider, it can feel like self-generalization, which disciplines deviance from these standards. So, it seems necessary to ask why people would self-generalize or essentialize themselves in this way. Invisibility is a form of hegemonic power. What is left unsaid is usually understood as the norm, and what is discursively marked is usually considered abnormal, for example, male figure skater, Korean American politician, woman president. This is true for Whiteness, too, as an unmarked category of difference, making it a slipperier target for resistance. It makes it difficult to advance anti-racist criticism when race itself is argued to be insignificant (Bonilla-Silva 2010). Indeed, Whiteness only names itself in moments of crisis (Artz and Murphy 2000; Lipsitz 1998). So, why would Koreans not also advance a similar strategy of ethnonational hegemony? One popular theory among some foreign residents is that it is akin to the explicit bigotry of White supremacy. I do not find that this is a satisfactory answer, however, because Koreanness is not constructed as the most superior. I contend that it is because of "defensive nationalism" that was mobilized during its history as a colonized state. One tactic of resistance was to declare itself different from Japan, and this meant marking Koreanness in explicit ways (Em 2013; Shin 2006; Cho 1998; Lie 2014; Nora Kim 2014; H. Kim 2006). This was especially necessary as Japan attempted to justify its hegemonic control by constructing Koreans as its subjects (Em 2013). As a postcolonial legacy, Koreanness, what it is and who belongs to it, is explicitly constructed, and its boundaries are regulated. This matters because it shapes how others are defined against this explicit norm and how Koreans view themselves in hierarchies of difference.

In the cultural mapping of anthrocategorism, I argue that there is a hierarchical ranking, marked in the figure by the vertical arrow, but that this intersects with concentric circles that indicate belonging and normality within the nation-state. This has some resonances to the Confucian Sino-centric understanding of the world (Tikhonov 2013), as well as to Japan's notion of citizenship, which is also constructed in concentric circles of belonging—Japan proper, *naichijin* (internal colonized people), and overseas colonized people (Tai 2004). Whether the reasons are because of the adoption of Confucian scholarly learning, internalized postcolonial frameworks, indigenous meaning making, or some combination of them, it is apparent that distance from imagined Koreanness that is explicitly negotiated in the cultural terrain constitutes degrees of foreignness and abjection.

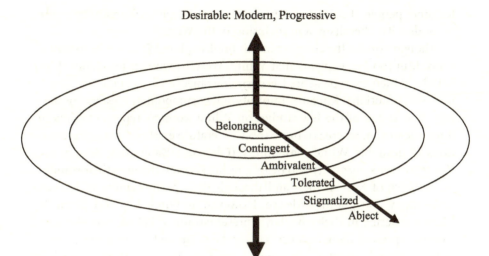

Fig. 1. Cultural logics of anthrocategorism

For instance, atop this hierarchy are (White) Americans and the (White) West. Because of its liberation of Korea from the brutality of Japanese colonial rule and its intervention against North Korea, the US is respected and admired as a powerful, advanced nation, even though there is some resentment for its treatment of the nation as an inferior partner. As Shome (1999) writes, Orientalism gets internalized by the colonized. While she is writing about the postcolonial condition, this is likely to be true for the neocolonial condition as well. Desire for the US, as a neocolonial presence in Korea (Höhn and Moon 2010), is internalized, and because of slippages between race, ethnicity, and nation in the local imagination, the US as the leading Western nation is imagined as a White nation (Nadia Kim 2006, 2014). Arguably, these slippages happen because (post)colonial articulations of *minjung* and the myth of ethnic homogeneity conflated nation and ethnicity; thus, in a predominantly homogeneous society, at least imagined as such, there are fewer reasons to make these distinctions. However, despite Western bodies signifying modernity and progress, they also signify difference. For instance, elsewhere, I argue that television shows like *Non Summit* construct White Westerners as a super-minority (Oh 2020). What this means is that while White people are presented as desirable, they are valued for their exotic difference. In other words, they are not super-Koreans; however, they are "super" because, unlike the model minority in the US, which acts as a disciplining object for other people of color, the super-minority disciplines Koreans to aspire to modernity, liberalism, and inclusion in the West.

Though none of the chapters in this book explore White US representations, Min Joo Lee explains that White, Western women in relationships with local men are represented as desirable objects, who paradoxically signify both traditional Korean femininity and cosmopolitan Western modernity. This is one of the few studies on White women's representations in domestic media, whereas a more robust literature exists on the representations of desirable White masculinity (Oh 2020; Kang 2018; Ahn 2015). White women's normality and belonging are secured through their romantic embrace of Korean men and through their performances of Korean authenticity and gratitude/desire. However, as Eunbi Lee and Colby Y. Miyose describe in their chapter, representations of White, non-Western women represent them as objects of sexual desire but without the cosmopolitan cultural capital of White people from the West. So, White desirability is moderated by its connection to Western nations' self-construction as bastions of high culture. Regional differences (e.g., Eastern Europe, the West) and the power of their countries of origin are configured into notions of desirability and belonging, and it is not reduced merely to race.

Although the elevation of Whiteness seems like a simple internalization of White supremacy, it is not as straightforward as it appears. First, I read Korea's affinity toward the US as linked to its compressed capitalism/modernity as it looked for models by which to judge its development and as a means of erasing its postcolonial ambivalence. The import bans on Japanese popular culture and the restrictions on the use of Japanese language were attempts to symbolically erase the legacies of its colonized condition. "To the intellectuals, Korean had been polluted by Japanese during the colonial period, and it was urgent to cleanse it of the impurities left by the occupiers" (Suh 2013, 147). An absence creates a vacuum by which that ideological void must be filled with something else. With the US's immediate neocolonial imprint and the existing Western racial discourses that had penetrated the peninsula in the late nineteenth century, the ideological shift was convenient. Thus, White supremacy has been internalized as a way of stamping out Korea's postcolonial relationship to Japan. So, in this way, White supremacy has been objectified to serve local purposes. Though the internalization of White supremacy causes harm, it also means that the investments in White supremacy are contingent upon its perceived meaning and value to Koreans. Thus, this is not, then, equivalent to the "possessive investments" in White supremacy as seen in the West (Lipsitz 1998).

It is for this reason that at the bottom of the hierarchy, there is not a simple replication of White supremacy's anti-Blackness. Instead, anti-Blackness is constitutive of a group of less desirable and undesirable others along with immigrant men from South Asia and Southeast Asia and *Joseonjok* (ethnic Koreans from China). It is in this category of the (un)tolerated minority that these complications become more exposed. The hierarchical mapping as well as the distance from the center is not based simply on race or ethnicity. Ethnic Koreans from China, and to a lesser extent from the former Soviet Bloc, are an oppressed minority despite sharing ethnic heritage ties and, of course, racial similarity (Seol and Seo 2014; Yang 2010; Yi and Jung 2015). Southeast Asian men, who primarily immigrate as economic migrants, are treated as a necessary but undesirable presence, despite their racial similarity (Nadia Kim 2014; Seol and Seo 2014; Lim 2014). In media representations, they are frequently depicted as a threat (Cha, Lee, and Park 2016; Jirn 2014). In the case of Koreans from former and current Communist nations, they are disadvantaged because of generalized beliefs about national development and, perhaps, the remnants of a Cold War logic. As such, *Joseonjok* are viewed as contaminated, despite their ethnic similarity, by the poverty and diminished status in their Communist home countries, and they are often represented as a criminal presence. Thus, abjection and undesirability are not reducible to race, which means that descriptions of discrimination are better understood through an anthrocategorism framework.

For Southeast Asian men, they are placed under restrictive conditions to discourage long-term stay. Though they share racial similarity with Koreans, there has not been a continental, racializing project in Asia as there was in Europe in which Europeans were encouraged to see themselves as belonging not only to their countries of origin but to the continent (Shohat and Stam 1994). Interestingly, Japan attempted to do the same to hegemonically justify colonialism (Fujitani 2011), but it did not take hold because, unlike Europe, which sought to dominate faraway, racially different others outside the continent in a shared, albeit competitive, colonial purpose, Japan sought to dominate and colonize other Asian nations (Tikhonov 2013). The point here is that racial similarity does not generate a sense of shared identity. Instead, regional differences are constructed in Asia. The Japanese and Chinese, though historical rivals, are represented as sharing affinities, while Southeast Asia is imagined as a regionally and culturally different other. That is, multiple cultural logics intermingle to construct notions of who is tolerated but undesirable—the anti-Blackness of White supremacy; the developmental hierarchies of neocolonial arrangements; anti-Communism within the diaspora; and the regional construction of human difference, such as Southeast Asia, the Middle East, Africa, Eastern and Western Europe, and North and Latin America. Othering cannot be reduced to racism, ethnocentrism, neo-nationalism, or to geopolitical power (by nation or region), and it is not simply hierarchical. Anthrocategorism combines all of these, complicating it not by conflating superiority with normality but by understanding these as separate dimensions.

In this book, Benjamin Han and Ji-Hyun Ahn both explore the conditional acceptance that is provided to those who are the most othered—hierarchy and distance from the center. Han's work on Sam Okyere and Han Hyun-min demonstrates that there is mediated acceptance of Black people in what he refers to as "strategic blackness," a representational move that allows the nation to claim that it is a cosmopolitan, progressive, and modern society. However, to be accepted requires overdetermined performances of Korean authenticity and belonging. Okyere's recent turn from the "most famous Black man in Korea" (a common moniker) to a controversial figure demonstrates his conditional popularity. After posting on Instagram his criticism of high school students whom he perceived as performing blackface, Okyere faced considerable backlash for shaming the students publicly and for what was argued to be his flaws, including anti-Asian racism. His popularity, though not yet resolved, was in jeopardy when he was perceived as overstepping, thereby not expressing sufficient gratitude for the fame and wealth he had gained. In Ahn's chapter, she, too, argues that the success of Baek Cheonggang, a *Joseonjok* performer, on a music competition program and his precipitous loss of popularity after the show ended are indicative of viewers' acceptance because his brief success flattered Korea/ns for providing the Korean Dream. Just as the US has figured prominently as a place for enterprising migrants to achieve the American Dream, for Korea to have become a receiving nation that provides socioeconomic mobility is understood as a sign of the nation's development (Oh and Oh 2016; Ahn 2014). In other words, Baek was elevated momentarily to hegemonically demonstrate Korea's place in the world.

The conditional nature of acceptance of the other points to their exceptional difference. That is, it implies that most Black Africans, Joseonjok, Southeast Asians, and mixed-race Black Koreans, especially with GI fathers, are not like these exceptional celebrities. It has resonances to the way the American Dream functions to argue that racism is unmeaningful to life outcomes; it blames the other rather than address systemic racism

(Cloud 1996). Where the Korean case differs is that abjection is not reducible to race and there is not the same dominant cultural belief in individualism. In anecdotal observations, Koreans openly recognize that these hierarchies exist, so there are fewer attempts to obscure and hide them as there are in the US, but the recognition of hierarchies motivates little social change. This could be perhaps linked to Confucian legacies of thought, which emphasize notions of self-improvement as individuals and as collectivities (K. Han 2007). The proper attitude, then, is for "less civilized" people to assimilate into the more desirable society. This helps to explain why there is a double othering—a self-othering desire to be more like the West and an othering expectation that those lower on the hierarchy and further from the center should endeavor to be more like Koreans (Oh and Oh 2016).

Below Koreans on this hierarchy are members of the Korean diaspora in the West and, arguably, mixed-race White Koreans. For Korean Americans, our status is contingent upon our ability to perform native Koreanness or upon success achieved in the West that reflects well upon the ethnic community. If so, we are easily folded into the fabric of Koreanness, but if not, we are seen as tainted. Because of the neocolonial fascination with the West, we are not devalued to the extent that the diaspora from China, Kazakhstan, or Sakhalin is, but we are seen as tainted, nonetheless, an impurity, which devalues Korean Americans, despite our shared ethnic identities. Though there are plenty of Korean television dramas that feature characters who are represented as Korean Americans, their fluency in the Korean language and culture, as well as the audience's extratextual knowledge of the actors' Koreanness, means that they are accepted not for their US American difference but for their Korean similarity. In their chapter in this book, Alice Nahyeon Kim and Sherry S. Yu make this point by examining the shifts in the news coverage of Yoo Seung-jun (aka Steve Yoo), who was represented favorably as a highly popular Korean American rapper but who became a national pariah after switching to US citizenship to avoid his pending military enlistment. His betrayal was marked in a discursive shift from being called Yoo Seung-jun, authentically Korean, to Steve Yoo, a tainted Korean American. For mixed-race White Koreans, their claims to Koreanness are more contingent because of their partial ethnic and racial difference, but if they perform Koreanness sufficiently, their Whiteness can be an asset, a combination of familiarity and modernity (Ahn 2015). Lie (2014) points out that while mixed-race (혼혈, honhyeol) Koreans are seen as tainted, Whiteness is redemptive, transforming stigma into desirable demarcation. The past several years have witnessed a number of successful Korean White celebrity models, K-pop idols, and actors, including Daniel Henney, Dennis Oh, Julien Kang, Somi, and Nancy.[2]

Lower on the hierarchy is a somewhat amorphous category of ethnic similarity, geopolitical power, historical relationships, and generalized perceptions of regional differences. Because of Korea's long historical relationship to China, it configures separately, as does Japan. The view of China is also complicated by its current geopolitical power and its historical influence in Korea, which grants it more esteem; however, the view is moderated by its Communist political system, its rivalry with the US, and its slower start to industrialization. Too little research on the representations of China and the Chinese is available, however, to be able to make confident claims, but stereotypes of Chinese as dirty, noisy, and dishonest exist (Lee, Jon, and Byun 2017). Korea's postcolonial relationship with its other neighbor, Japan, produces ambivalence. Japanese, who are represented as sympathetic to Korea, are portrayed in humane, sometimes heroic, and desirable ways. Though Japanese people may be understood as threatening or condescending, they are not represented as inferior to Koreans, perhaps reflecting a postcolonial internalization of inferiority for being colonized (Em 2013). As Russell Edwards points out in his chapter, the usual dichotomy of bad Japanese and good Koreans is ambivalently presented in local films. Further, even a cursory glance at K-pop shows that many of the most popular women performers are from Japan. That said, *Zainichi* (Japan-residing ethnic Koreans) often suffer from a lack of social acceptance because of their perceived impurity as co-ethnics (Lie 2014). Min Wha Han, in her chapter, points out that documentaries have constructed *Zainichi* as sympathetic victims of Japanese oppression and as part of the Korean people. This is to again point out that simple notions of ethnocentrism do not make sense in local articulations of anthrocategorism because co-ethnics are valued differently and are seen as having stronger or more tenuous claims to inclusion in the national imaginary.

This is why North Korean refugees, despite being from a Communist state and an underdeveloped nation, are viewed relatively favorably. North Korean refugees are seen as part of a divided nation but still part of the Korean people (Nora Kim 2016). In her chapter, Miseong Woo points out that North Korean refugees are represented as sympathetic, humanized figures in theater. Their poverty is not a reason to cast aspersions but a reason to reflect upon the harms of neoliberal South Korea and oppressive North Korea. North Korean refugees are victims of oppressive systems, but they are not the agents of them. This is also demonstrated in Myoung-

Sun Song's chapter on the film *The Bacchus Lady*, which sympathetically represents a North Korean refugee as a victim of Korean patriarchy. In JongHwa Lee's chapter, he shows that films represent North Koreans as humanized figures, who are often played by attractive actors to strengthen their appeal. Though North Koreans are represented as living very different lives, North and South Koreans pull together in times of need because they are connected as the same people (*minjok*). Despite these humanizing portrayals, North Koreans are received more ambivalently in everyday culture. Because of neoliberal logics, they are seen as a burden for not adapting and becoming self-sufficient subjects within capitalist arrangements (Jung 2014; Seol and Seo 2014). North Koreans are sometimes vilified as untrustworthy and as bilking the system (Nora Kim 2016). So, despite their very different ideological perspectives and worldviews, North Koreans are seen as having strong claims to Koreanness but are devalued for their inability to adjust to neoliberal capitalism.

In research about *damunhwa* (multiculturalism), perhaps the group that has been studied the most are women who move to Korea as international marriage migrants. Indeed, it is arguably because of the societal need to integrate large numbers of migrant women into local households (and, by extension, the larger society) that the government took up gendered *damunhwa* policies (Nora Kim 2014; Lim 2014; Cheng 2011; Chung and Kim 2012; Prey 2011). Despite these top-down efforts, multicultural children are stereotyped as less intelligent because of their struggles in school and are bullied (Lee 2009; Lee, Jon, and Byun 2017), particularly if they have darker skin color (Shin 2006). There are no serious attempts at multicultural inclusion as governmental programs emphasize assimilation into the nation-state (Kang 2018; Lim 2014; G. Han 2007; Kim and Oh 2012). This is because while Southeast Asian women are positioned higher on the hierarchy than their male counterparts, they are still presented as distant from the center, an unusual presence that has avenues to gain proximity to Koreanness but only by assimilating and performing Koreanness and filling societal needs. Media tend to represent marriage migrants and their children as sympathetic, but the sympathy is dependent upon their demonstrations of assimilation. In their chapter, Eunbi Lee and Colby Miyose point to the ways a Southeast Asian widow is represented as an idealized, faithful wife and daughter-in-law who heroically investigates her husband's suspicious death and who continues to take care of her ailing mother-in-law. In other news and documentary reports, the focus is on love as a way to ameliorate structural barriers faced by multicultural families, ignoring cultural isolation, ethnic bigotry, and domestic violence (Cha, Lee, and Park 2016). Representations of "pure" Southeast Asian women also function to discipline feminism by suggesting that local women have abandoned traditional femininity and endanger societal order (S. Kim 2009).

Notably, this book has not included large swaths of the world, such as Latin America and the Middle East, in its examination of otherness in South Korea media. None of the chapters in this book examined media representations of groups from these regions, and I am unaware of existing literature explaining the portrayals of the people or places of Latin America and the Middle East. I would suspect, however, that individuals from the Middle East are generally viewed as lower on the hierarchy and quite distant from the center if the reaction to Yemeni refugees in Jeju island are an indication. At best, the Yemeni migrants were viewed sympathetically but still as a foreign, tolerated presence. Given these absences, it is important that ongoing studies of *damunhwa* continue to build upon the conclusions of this book and to build upon and/or challenge the notion of anthrocategorism articulated here in the conclusion.

It is important to also recognize that these logics are arbitrary and changeable. For instance, popular reports have noted not only Koreans' surprise at the US's bungled response to COVID-19 but also East Asia's better outcomes in managing public health. The Black Lives Matter protests have also made the US's systemic racism and brutal police practices hyper-visible, challenging notions of Western progressiveness and modernity. It is also not insignificant that K-pop, especially the group BTS, has made widely reported, visible inroads into the US. With changes to Korea's desirability and the West's punctured image, this may alter the ways in which specific groups are organized in anthrocategorism, though it is unlikely to change this view of human difference itself.

NOTES

1. Current iterations of White supremacy are often explained through the work of critical Whiteness studies, which generally argue that Whiteness is an invisible, ex-nominated racial category (Dyer 1997; Nakayama and Krizek 1995). That is, it is constructed by what it is not—not Black, not Asian, not Native.

2. Nancy and Somi's stage names only include their first names.

REFERENCES

Ahn, Ji-Hyun. 2014. "Rearticulating Black Mixed-Race in the Era of Globalization: Hines Ward and the Struggle for Koreanness in Contemporary South Korean

Media." *Cultural Studies* 28 (3): 391–417. https://doi.org/10.1080/09502386.2013.84
0665
Ahn, Ji-Hyun. 2015. "Desiring Biracial Whites: Cultural Consumption of White Mixed-Race Celebrities in South Korean Popular Media." *Media, Culture & Society* 37 (6): 937–47. https://doi.org/10.1177/0163443715593050
Artz, Lee, and Bren Ortega Murphy. 2000. *Cultural Hegemony in the United States*. Thousand Oaks, CA: Sage.
Bloch, Katrina Rebecca. 2014. "'Anyone Can Be an Illegal': Color-Blind Ideology and Maintaining Latino/Citizen Borders." *Critical Sociology* 40 (1): 47–65. https://doi.org/10.1177/0896920512466274
Bonilla-Silva, Eduardo. 2010. *Racism without Racists: Color-Blind Racism and Racial Inequality in Contemporary America*. Lanham, MD: Rowman & Littlefield.
Cha, Na Young, Claire Shinhea Lee, and Ji Hoon Park. 2016. "Construction of Obedient Foreign Brides as Exotic Others: How Production Practices Construct the Images of Marriage Migrant Women on Korean Television." *International Journal of Communication* 10:1470–88.
Cheng, Sealing. 2011. "Sexual Protection, Citizenship and Nationhood: Prostituted Women and Migrant Wives in South Korea." *Journal of Ethnic and Migration Studies* 37 (10): 1627–48. https://doi.org/10.1080/1369183X.2011.613335
Cho, Hae-Joang. 1998. "Constructing and Deconstructing 'Koreanness.'" In *Making Majorities: Constituting the Nation in Japan, Korea, China, Malaysia, Fiji, Turkey, and the United States*, edited by Dru C. Gladney, 73–91. Stanford: Stanford University Press.
Chung, Erin Aeran, and Daisy Kim. 2012. "Citizenship and Marriage in a Globalizing World: Multicultural Families and Monocultural Nationality Laws in Korea and Japan." *Indiana Journal of Global Legal Studies* 19 (1): 195–219.
Cisneros, J. David, and Thomas K. Nakayama. 2015. "New Media, Old Racisms: Twitter, Miss America, and Cultural Logics of Race." *Journal of International and Intercultural Communication* 8 (2): 108–27. https://doi.org/10.1080/17513057.2015.1025328
Cloud, Dana L. 1996. "Hegemony or Concordance? The Rhetoric of Tokenism in 'Oprah' Winfrey's Rags-to-Riches Biography." *Critical Studies in Mass Communication* 13 (2): 115–37. https://doi.org/10.1080/15295039609366967
Dyer, Richard. 1997. *White*. New York: Routledge.
Em, Henry H. 2013. *The Great Enterprise: Sovereignty and Historiography in Modern Korea*. Durham: Duke University Press.
Fujitani, Takashi. 2011. *Race for Empire: Koreans as Japanese and Japanese as Americans during World War II*. Berkeley: University of California Press.
Gage, Sue-Je L. 2014. "Almost Korean: Korean Amerasians in an Era of Multiculturalism." In *Multiethnic Korea? Multiculturalism, Migration, and Peoplehood Diversity in Contemporary South Korea*, edited by John Lie, 244–76. Berkeley, CA: Institute of East Asian Studies.
Han, Benjamin. 2017. "K-Pop in Latin America: Transcultural Fandom and Digital Mediation." *International Journal of Communication* 11:2250–69.
Han, Geon-Soo. 2007. "Multicultural Korea: Celebration or Challenge of Multiethnic Shift in Contemporary Korea?" *Korea Journal* 47 (4): 32–63.
Han, Kyung-Koo. 2007. "The Archaeology of the Ethnically Homogeneous Nation-State and Multiculturalism in Korea." *Korea Journal* 47 (4): 8–31.
Herakova, Liliana L., Dijana Jelaca, Razvan Sibii, and Leda Cooks. 2011. "Voicing Silence

and Imagining Citizenship: Dialogues about Race and Whiteness in a 'Postracial' Era." *Communication Studies* 62 (4): 372–88. https://doi.org/10.1080/10510974.2011.588072

Höhn, Maria, and Seungsook Moon. 2010. "Introduction: The Politics of Gender, Sexuality, Race, and Class in the U.S. Military Empire." In *Over There: Living with the U.S. Military Empire from World War Two to the Present*, edited by Maria Höhn and Seungsook Moon, 1–36. Durham: Duke University Press.

Jhally, Sut, and Justin Lewis. 1992. *Enlightened Racism: The Cosby Show, Audiences, and the Myth of the American Dream*. Boulder: Westview Press.

Jirn, Jin Suh. 2014. "'Happy Seoul for Foreigners': Scenes from Multicultural Life in South Korea." *Inter-Asia Cultural Studies* 15 (2): 315–22. https://doi.org/10.1080/14649373.2014.918683

Jung, Jin-Heon. 2014. "North Korean Migrants in South Korea: From Heroes to Burdens and First Unifiers." In *Multiethnic Korea? Multiculturalism, Migration, and Peoplehood Diversity in Contemporary South Korea*, edited by John Lie, 142–64. Berkeley: Institute of East Asian Studies.

Kang, Kyoung-Lae. 2018. "Talking Hospitality and Ethno-national Boundaries in Contemporary Korea: Considering Korean TV Shows Featuring Foreigners." *Television & New Media* 19 (1): 59–74. https://doi.org/10.1177/1527476417697196

Kim, Hyuk-Rae, and Ingyu Oh. 2012. "Foreigners Cometh! Paths to Multiculturalism in Japan, Korea, and Taiwan." *Asian & Pacific Migration Journal* 21 (1): 105–33.

Kim, Hyun-Sook. 2006. "Hanmal 'minjok'ui tansaenggwa minjokjuui damnonui changchul minjokjuui yeoksaseosureul jungsimeuro." *Hangukdongyangjeongchisasangsayeongu* 한국동양정치사상사연구 [*The Review of Korean and Asian Political Thought*] 5 (1): 117–40.

Kim, Nadia Y. 2006. "'Patriarchy Is So Third World': Korean Immigrant Women and 'Migrating' White Western Masculinity." *Social Problems* 53 (4): 519–36. https://doi.org/10.1525/sp.2006.53.4.519

Kim, Nadia Y. 2014. "Race-ing toward the Real South Korea: The Cases of Black-Korean Nationals and African Migrants." In *Multiethnic Korea? Multiculturalism, Migration, and Peoplehood Diversity in Contemporary South Korea*, edited by John Lie, 211–43. Berkeley: Institute of East Asian Studies.

Kim, Nora Hui-Jung. 2014. "Korea: Multiethnic or Multicultural?" In *Multiethnic Korea? Multiculturalism, Migration, and Peoplehood Diversity in Contemporary South Korea*, edited by John Lie, 58–78. Berkeley: Institute of East Asian Studies.

Kim, Nora Hui-Jung. 2016. "Naturalizing Korean Ethnicity and Making 'Ethnic' Difference: A Comparison of North Korean Settlement and Foreign Bride Incorporation Policies in South Korea." *Asian Ethnicity* 17 (2): 185–98. https://doi.org/10.1080/14631369.2016.1151234

Kim, Sumi. 2009. "Politics of Representation in the Era of Globalization: Discourse about Marriage Migrant Women in Two South Korean Films." *Asian Journal of Communication* 19 (2): 210–26. https://doi.org/10.1080/1292980902827086

Lee, Jenny, Jae-Eun Jon, and Kiyong Byun. 2017. "Neo-racism and Neo-nationalism within East Asia: The Experiences of International Students in South Korea." *Journal of Studies in International Education* 21 (2): 136–55. https://doi.org/10.1177/1028315316669903

Lee, Mary. 2009. "Mixed Race Peoples in the Korean National Imaginary and Family." *Korean Studies* 32:56–85. https://doi.org/10.1353/ks.0.0010

Lie, John. 2014. "Introduction: Multiethnic Korea." In *Multiethnic Korea? Multiculturalism, Migration, and Peoplehood Diversity in Contemporary South Korea*, edited by John Lie, 1–27. Berkeley: Institute of East Asian Studies.

Lim, Timothy C. 2014. "Late Migration, Discourse, and the Politics of Multiculturalism in South Korea." In *Multiethnic Korea? Multiculturalism, Migration, and Peoplehood Diversity in Contemporary South Korea*, edited by John Lie, 31–57. Berkeley: Institute of East Asian Studies.

Lipsitz, George. 1998. *The Possessive Investment in Whiteness: How White People Profit from Identity Politics*. Philadelphia: Temple University Press.

Moon, Katharine H. S. 1997. *Sex among Allies: Military Prostitution in U.S.-Korea Relations*. New York: Columbia University Press.

Moon, Seungsook. 2010. "Camptown Prostitution and the Imperial SOFA: Abuse and Violence against Transnational Camptown Women in South Korea." In *Over There: Living with the U.S. Military Empire from World War Two to the Present*, edited by Maria Höhn and Seungsook Moon, 337–65. Durham: Duke University Press.

Nakayama, Thomas K., and Robert L. Krizek. 1995. "Whiteness: A Strategic Rhetoric." *Quarterly Journal of Speech* 81:291–309. https://doi.org/10.1080/00335639509384117

Oh, David C. 2012. "Black-Yellow Fences: Multicultural Boundaries and Whiteness in the *Rush Hour* Franchise." *Critical Studies in Media Communication* 29 (5): 349–66. https://doi.org/10.1080/15295036.2012.697634

Oh, David C. 2020. "Representing the Western Super-Minority: Desirable Cosmopolitanism and Homosocial Multiculturalism on a South Korean Talk Show." *Television & New Media* 21 (3): 260–77. https://doi.org/10.1177/1527467418789895

Oh, David C., and Chuyun Oh. 2016. "'Until *You* Are Able': South Korean Multiculturalism and Hierarchy in *My Little Hero*." *Communication, Culture, & Critique* 9 (2): 250–65. https://doi.org/10.1111/cccr.12104

Palumbo-Liu, David. 1999. *Asian/American: Historical Crossings of a Racial Frontier*. Palo Alto: Stanford University Press.

Parameswaran, Radhika. 2009. "Facing Barack Hussein Obama: Race, Globalization, and Transnational America." *Journal of Communication Inquiry* 33 (3):195–205. https://doi.org/10.1177/0196859909333896

Pieterse, Jan Nederveen. 1992. *White on Black: Images of Africa and Blacks in Western Popular Culture*. Translated by Jan Nederveen Pieterse. New Haven: Yale University Press.

Prashad, Vijay. 2001. *Everybody Was Kung Fu Fighting: Afro-Asian Connections and the Myth of Cultural Purity*. Boston: Beacon Press.

Prey, Robert. 2011. "Different Takes—Migrant World Television and Multiculturalism in South Korea." *Global Media Journal—Canadian Edition* 4 (1): 109–25.

Seol, Dong-Hoon, and Jungmin Seo. 2014. "Dynamics of Ethnic Nationalism and Hierarchal Nationhood: Korean Nation and Its Otherness since the Late 1980s." *Korea Journal* 54 (2): 5–33.

Shin, Gi-Wook. 2006. *Ethnic Nationalism in Korea: Genealogy, Politics, and Legacy*. Stanford: Stanford University Press.

Shohat, Ella, and Robert Stam. 1994. *Unthinking Eurocentricism: Multiculturalism and the Media*. New York: Routledge.

Shome, Raka. 1999. "Whiteness and the Politics of Location: Postcolonial Reflections." In *Whiteness: The Communication of Social Identity*, edited by Thomas K. Nakayama and Judith N. Martin, 107–28. Thousand Oaks, CA: Sage.

Siapera, Eugenia. 2019. "Right-Wing Populism and Mediated Activism: Creative Responses and Counter-Narratives." *Open Library of Humanities* 5 (1) (13):1–34. https://doi.org/10.16995/olh.405

Sorby, Stella. 2008. "Translating News from English to Chinese: Complimentary and Derogatory Language Usage." *Babe* 54 (1): 19–35. https://doi.org/10.1075/babel.54.1.03sor

Suh, Serk-Bae. 2013. *Treacherous Translation: Culture, Nationalism, and Colonialism in Korea and Japan from the 1910s to the 1960s, Seoul-California Series in Korean Studies*. Berkeley: University of California Press.

Supriya, K. E. 1999. "White Difference: Cultural Constructions of White Identity." In *Whiteness: The Communication of Social Identity*, edited by Thomas K. Nakayama and Judith N. Martin, 129–48. Thousand Oaks, CA: Sage.

Tai, Eika. 2004. "'Korean Japanese': A New Identity Option for Resident Koreans in Japan." *Critical Asian Studies* 36 (3): 355–82. https://doi.org/10.1080/1467271042000241586

Tikhonov, Vladimir. 2013. "The Race and Racism Discourses in Modern Korea, 1890s-1910s." *Korean Studies* 36:31–57.

Watts, Eric King. 2017. "Postracial Fantasies, Blackness, and Zombies." *Communication and Critical/Cultural Studies* 14 (4): 317–33. https://doi.org/10.1080/14791420.2017.1338742

Yang, Eun-Kyung. 2010. "Minjogui yeogijuwa wigyejeok minjokseongui damnon guseong joseonilboui joseonjok damnon bunseok" 민족의 역이주와 위계적 민족성의 담론 구성 조선일보의 조선족 담론 분석 [Ethnic return migration and the discursive construction of hierarchical nationhood: The case of Korean-Chinese discourse on Chosun Ilbo]. *Hangukbangsonghakbo* 한국방송학보 [*Korean Journal of Broadcasting and Telecommunication Studies*] 9:194–237.

Yi, Joseph, and Gowoon Jung. 2015. "Debating Multicultural Korea: Media Discourse on Migrants and Minorities in South Korea." *Journal of Ethnic and Migration Studies* 41 (6): 985–1013. https://doi.org/10.1080/1369183X.2014.1002202

Contributors

Ji-Hyun Ahn is Associate Professor of Communication in the School of Interdisciplinary Arts and Sciences at the University of Washington Tacoma. Her research interests include critical mixed-race studies, global media studies, national identity, and racial politics in contemporary South Korean media and popular culture. She is the author of *Mixed-Race Politics and Neoliberal Multiculturalism in South Korean Media* (2018).

Russell Edwards teaches Asian Cinemas at RMIT University in Melbourne, where he is currently researching representations of Japan in contemporary South Korean cinema. Edwards is the founding reviews editor at *Empire* (Australia ed.) (2001–3); has covered film festivals for the international trade publication *Variety* (2003–12); was president of the Film Critics Circle of Australia (2004–6); and is currently an adviser to the Busan International Film Festival. He has also made short films, notably, *The Agreement* (2007), which played at several international film festivals and was screened on SBS-TV.

Benjamin M. Han is Assistant Professor in the Department of Communication at Tulane University. His research focuses on television theory and history and on global media. His work has been published in the *Journal of International Communication*, *Television & New Media*, and *Media, Culture & Society*. He is the author of *Beyond the Black and White TV: Asian and Latin American Spectacle in Cold War America* (2020).

Min Wha Han is Adjunct Professor in the Department of Communication and Media Studies at Angelo State University in Texas. Influenced by critical rhetorical scholarship, she examines the arenas of multicultural contacts where diverse voices, memories, and identities are represented, negotiated, and silenced. Han is editing a book on the cultural identities of the Korean diaspora community in Japan, integrating oral and life histories into the project. She has published in the journals *Communication Theory*, the *International Communication Gazette*, the *Review of Communication*, *Keio Communication Review*, and *Language and Intercultural Communication*.

Alice Nahyeon Kim is a PhD student at the Faculty of Information at the University of Toronto. She is interested in intercultural communication, diasporic media, and social media. Her co-authored research is published in *Information Research*. She has also presented at multiple conferences, including the International Association for Media and Communication Research, the Association for Information Science and Technology, and Social Media & Society.

Eunbi Lee is a doctoral candidate in the Department of Communication at the University of Massachusetts, Amherst. Her research focuses on identity, surviving, belonging, and coalition in the context of human migration and border politics in communication and performance studies. Her works have revolved around performance in (digital) storytelling and activism that embody voices and actions of migrants and refugees of color. She also researches critical media literacy and critical pedagogy for community media.

JongHwa Lee is Associate Professor in the Department of Communication and Mass Media at Angelo State University in Texas. His research interests include activism and historical justice, collective memory and visual rhetoric, tourism and global citizenship, and Cold War rhetoric in Northeast Asia. Some of his recent works include the co-edited books *Activism and Rhetoric: Theories and Contexts for Political Engagement* (2019); *Korean Diaspora across the World: Homeland in History, Memory, Imagination, Media, and Reality* (2019); and *Candlelight Movement, Democracy, and Communication in Korea* (2022).

Min Joo Lee is a Visiting Lecturer in the Department of Women's and Gender Studies at Wellesley College. She received her PhD in Gender Studies from UCLA. Her dissertation analyzed how the transnational popularity of South Korean television dramas inspires Western fans to travel to South Korea to form intimate relations with South Korean men. Lee's research interests include transnational media, tourism, and contemporary South Korean gender and race relations.

Colby Y. Miyose is an Instructor at the University of Hawaiʻi, Hilo. He is interested in portrayals of masculinity and how they intersect with ideas of love, romance, and sexuality in Southeast and East Asian film and television, such as the K-drama (Korean drama). He is also interested in how Native Hawaiʻian culture is displayed in film and television and how these portrayals influence Native Hawaiian identity formation.

David C. Oh is Associate Professor of Communication Arts at Ramapo College of New Jersey. He is the author of *Second-Generation Korean American Adolescent Identity and Media: Diasporic Identifications* (2015) and *Whitewash: White Subjectivity and Asian Erasure in US Film Culture* (2022). He has published a few dozen articles on Asian/American representation vis-à-vis Whiteness, intersectional representations of multiculturalism in South Korean popular media, and the transnational audience reception of Korean media.

Myoung-Sun Song is Assistant Professor in the Department of East Asian Languages and Culture at the University of Illinois, Urbana-Champaign. She received her PhD in Communication from the University of Southern California. Her research focuses on the intersections of race, gender, sexuality, class, and (national) identity in Korean media and popular culture. She is the author of *Hanguk Hip Hop: Global Rap in South Korea* (2019), and her work on the representation of female marriage migrants in South Korean film and television has been published in the *International Journal of Media & Cultural Politics*.

Miseong Woo is Professor in the Department of English Language and Literature and the Director of the Institute of East and West Studies at Yonsei University in Seoul, South Korea. Her research interests include race, gender, modernity in modern drama, the literary and visual history of Asian diaspora, and cultural encounters between the East and West in popular culture. She published *Representation of Asian Women in the West* (2014) with Sam & Parkers, which won the 2014 Korea Research Foundation Achievement Award. She received a Fulbright Scholar Award for the 2011–12 academic year, taught at Cornell University as a distinguished visiting professor in Korean Studies in 2016, and was the first scholar selected as the Fulbright Korea Distinguished Chair at Emory University in 2020.

Sherry S. Yu is Assistant Professor in the Department of Arts, Culture, and Media and the Faculty of Information at the University of Toronto.

Her research explores multiculturalism, media, and social integration and demonstrates a special interest in diasporic media in relation to cultural literacy, intercultural dialogue, and civic engagement in a multicultural society. She is the author of *Diasporic Media beyond the Diaspora: Korean Media in Vancouver and Los Angeles* (2018) and the co-editor of *Ethnic Media in the Digital Age* (2019). Her research also has been published in several leading scholarly journals.

Index

Abe, Shinzo, 174
Africa Development Initiative, 47
African Americans: Black Lives Matter movement, 228; media preference for Africans over, 46, 50; as reminder of US occupation, 50–51, 125; social status in Korea, 5, 218; and strategic ambiguity, 48; in World War II, 3, 51. *See also* blackface; strategic blackness
Africans: in anthrocategorism hierarchy, 218, 224; and desirability, 61; immigration areas, 54; and Korean foreign policy, 47, 54–55, 60; Korean identity and othering of, 50, 51, 54–55; marginalization of in film, 123, 131–32; media preference for, 46, 50; numbers of in Korea, 47; and strategic blackness, 15, 46–63, 131–32, 224. *See also* blackface
age and marginalized identity of women, 123–37
agent/agency and Cold War rhetoric in films, 166–68, 169–72, 173
The Age of Shadows (2016), 103
Always a Guest, 36, 38
ambiguity, strategic, 48–49
American Idol, 66, 67, 68, 69
America's Next Top Model, 67
Anarchist from Colony (2017), 16, 104, 112–17
annihilation, symbolic, 100
anthrocategorism: compared to White supremacy hierarchy, 218–22; hierarchies in, 7–8, 217, 223–28; as intertwined with racism, 217; and intertwining of identities, 136–37; as term, 7–8, 216
anti-immigration sentiment: and Chinese Koreans *(Joseonjok)*, 79; in Europe, 218
anti-Japanese sentiment and ethnic Koreans in Japan *(Jaeil)*, 185, 189
Asian American term, 219
Assassination (2015), 103, 116
assimilation: and double othering, 225; lack of as reason for othering, 6–7; and marriage immigrants, 12, 34, 89, 93–94, 227; and multicultural policies, 11–12, 46–47, 227; and nationalism, 46–47; of North Koreans, 142; of White women, 34. *See also* strategic blackness

The Bacchus Lady (2016), 16, 123–37, 237
The Bachelor, 67
Baek, Cheonggang, 15–16, 66–81, 224
Baek, Nam-Gi, 138n12
Baek, Seeun, 71
Bang, Sihyuk, 81n6
Banjjokbari term, 179
The Battleship Island (2017), 104, 110
Bbalgaengi term, 179
beauty and appearance: and audition shows, 76–77; and multicultural children, 39; and White women, 39, 92
Beenzino, 27, 32–35
The Birth of a Great Star, 15–16, 66–81, 224
Black Americans. *See* African Americans
blackface, 5, 51–52, 62, 224
Black Koreans. *See* multiracial Koreans

blackness, strategic, 15, 46–63, 131–32, 224
Bodhisattva Avalokiteshvara, 134–35
bodies: commodification of in sex work, 126–27; marginalization of disabled bodies, 16, 123, 133, 138n11; one body concept *(naeseon ilche)*, 104, 114; women's bodies as in service to others, 16, 88, 91–94
Bolton, John, 174
Brokeback Mountain (2005), 116
bromance, 172
Bukhanitaljoomin term, 141
Burke, Kenneth, 161, 162, 164, 184–85, 189

cameras, as symbol of Japan, 106, 107
camptowns, 3, 125–26, 217
capitalism. *See* neoliberal capitalism
Central Asian women: *Rosa* (2012), 16, 85–100; and sex work, 87, 88, 92
child-rearing, 40–41
children. *See* multicultural children
China: affinities with Japan, 223–24; in anthrocategorism hierarchy, 226; Chinese as different race, 4–5; marriage immigrants from, 12, 72
Chinese-Koreans. *See* Korean minority in China *(Joseonjok)*
Chongryeon, 17, 179, 184–92
Choo, Shin-Soo, 209
Christianity, 2, 106, 110–11
Chung, Mia, 17, 141
citizenship: dual citizenship, 199; in Japan and circles of belonging, 220; and military service, 17–18, 197–211, 225
clothing, 109, 126
co-ethnic othering: of Korean minority in Japan *(Jaeil)*, 17, 178–92, 226; of Koreans from China *(Joseonjok)*, 6, 72–73, 223; and lack of shared identity, 223–24; and national weakness, 6; of North Koreans, 6, 17, 141–56, 159–75, 227
Cold War: enemy-making rhetoric in, 162–63; and Korean minority in Japan *(Jaeil)*, 182; and Koreans from China *(Joseonjok)*, 223; rhetoric and North Koreans in film, 17, 159–75
colonialism: and African policy, 55, 59, 60; as corrupting Korean identity, 16, 103–17, 222; and ethnic Koreans in Japan *(Jaeil)*, 17, 179–81, 186, 189–91; homogeneity as reaction to, 4, 220; and internalization of Orientalism, 221; and Itaewon, 131; Korea as both postcolonial and neocolonial state, 8–9, 10; as merging with Cold War, 163–64, 171, 174; and positioning of identity, 160; and racial hierarchies, 2–4, 51, 218–22; and relationships between Korean women and Japanese men, 29; and White desirability, 92, 93–94; and White supremacy, 218
colorblindness, 218
comfort women, 110, 111, 116
communism: and Chinese Koreans *(Joseonjok)*, 223–24; and Koreans in Japan *(Jaeil)*, 179, 181, 190, 191; and North Korean defectors, 154, 226. *See also* Cold War
Confalonieri, Christina, 27, 35–38, 42
Confidential Assignment (2017), 17, 161, 164, 168–73
consumerism. *See* materialism and consumerism
cosmopolitanism: and English language, 34; globalization's pressure for, 9; of Korean identity, 31, 42; of Korean men in relationships with White women, 15, 27–43, 222; markers of, 31; and strategic blackness, 224; of White women, 38–42, 222
criminality: and Chinese Koreans *(Joseonjok)*, 13–14, 73, 74, 217; and ethnic Koreans in Japan *(Jaeil)*, 182
cultural policy. *See* multicultural policy *(damunhwa)*

damunhwa. See multicultural policy *(damunhwa)*
Dear My Friends, 138n14
Dear Pyeongyang (2005), 183
death: assisted deaths in film, 130, 133–35; *muyeongo*, 125, 136; of sympathetic gay characters, 116; of sympathetic Japanese characters, 116, 117; women's service in, 134–35

Index | 239

defections: double defections, 143–47; and identity, 17, 141–56; numbers of, 142–43; terms for defectors, 141, 142
desirability: of African women, 61; in anthrocategorism, 221–23, 225, 228; of Japanese women, 113; of Korean men, 15, 31, 38, 42, 43, 222; of White masculinity, 9–10; of White women, 27–43, 92, 93–94, 222
developmentalism filter and ethnic Koreans in Japan *(Jaeil)*, 181
diaspora: and anthrocategorism hierarchy, 217, 223–24; of foreign workers, 97; and impurity, 4, 225; as increasing, 155–56; Korean diasporic media, 202–3, 207–11; and Korean minority in Japan *(Jaeil)*, 179–92; of marriage immigrants, 98; and North Korean defections, 141–56, 222; and reality shows, 53, 70; and songs, 185, 187–88, 189–90; and sports, 185, 187, 189; as term, 155
disabled bodies, 16, 123, 133, 138n11
discrimination: against Black Koreans, 3, 10, 55–56, 224, 225; against Chinese Koreans *(Joseonjok)*, 73, 79–80, 81; against ethnic Koreans in Japan *(Jaeil)*, 188–89; against Korean Americans in US, 201; against multicultural children, 10, 40, 55–56, 227; against North Koreans in West, 151
doenjang-nyeo term, 28, 33
domestic violence and marriage immigrants, 16, 91, 95–96, 98
double defections, 143–47
double othering, 225
Dr. Strangelove Or: How I Learned to Stop Worrying and Love the Bomb (1964), 106
Dugard, Jaycee, 148–49

E-6 visa, 87
E-9 visa, 87
education: competition in, 147; 4.24 Education Fight, 188–89; Korean schools in Japan, 17, 178–92; and multicultural policies, 11
empathy, unsympathetic, 135

enemy concept and Cold War rhetoric, 159–75
English language: as cosmopolitan, 34; and Filipinos, 87, 129; and Korean Americans, 202; selective use of in media, 10, 34, 78; and White teachers, 5; and White women, 34
ethnic nationalism and ethnic Koreans in Japan *(Jaeil)*, 181, 189–90
Europe: anthrocategorism in, 218; anti-immigration sentiment in, 218; child-rearing style, 40; and cosmopolitanism, 9; and hierarchies of race, 2–4, 51, 217, 218, 223; North Koreans in, 156

F-4 visa, 200, 206, 207
F-6 visa, 87
Failan (2001), 89
families: alternative family construction in film, 16, 124, 129–33; family-ism in spy films, 172; multicultural family support centers, 10, 132–33; portrayals of multicultural families, 12–13; *sikgu* term, 138n9. *See also* multicultural policy *(damunhwa)*
farm labor and female immigrant workers, 85, 87, 88
fathers: abandonment of multicultural children, 124, 129; Black, 52
femininity: and feminists, 28–29; feminization of poverty, 133; of Korean women, 13, 28–29, 33–35, 43, 222, 228; of marriage immigrants, 13, 88–89, 93–94, 95, 97–98, 228; and patriarchy, 28–29, 42, 43, 88–89, 91, 93–100, 228; of White women, 9, 28–29, 33–35, 42–43, 88–89, 96–97, 98, 222
feminists: and femininity, 28–29; military service and anti-feminism, 33–35
fertility and birth rates, 34, 87
food and cooking: and alternative family formation, 132–33; and performance of Korean identity, 57, 61; self-feeding, 151–52; and White women in relationships with Korean men, 41
foreign policy: and Africa, 47, 54–55, 60; Sunshine Policy, 142, 182

4.24 Education Fight, 188–89
Four Weddings and a Funeral (1994), 116

gender: and alternative family formation, 132–33; and Black entertainers, 62–63; and expectations of caregiving, 127–28; and marriage immigrants, 12; multicultural policies as gendered, 12–13, 87; ratio of defectors, 147; and trans marginalization in film, 123, 131, 138n11. *See also* femininity; masculinity
globalization: as based on difference, 67; and cultural policy, 9, 48, 182; of K-pop, 66, 69–70, 78, 80, 228
Global Korea policy, 9
Goodbye to Goodbye, 62
Graham, Lindsey, 173
guisoonyongsa term, 142

Hallyu. *See* Korean Wave
Han, Donggeun, 75
Han, Hyun-min, 15, 46, 47, 52–58
Hanshin Education Fight, 188–89
Hello Counselor, 46
Heo, Gak, 75
hero narrative in audition shows, 68, 74–75
Herstory (2018), 105
hierarchies: in anthrocategorism, 7–8, 217, 223–28; and Chinese Koreans *(Joseonjok)*, 5, 72–73, 217, 223–24; as explicit in Korea, 219, 225; local hierarchy of migrants, 10; of masculinity, 29–30; racial hierarchies in Europe, 2–4, 51, 217, 218, 223; racial hierarchies in US, 7–8, 14–15, 51, 201; and White supremacy, 2–4, 218–22
hipster racism, 49, 58–59
homogeneity: of Japan, 4; as reaction to colonialism and neocolonialism, 4, 220, 221; and xenophobia, 6
honhyeol. *See* multicultural children; multiracial Koreans
horror films and Japanese othering, 16, 103, 104–12, 117
Hwang, Jung-Min, 108

I Can Speak (2017), 105, 110
identity: concept of identification, 184–85, 189; and defection, 17, 141–56; hybrid identity of Korean Americans, 197–98, 202, 205–11; intertwining of in anthrocategorism, 136–37; marginalized identities in film, 123–37; as positioned, 160–61, 179. *See also* Korean identity; national identity
ideographs, 180, 185–91
immigrants: and Korean language use, 10, 46, 54, 55; othering of despite race, 5–6; status of male immigrant workers, 13, 223; type of work and race/ethnicity, 87–88; US immigration, 200–201, 210. *See also* Korean minority in China *(Joseonjok)*; Korean minority in Japan *(Jaeil)*; marriage immigrants; multicultural policy *(damunhwa)*; North Koreans
individualism and North Koreans, 154–55
injongchabyeol/injongjuui term, 1, 7, 216. *See also* anthrocategorism
innocence, corruption of, 110, 111
intimacy, performance of in K-pop, 61
Itaewon, changes in, 131
Itaewon Class, 62

Jaeil. *See* Korean minority in Japan *(Jaeil)*
Japan: affinities with China, 223–24; in anthrocategorism hierarchy, 226; anti-Japanese sentiment, 185, 189; cameras as symbol of, 106, 107; citizenship and circles of belonging, 220; and comfort women, 110, 111, 116; as corrupting Korean identity, 16, 103–17, 222; homogeneity of, 4; Japanese as different race, 4–5; Japanese as same race, 3–4; Japanese othering in film, 16, 103–17; Japanese women as ally in film, 16, 104, 112–17; Korean minority in *(Jaeil)*, 17, 178–92; marriage immigrants from, 12; racial slurs for, 106; restrictions on Japanese language and cultural products, 222; World War II treaty negotiations, 8. *See also* colonialism
jareuda term, 138n11

jeong and mentoring, 76
Jewel in the Palace, 41
Jin, Longguo, 66
Joint Security Area (2000), 17
Joseonjok (Korean minority in China). See Korean minority in China *(Joseonjok)*
Joseon term, 186, 192n1. *See also* Korean minority in Japan *(Jaeil)*
JSA (2000), 182
Juche ideology, 152–53
jugyeojuneun term, 124
Jun, Kunimura, 104
J-Yong, E, 123, 137n2, 138n11

Kaneko, Fumiko, 104, 113–16
Kangnam, 58
Kim, Eun-sung, 17, 141, 143, 148
Kim, Hyun-joon, 27, 35–38
Kim, Il-sung: and Juche ideology, 152–53; in plays about defectors, 143, 150
Kim, Jung-il: and Cold War rhetoric in films, 165–66, 168; and Juche ideology, 153
Kim, Taewon, 76–77
Kim, Yuna, 81n6
kimchi-nyeo term, 28, 33
Korea International Cooperation Agency, 47
Korean Americans: in anthrocategorism hierarchy, 217, 225; diasporic media, 202–3, 207–11; discrimination against in US, 201; and English language, 202; as fortunate/cultural capital of, 201, 217; generational differences in, 208, 210; hybrid identity of, 197–98, 202, 205–11; Korean immigration rates, 201; and Korean language, 181, 225; and military service, 17–18, 197–211, 225; terms for, 201–2; as traitors/tainted, 201, 207, 208, 225
Korean Dream: global reach of, 74, 77–79; impossibility of and Chinese Koreans (Joseonjok), 15, 66–81, 224; impossibility of and female immigrants, 86, 94–99
Korean Filipino children, 16, 124, 129–30

Korean identity: as corrupted by Japan, 16, 103–17, 222; homogeneity of as reaction to colonialism/neocolonialism, 4, 220, 221; Japanese identification with in film, 114–16; and Korean Americans, 17–18, 197–98, 205, 206, 225; and Korean diasporic media, 202–3, 211; and Koreans in Japan *(Jaeil)*, 178–92; and military service, 209; as modern, 10, 41–42, 47, 57–58, 60; and North Koreans, 17, 141–42, 152, 153, 154, 160–75; performance of by Korean minority in China *(Joseonjok)*, 15–16, 66–81, 224; performance of by multiracial Koreans, 52, 53, 54, 57, 61, 62; and self-generalization, 219–20; and state power and othering of migrant women, 91, 95–98; and strategic blackness, 15, 46–63, 131–32, 224
Korean language: expectations for immigrants in media, 10, 46, 54, 55; expectations for Koreans in Japan *(Jaeil)*, 181; honorifics in, 40–41, 219; and Korean Americans, 181, 225; and multicultural children, 40–41, 130; performance of by Black Koreans, 15, 54; requirements on audition shows, 70; use by Japanese women in film, 114
Korean minority in China *(Joseonjok)*: in anthrocategorism hierarchy, 217, 223–24; and Chinese identity, 73; co-ethnic othering of, 6, 72–73, 223; and criminality, 13–14, 73, 74, 217; history of, 72–73; as immigrant workers, 72, 89; and impossibility of Korean Dream, 15–16, 66–81, 224; numbers of, 72; status of, 5, 72–73, 217, 223–24
Korean minority in Japan *(Jaeil)*: in anthrocategorism hierarchy, 226; on audition shows, 71; co-ethnic othering of, 17, 178–92, 226; and *Joseon* nationality, 179; media filters, 181; terms for, 179, 192n3
Koreans, multicultural. *See* multicultural children
Koreans, multiracial. *See* multiracial Koreans

242 | Index

Korean War, 51, 62, 159–60, 164, 172
Korean Wave: and Africa, 60–62; and Cold War rhetoric in film, 17, 159–75; and strategic blackness, 48, 49; and success of K-pop, 69–70, 78, 79, 80
K-pop: globalization and hybridization of, 66, 69–70, 78, 80, 228; and military service, 17–18, 197–211, 225; performance of intimacy in, 61; success of, 69–70, 78, 79, 80
K-Pop Star, 69, 70
Kwon, Rise, 71

Lan Ngoc, Ninh Duong, 86
Lee, Euna, 148
Lee, Taegon, 76, 77
LGBT people: and alternative families, 131; death of sympathetic gay characters in media, 116; as marginalized in film, 123, 131, 138n11
Lim, Ji-hyun, 147
Ling, Laura, 148

marriage immigrants: in anthrocategorism hierarchy, 227; and assimilation, 12, 34, 89, 93–94, 227; child-rearing by, 40; and domestic violence, 16, 91, 95–96, 98; ethnicities of, 12, 72–73; femininity of, 13, 88–89, 93–94, 95, 97–98, 228; forced labor by, 86; numbers of, 87; portrayals of, 12–13, 85–100; as service body, 16; victim narrative, 13, 129; visas for, 87. *See also* multicultural policy *(damunhwa)*
masculinity: of Black Koreans, 57; crisis of and costs to women, 135; and disabled bodies, 133; emasculation of Korean men, 107; hierarchy of, 29–30; and nationalism, 29; and sexualization of White women, 92, 93, 94–95, 98, 217; White, 9–10
materialism and consumerism: and Itaewon, 131; of Korean women, 28, 33; of South Korea to North Koreans, 144–47
media, Korean diasporic, 202–3, 207–11
men: abandonment of multicultural children, 124, 129; desirability of Korean men, 15, 31, 38, 42, 43, 222; emasculation of Korean men, 107; Japanese men as malignant other in film, 16, 103, 104–12; Korean men with Japanese women, 16, 104, 112–17; Korean men with White women, 15, 27–43, 222; White men and masculinity, 9–10; White men as romantic, 32; White men in relationships with Asian women and disciplining of femininity, 28–29; White men in relationships with women of color on US TV, 66. *See also* masculinity
mentoring and audition shows, 15, 68, 71, 75, 76–77
Michova, Stephanie, 27, 32–35
military service: and anti-feminism, 33–35; by Beenzino, 34–35; changes in for citizens outside Korea, 209–10; and citizenship, 17–18, 197–211, 225; dodging of, 197, 198, 200; and Korean Americans, 17–18, 197–211, 225; and Korean identity, 209
minjok, 57–58, 227
Mizuno, Rentaro, 113
modernity and modernization: compressed modernity term, 146; interracial relationships as modern, 27; Korean identity as, 10, 41–42, 47, 57–58, 60; marriage immigrants as inadequately modern, 40; and North Korean defectors, 146–47; push for, 3–4, 146; romance as modern, 32, 41–42; and strategic blackness, 57–58, 224; and Whites as super-minority, 221; of White women, 35, 39–40, 92
Moore, Brad, 66
morality: and Cold War rhetoric in films, 162, 167, 171; and enemy-making, 162; Japan as immoral, 16; South Korea as immoral, 144–47; West as immoral, 149; of Western women, 37; and White supremacy, 218
mothering: and sex work, 16, 125, 127–30; white women as, 38–42
multicultural children: abandonment of, 124, 129; in anthrocategorism hierarchy, 227; and assimilation, 12; and

beauty, 39; and cosmopolitanism, 38–42; discrimination against, 10, 40, 55–56, 227; dual citizenship of, 199; and language use, 39, 40–41, 130; as marginalized in film, 16, 124, 129–30; and military service, 198–99; mothering of, 16, 38–42, 125, 127–30; terms for, 11; victim narrative, 13, 129

multicultural family support centers, 10, 132–33

multicultural policy *(damunhwa)*: and assimilation, 11–12, 46–47, 227; and ethnic Koreans in Japan *(Jaeil)*, 181–82; family support centers, 10, 132–33; as gendered, 12–13, 87; globalization pressures for, 9, 48, 182; and nationalism, 4; and North Koreans, 153; rise of, 10–11; Sunshine Policy, 142, 182; and xenophobia, 6

multiracial Koreans: in anthrocategorism hierarchy, 218, 224–25; association with national trauma, 10, 50–51, 125; commodification of, 56–57; discrimination against, 3, 10, 55–56, 224, 225; gender and media, 62–63; increase in media, 47; and multicultural policies, 11; performance of Korean identity by, 52, 53, 54, 57, 61, 62; and racism, 3, 5, 11, 55–56; and strategic Blackness, 15, 46, 47, 52–58; White Koreans, 10, 225–26

Mutually Assured Destruction rhetoric, 162–63

muyeongo death, 125, 136

My Little Old Boy, 58–62

names: format and inversion of, 18n2, 137n1; and marriage immigrants, 34; and schools for ethnic Koreans in Japan *(Jaeil)*, 185–87; sex work and changing of, 90, 94, 125, 136, 147; terms for women, 28, 30; Yoo coverage, 204, 205, 206, 207–8, 225

narrative and Cold War rhetoric in films, 166, 168, 171–73

national identity: Chinese Koreans *(Joseonjok)* as Chinese, 72–73; and enemy-making, 162–63; and *Idol* type shows, 67, 68, 69; status of individuals as reflecting status of country, 6. *See also* Korean identity

nationalism: and assimilation, 46–47; ethnic nationalism and ethnic Koreans in Japan *(Jaeil)*, 181, 189–90; and *minjok*, 57–58, 227; misogyny in, 29; and multicultural policies, 4; and relationships with foreigners, 29–30; transnationalism, 53, 60–62, 142, 156

neoliberal capitalism: and assimilation, 6–7; and Black entertainers, 50, 56–57; of border crossings, 145–47; and commodification of culture, 67; and cosmopolitanism, 9; and ethnic Koreans in Japan *(Jaeil)*, 179, 182; and North Korea market economy, 153–54; and North Koreans, 17, 145–47, 150–56, 227

neo-racism, 6

Nigerian immigrants, 47, 54

Non Summit, 221

normality in anthrocategorism, 7

North Koreans: in anthrocategorism hierarchy, 217, 223–24, 226–27; assimilation of, 142; co-ethnic othering of, 6, 17, 141–56, 159–75, 227; and Cold War rhetoric, 17, 159–75; defections, numbers of, 142–43; defections and identity, 17, 141–42, 152, 153, 154; double defections, 143–47; and ethnic Koreans in Japan *(Jaeil)*, 17, 178–92; and Korean identity, 17, 141–42, 152, 153, 154, 160–75; market economy in North Korea, 153–54; sex work by, 16, 125, 143–44, 145; status of, 5, 6, 217, 223–24, 226–27; Sunshine Policy, 142, 182; and Zainichi cinema, 183–84

Oh, David, 71, 78

Okyere, Sam, 15, 46, 47, 54–62, 224

one body concept *(naeseon ilche)*, 104, 114

Orientalism, internalization of, 221

Orok, Shayne, 71, 78

othering: as anthrocategorism, 7–8, 216–28; double othering, 225; of immigrants despite race, 5–6; as more than racism, 1–7, 216; and xenophobia, 5–6

Park, Anna, 27, 38–42
Park, Hae-sung, 150
Park, Joo-ho, 27, 38–42
Park, Naeun, 38–41
Park, Yeol, 104, 113–16
Park Yeol (2017). See *Anarchist from Colony* (2017)
patriarchy: and disabled bodies, 133; and femininity, 28–29, 42, 43, 88–89, 91, 93–100, 228; and maternal giving, 128; romance as anti-patriarchy, 32
pentadic cartography, 161, 164, 166–68, 169–71, 173
Philadelphia (1993), 116
Philippines: as destination, 129; and English language, 87, 129; Kopino children in film, 16, 124, 129–30; marriage immigrants from, 12; and type of work for women immigrants, 87
Produce 101, 66
purpose and Cold War rhetoric in films, 166–68, 169–72

race: Chinese as different race, 4–5; European hierarchies, 2–4, 51, 217, 218, 223; inter-racial relationships as aspirational, 15, 27–43; Japanese as different race, 4–5; Japanese as same race, 3–4; racial inferiority complex, 30–31, 92; strategic blackness, 15, 46–63, 131–32, 224; and type of work, 87–88; US hierarchies, 7–8, 14–15, 51, 201. See also African Americans; Africans; multiracial Koreans; Whites
racism: and anthrocategorism, 217; as based on White supremacy, 2–4, 218–22; blackface, 5, 51–52, 62, 224; and Black Lives Matter movement, 228; against Chinese Koreans (Joseonjok), 81; against ethnic Koreans in Japan (Jaeil), 188–89; hipster racism, 49, 58–59; introduction into Korea, 3, 51; and multiracial Koreans, 3, 5, 11, 55–56; neo-racism, 6; power of term, 216–17; reducing othering to as problematic, 1–7; and strategic ambiguity, 48; as translation of *injongjuui/injongchabyeol*, 1, 216; as Western concept, 1, 10

Radio Star, 35, 38
reality television and performance of Korean identity by Chinese Koreans (Joseonjok), 15–16, 66–81, 224
The Real World, 67
reentry shock, 202
Return of Superman, 38–42
romance, 32–33, 41–42, 169, 171
Romper Stomper (1992), 106
Rosa (2012), 16, 85–100
Russian women and sex work, 88, 217

saeteomin term, 142
San Francisco Peace Treaty, 8
sayeon term, 138n11
scene and Cold War rhetoric in films, 166–68, 169–70, 172, 173
The Sea Knows (1961), 112
segyehwa economic policy, 9
self-reliance and Juche ideology, 152–53
sex and sexuality: Asian women as oversexual, 37–38, 94; and desirability of Korean men, 15, 31, 38, 42, 43, 222; of Korean women, 29–30, 35–38; of marriage immigrants, 89; and public displays of affection, 36–37; and vulnerability to sexual harassment, 144, 145; of White women, 16, 35, 36–38, 89, 91–95, 98, 217
sex work: association with national trauma, 10, 50–51, 124–27; and capitalism, 146; and comfort women, 110, 111, 116; and ethnicity, 87; as marginalized identity, 16, 123–37; and mothering, 16, 125, 127–30; by North Koreans, 16, 125, 143–44, 145; by older women, 16, 124; terms for workers, 125–26; as Third World Women's work, 88; and White women, 16, 85–100, 217; and World War II, 3, 110, 111
shamanism in film, 105, 107–12
Shin, Seonghoon, 81n6
Shiri (1999), 142, 182
sikgu term, 138n9
Sister Mok-rahn (Kim), 17, 141–48, 154, 155, 156
soccer and ethnic Koreans in Japan (Jaeil), 185, 187, 189
social harmony and assimilation, 12

social welfare, 155
Son, Jinyoung, 76, 77
songs and ethnic Koreans in Japan *(Jaeil)*, 185, 187–88, 189–90
South Asians in anthrocategorism hierarchy, 223
Southeast Asians: in anthrocategorism hierarchy, 223, 227; assimilation expectations, 34, 227; passing as Korean, 93; sexuality of in West, 94; social status, 5, 13, 223, 227; and type of work for women immigrants, 87. *See also* marriage immigrants
The Spanish Prisoner (1999), 106
Spirits' Homecoming (2016), 110, 116
sports and ethnic Koreans in Japan *(Jaeil)*, 185, 187, 189
The Spy Gone North (2018), 17, 161, 164, 165–68, 173
state power and othering of migrant women, 91, 95–98
stereotypes: and marginalized people in films, 130; use in media, 99–100
Strange, 53–57
strategic ambiguity, 48–49
strategic blackness, 15, 46–63, 131–32, 224
Sunshine Policy, 142, 182
super-minorities, 10, 221–22
Super Star K, 66, 69, 70, 75
Survivor, 67
Swing Kids (2018), 62
symbolic annihilation, 100

Taegukki (2004), 182
Thailand and type of work for women immigrants, 87
Third Space, 202, 211
Thuy (2013), 16, 85–100
Tona, Jonathan, 46
Top Band, 69
transnationalism: and defections, 142, 156; of Korean Wave and Africa policy, 60–62; of multiracial Koreans, 53
Trump, Donald, 173–74

United States: American Dream, 74, 224; Black Lives Matter movement, 228; and Cold War rhetoric, 162–63, 171, 173–75; immigration laws, 200–201; multiracial Koreans as reminder of occupation by, 10, 50–51, 125; neocolonial domination by, 4, 8–9, 10; and North Korean defectors, 17, 149, 150–51; racial hierarchies in, 7–8, 14–15, 51, 201; and sex work in Korea, 3, 10, 87, 125–26; television culture in Korea, 118n6; White supremacy hierarchies, 218–22; World War II and introduction of racism, 3, 51; World War II treaty negotiations, 8
unsympathetic empathy, 135
Uri-Hakkyo (2006), 17, 179, 183–92
uri ideograph, 17, 180, 185–91
Uzbek women and sex work, 16, 85, 86, 89–100

victim narrative, 13, 129
Video Star, 32–33
Vietnam: audition show contestants from, 71; marriage immigrants from, 12, 72; marriage immigrants in film, 16, 85–100
visas, 87, 200, 206, 207

WAGS (wives and girlfriends of sports stars), 31
The Wailing (2016), 16, 104–12, 117
Ward, Hines, 11, 53
Wedding Campaigns (2005), 89
Welcome to Dongmakgol (2005), 182
white (color), 109
White men: masculinity, 9–10; in relationships with Asian women and disciplining of femininity, 28–29; in relationships with women of color on US TV, 66; as romantic, 32
Whites: in anthrocategorism hierarchy, 221–22; beauty and appearance, 39, 92; and immigration law, 210; and neoracism, 6; as super-minority, 221–22; White Koreans, 10, 225–26; Whiteness as beneficial, 5, 217, 225–26; Whiteness as invisible, 220; White supremacy hierarchies, 2–4, 218–22

White women: desirability of, 27–43, 92, 93–94, 222; femininity of, 9, 28–29, 33–35, 42–43, 88–89, 96–97, 98, 222; as innocent, 93; and Korean men relationships as aspirational, 15, 27–43; as modern, 35, 39–40, 92; as mothers, 38–42; and multilingualism, 39; sexuality of, 16, 35, 36–38, 85, 91–95, 98, 217; and sex work, 16, 85–100, 217; as unmaterialistic, 33

wives and girlfriends of sports stars (WAGS), 31

World War II: enemy-making and war rhetoric, 162; and introduction of racism, 3, 51; treaty negotiations, 8

women: age and marginalized identity of, 123–37; comfort women, 110, 111, 116; and expectations of caregiving, 127–28; Japanese women as ally in film, 16, 104, 112–17; as in service to others, 16, 88, 91–94, 134–35. *See also* Central Asian women; marriage immigrants; White women

women, Korean: age and marginalization of, 123–37; comfort women, 110, 111, 116; femininity of, 13, 28–29, 33–35, 43, 222, 228; as materialistic, 28, 33; sexuality of, 29–30, 35–38; terms for, 28, 30

xenophobia, 5–6

Yang, Jeongmo, 76
Yemeni refugees, 228
Yoo, Steve/Seung Jun, 17–18, 197–200, 203–11, 225
You for Me for You (Chung), 17, 141–42, 148–56
Youn, Yuh-Jung, 126
Yu, Se-yoon, 29

zainichi: as term, 192n6. *See also* Korean minority in Japan *(Jaeil)*
Zainichi cinema, 183–84